# VICTORY
# THROUGH
# AIR
# POWER

GENERAL WILLIAM (BILLY) MITCHELL

This book I dedicate in gratitude to the memory of my superior, my colleague, my friend—

GENERAL WILLIAM MITCHELL

—and, through him, to the gallant airmen of all our American armed forces.

General Mitchell's stature has grown with the passage of time. Every crowded year of this crucial epoch in history has added dimensions to his prophetic vision. He has emerged not merely as the clearsighted and farsighted apostle of true air power, but as the human symbol of America's air age.

The good fight which General Mitchell fought has been continued courageously and unselfishly by countless American aviators. They have been not only willing but eager to risk their lives to demonstrate the efficacy of true air power. And they are carrying General Mitchell's epic campaign of enlightenment to a victorious conclusion.

My close association with General Mitchell and with so many other members of our military aviation personnel for nearly a quarter of a century emboldens me to believe that I speak, in some measure at least, for them all in the pages that follow.

In particular I believe that I voice their beliefs in conveying a message of sober optimism, of hope based on scientific fact, to the American people. In a war in which air power is the decisive factor, America can win, must win, and will win.

The inventive and technological genius of our country gave modern aviation to mankind. General Mitchell sought to make this American weapon the instrument of American security. His prophetic words and thoughts today, in the hour of supreme crisis and supreme test, point clearly and optimistically to the road of VICTORY THROUGH AIR POWER.

# VICTORY
# THROUGH AIR POWER

BY

MAJOR ALEXANDER P. DE SEVERSKY

SIMON AND SCHUSTER · NEW YORK · 1942

NOTE: Some of the material in this book has appeared, in an earlier form, in the *American Mercury, The Atlantic Monthly, The American Magazine, Flying and Popular Aviation, Look, Coronet, Reader's Digest, Town and Country*. To these magazines the author acknowledges his grateful appreciation for permission to edit, elaborate and bring up to date the writings which first appeared in their pages.

DIAGRAMS RENDERED BY I. N. STEINBERG

MANUFACTURED IN THE UNITED STATES OF AMERICA
BY H. WOLFF BOOK MFG. CO., INC., NEW YORK, N. Y.

# CONTENTS

# ILLUSTRATIONS

# VICTORY
# THROUGH
# AIR
# POWER

# CHAPTER I

# THE CHALLENGE TO AMERICA

### 1

THE MOST significant single fact about the war now in progress is the emergence of aviation as the paramount and decisive factor in warmaking. There is still some difference of opinion as to the precise role of aviation in the immediate future, its relation to the older military services, its role in this or that specific battle or campaign. But there are no two opinions on the fundamental fact that aviation has altered the traditional textbook conceptions of strategy and tactics. All experts agree that air power will play an ever more decisive part in determining the power balance among the nations of the earth. But it does not need an expert to recognize this towering truth. It is inescapable in the day-to-day news from every theater of conflict.

Since world empires have depended throughout history on the available weapons of domination, the advent of this new weapon—swifter and more destructive than any in the past, equally potent on land or at sea—must affect fundamentally the pattern of life on our planet. It has already, indeed, gone far toward smashing the accustomed power designs and toward sketching the future picture.

This process, it is self-evident, involves the United States as intimately as it does any other great nation. A realistic understanding of the new weapon, of its implications in terms of national security, of its challenge to America, is not a matter of choice. It is the very condition of national survival.

At the outbreak of the Second World War and for at least
two years thereafter, the United States lagged dismally in
military aviation—not only absolutely, considering the technical potentialities of aeronautics, but even relatively, compared with the achievements of other nations, especially
Germany and Great Britain. Despite bureaucratic attempts
to blur its outlines, the record is clear. American military aviation, when the European war started, was primitive and
haphazard, whether measured by the yardstick of military
performance—range, armament, fire power, speed—or by the
yardstick of planned strategy, tactics, and organization.

As dramatically as though it had been staged by provi-
dence as a warning to the American people, our own entry
into the war, on December 7, 1941, was signalized by a humiliating defeat through enemy air power. The tragedy at
Pearl Harbor, on that day, underlined soon thereafter by the
sinking of the British battleships *Prince of Wales* and *Repulse*
from the air, cut through national complacency and brass-
hat smugness. The terrific danger was exposed for all to see.
That initial week shocked the American people even as the
French people had been shocked when German aviation and
Panzer divisions ignored their Maginot Line.

The challenge of air power cannot be met by merely "admitting" our failures and undertaking to "catch up" with more
advanced countries. The tempo of air-power expansion is
much too swift. A nation content to imitate and "catch up"
must in the nature of the case remain backward, trailing
foreign leaders. The method of trial-and-error is ruled out because the penalty for error may be loss of national independence. We cannot afford to wait and see, to suspend judgment; we may not have a second chance. The challenge can
be met only by exploring the physical and psychological
causes of our tardiness and weakness in the air, applying

radical surgery rather than surface cures, and preparing for nothing less than undisputed first place in the epochal race for aerial supremacy.

The rapid obsolescence of aeronautical equipment, especially now under the impetus of a great war, enables us to overtake and outstrip other nations, provided we take advantage of it without delay. It offers us the chance *to skip intermediary stages of development* and reach out boldly beyond the present confines of aviation types. As far as the aircraft of tomorrow is concerned, all nations are starting from scratch. America is more richly endowed with the resources of brains, materials, personnel, and industrial efficiency than any other country on earth. Whether it utilizes these potentialities, or once more allows itself to trail along imitatively, depends on how quickly and thoroughly we comprehend the nature of the new weapon—and on how quickly and thoroughly we cleanse our air power from the accretions of conservatism, timidity, and astigmatic leadership.

In this book I hope to contribute toward that emancipation of American air power. I want to focus attention on the new principles of warfare shaped by the emergence of military aviation and demonstrated by the experience of the present war. Above all, I hope to convey the sense of air power as a dynamic, expanding force, the growth of which must be anticipated by courageous minds. It happens to be a force that eludes static, orthodox minds no matter how brilliant they may be. Air power speaks a strategic language so new that translation into the hackneyed idiom of the past is impossible. It calls not only for new machines and techniques of warmaking but for new men unencumbered by routine thinking.

We must not merely outbuild any potential enemy or combination of enemies—that is the lesser half of the job for a machine-age nation like the United States. We must out*think* and out*plan* them, in a spirit of creative audacity. As long as aeronautics remains merely another industry, or just another adjunct of national defense, America will be foredoomed to a secondary position among the air-power nations. Aviation must be apprehended by the whole American people as the essential expression of the present-day world and given unbounded room for development. All those gifts of mechanical ingenuity, industrial efficiency, and, above all, imaginative daring which have made America the first nation of the industrial era must be given full play in American air power.

Let me at the outset summarize my basic convictions, in the simplest terms:

1. The rapid expansion of the range and striking power of military aviation makes it certain that the United States will be as exposed to destruction from the air, within a predictable period, as are the British Isles today.

2. Those who deny the practical possibility of a direct aerial attack on America are lulling the American people into an utterly false sense of safety which may prove as disastrous to us as the "Maginot Line mentality" proved to France.

3. To meet this threat to the existence and independence of our country we must begin immediately to prepare for the specific kind of war conditioned by the advent of air power. That can mean only an interhemispheric war direct across oceans, with air power fighting not over this or that locality, but by longitude and latitude anywhere in the uninterrupted "air ocean." Such preparedness calls not merely for more aviation but for new military organization and new strategic conceptions.

4. Despite immediate shortcomings, there is no excuse for a defeatist approach to the problem. On the contrary, America has all the prerequisites for victory in the race for domi-

nation of the skies. It has all that is required to make it the
dominant air-power nation, even as England in its prime was
the dominant sea-power nation of the world.

The pressing immediate need is for a national awakening
to the threat implicit in air power—and to the urgency of
preparing not merely to meet it but to take the offensive
initiative. Autonomous and specialized organization for air
power, freed from the restraints and inertias of long-estab-
lished army and naval organizations, is almost axiomatic. It
will follow, I believe, just as soon as the American people
break through their present lethargy.

If we continue to ignore these looming aeronautical facts,
if we remain stubbornly committed to pure Army and Navy
strategy, we shall be helpless when the interhemispheric
*aerial conflict* catches up with us. I do not relinquish the
hope that we shall be amply prepared long before that happens. But for the sake of emphasis—as a warning rather than
a prophecy—I visualize a contingency as melodramatic as
this:

———————————— 2 ————————————

FROM EVERY point of the compass—across the two oceans and
across the two Poles—giant bombers, each protected by its
convoy of deadly fighter planes, converge upon the United
States of America. There are thousands of these dreadnaughts
of the skies. Each of them carries at least fifty tons of streamlined explosives and a hailstorm of light incendiary bombs.
Wave after wave they come—openly, in broad daylight, mag-
nificently armored and armed, surrounded by protective
aircraft and equipped to fight their way through to their appointed targets. Aerial armadas now battle boldly and fiercely,
just as great naval armadas used to do in the past, only with
a destructive fury infinitely more terrifying.

With the precision of perfect planning, the invading aerial
giants strike at the nerve centers and jugular veins of a great
nation. Unerringly they pick their objectives: industrial centers and sources of power, government seats and fuel concentrations, especially the American aviation setup of airdromes
and factories.

The havoc they wreak is beyond description. New York,
Detroit, Chicago, and San Francisco are reduced to rubble
heaps in the first twenty-four hours. Washington is wiped out
before the government has a chance to rescue its most treas-
ured records. A dozen crucial power plants like Muscle
Shoals, Niagara Falls, and Boulder Dam are wrecked, crippling a great section of American industrial life at a single
blow. A thousand tons of explosives deposited expertly on a
few great railroad depots like those at Chicago dislocate the
country's transportation system.

Scarcely five years have passed since the bombardment of
Warsaw, Rotterdam, London, Hamburg, Coventry, and other
European cities. Yet they seem a mere rehearsal for this
massive and cataclysmic attack on America. Every one of the
new bombers carries more destructive force than a hundred
of the once-dreaded Stuka dive-bombers or two dozen of the
largest horizontal bomber planes used in those milder years.
A single assault now inflicts as much death and damage as
two or three months of the famous Nazi air attacks on the
British Isles back in 1941. One expedition now lays waste a
hundred cities like Coventry.

In this first concentrated aerial assault on the nation, the
enemy attacks not only vital strategic objectives, but objectives of a sentimental character. The purpose is to stir up
every ounce of patriotism and induce a mood of sacrifice and
desperation which coaxes the entire air force of the nation
to rise for combat despite the odds. Our "purely defensive"

aviation accepts the challenge and gallantly takes to the air. But it proves sadly inadequate. Its military characteristics, the tactical ideas on which it has been nurtured, are wholly unsuited to the task. The entire force is quickly smashed and reduced to impotence.

Then begins the tedious, unceasing process of total destruction of a great nation from the air. It resolves into the kind of "three-dimensional aerial blockade" which was dismissed as "visionary" when described in the past by aviation men. The merciless blockade not only cuts all external lines of communication, as in the orthodox blockade of the pre-aviation era; it destroys internal lines of communication and primary centers of national life. If the blockade of the past was a wall or fence around the enemy, the new type may be compared to an inverted bowl or dome, under which the enemy is gradually suffocated.

Not until this all-out offensive by a combination of enemies on both sides of the world got under way did the American people realize their country's vulnerability. They had been put to sleep by the lullabies of optimists. Did they not enjoy the blessings of vast "ocean ramparts" and of thousands of rolling miles between the Atlantic and the Pacific? Were they not "isolated" by nature itself? The first genuine all-out transoceanic air attack shatters such illusions of size and distance. The new air weapon is contemptuous of miles. With the circumference of the earth annihilated by sustained flight, the old concepts of space have simply evaporated.

Now the American people discover too late that the most highly industrialized nation is the most exposed to the ravages of the new air menace. Backward and primitive peoples can take to the woods and the caves and there survive a rain of air bombs. But Americans, proud heirs of the most advanced machine-age civilization, depend on their industry

and their power resources and their urban population centers
—all of which are of necessity highly centralized and crowded
into comparatively small congested areas, offering ideal targets for the raiders of the skies. A few well-placed bombs
blot out public utilities, cut off water supplies, bury a million
city dwellers under the debris of their skyscrapers, disrupt
industrial life, and interrupt the flow of food and supplies.

As the cyclones of aerial devastation sweep through the
land, hour after hour, day after day, only one thing proves
more shocking and demoralizing than the physical destruction and the fantastic loss of life. It is the sudden and incredible realization that the immense program of defense to
which the country gave its best efforts and billions of dollars
in the preceding five or six years is largely irrelevant to this
total war from the skies. True, there are millions of trained
and well-equipped soldiers on tap; an army superbly mechanized and brilliantly commanded. But they all become mere
frustrated onlookers. True, our two-ocean navy is almost
completed; by general acclaim it adds up to the finest and
strongest naval force the world has ever seen. Yet it can now
do nothing, literally nothing, against the locust swarms of
giant airplanes. The multibillion navy is itself as pathetically
exposed to the onslaught as any other surface target.

As the air attack proceeds, as the country begins to writhe
under the suffocating blockade, a panic-stricken nation wonders when the invasion by millions of enemy troops will begin. Our own mechanized land forces are hastily deployed
to meet them head on. Every inch of our coastlines and land
frontiers has been elaborately fortified for miles and miles
inland. After the first horrifying week of the aerial devastation the country begins to *wish* for the land invasion that it had
feared—anything seems preferable to the relentless pounding from on high.

Then the stricken people begin to understand that there will be no "invasion" in the old-fashioned sense of the word. The enemies have no intention of undertaking a slow and costly mile-by-mile conquest of America on the ground. They prefer to hammer the nation into a writhing mass of ruins from overhead. They prefer to bleed America to the point of utter exhaustion and helplessness, demolishing its cities and its industries, wrecking its complicated machinery of existence and its national morale, smashing all inside and outside communication lines to tighten the stranglehold of an aerial blockade.

In the past, too, there had been talk of "total war." But now it is being demonstrated for the first time. America is not being attacked piecemeal but *as a totality*. There is just one target: the whole country. A few farsighted aviation strategists had foreseen this type of third-dimensional warfare. Only now, with the disaster upon them, do people begin to grasp the fact that the epoch of troop landings and war "fronts" and struggles for a few miles of disputed soil has ended forever. The key word is no longer *occupation* but *destruction*.

And the destruction is now systematic, scientific—the planned wrecking of a great nation. It becomes clear even through the panic and the rising tides of death that the enemy's purpose is not merely to force us to surrender. It is to break our strength, destroy our civilization, lay low our cities, decimate our population, and leave us to dig out of the debris slowly and painfully.

After the nation has been paralyzed by bombing and incendiarism and wholesale slaughter, and starved through the disruption of all transport, the futility of resistance becomes apparent. The government offers to give up the hopeless struggle. But the attackers ignore the offer. The aim of total war is total destruction: to obliterate the United States as a modern nation. The enemy continues the macabre job of superwrecking to achieve that purpose, to eliminate this nation as a world factor, economically and politically, for generations to come.

---

3

---

THE PICTURE, I am fully aware, will seem fanciful at first blush. Those who dare to visualize it so vividly and to paint it as an emerging reality lay themselves open to the charge of being alarmists and panicmongers. Even thus General de Gaulle and other Frenchmen were branded as alarmists when they warned that frontier fortifications and huge armies were not enough in this age of aviation. Yet there is nothing remotely fanciful about the nightmarish picture. Technically it has been within the limits of reality for some time. Only psychological meekness and deficient military imagination have prevented the transfer of the technical potentials into functioning facts.

Under the terrific pressures of our war for self-preservation, however, timidity is being changed into courage. The full possibilities of aviation will inevitably be utilized. No such disaster as I have sketched out will overtake America—not because it is impossible, but because we shall be prepared to prevent it. American air power equal to the fearful challenge will be on hand. It will not only frustrate the enemy's attack on America; it will carry the "total aerial war" to the attacker's home grounds.

Present-day aviation—through military shortsightedness rather than aeronautical limitations—lacks only one element to make the awe-inspiring picture of America under aerial onslaught wholly realistic. That element is aviation "reach"

or range that will expose the continent of North America to
direct blows from other continents. The fact that such range
has not been incorporated in equipment thus far exhibited
in the world struggle does not imply any technical limitation in the science of aeronautics. It is due simply to the failure of all nations to grasp the full implications of the aerial
weapon—to the inertia which keeps principles of warfare in-
violate long after they have outlived their usefulness. Admiral Mahan, our great theorist of sea power, long ago noted
the lapse of time between technical advances and their strategic exploitation for sea power.

His words apply no less to air power. It is only this time
gap which has postponed for a while longer the kind of aerial
operation that I have tried to describe. As soon as hostile air
power can strike across oceans as readily as it now does
across narrower waters, the United States will become every
bit as vulnerable as England. Broad oceans will then be just
so many English Channels, Skagerraks, and Sicilian Straits.
Whether they are barriers to shield a nation or highways of
destruction will then depend entirely on the size and effectiveness of our own air power.

The fact that the enemy must travel a few hours longer
to reach its goal and to return to its home base after unload-
ing cargoes of death will not diminish the destructive force
in the slightest. It will matter nothing that the armadas of
bombers will fly ten hours or more before reaching American
objectives. They will be crossing at substratospheric altitudes, with relief crews, under ideal conditions of comfort.
On arrival at their targets, the crews will be as fresh and
rested as if they had stepped out of their homes after break-
fast. In modern planes, after all, what is the difference between flying three hours to the interior of Germany or Italy
and flying ten hours across the ocean to the interior of the

United States? *Of all the elements involved in the undertaking, the period of approach is the least hazardous and the least exhausting.* Normally it is the least dangerous if only because the initiative lies with the attacker.

Once the bomber is over enemy territory, whether it is the Ruhr or Pennsylvania, the English Midlands or Chicago, London or New York, makes not the slightest technical difference. The procedure after arrival is identical—and so are the disastrous consequences upon the victimized area. Continuous waves of air power from overseas will mean continuous bombardment despite the longer interval of approach—just as the flow of a river remains unbroken although its point of origin may be thousands of miles away.

*We need only make the assumption of a vastly expanded aviation range—an assumption fully justified by the scientific aeronautical facts—and instantly the exposed position of America becomes evident. Imagine the reach of air power multiplied three to five times, and the tactical position of the United States becomes precisely the same as that of the British Isles today.*

The range of military aviation is being extended so rapidly that the Atlantic will be canceled out as a genuine obstacle within two years, the Pacific within three years. After that, in five years at the outside, *the ultimate round-the-world range of 25,000 miles becomes inevitable.* At that point any nation will be able to hurl its aerial might against any spot on the face of the globe without intermediary bases. By the same token every country will be subject to assault from any direction anywhere in the world. The blows will be delivered from the home bases, regardless of distance, with all oceans and bases in between turned into a no-man's land. Indeed, in order to dominate the world from the air, a nation does not need to wait for the ultimate 25,000-mile range. The possession of air power of a 15,000-mile range—which means a striking radius of about 6000 miles—would bring all the major nations, their capitals and key cities and strategic industrial centers, within a country's reach. Anyone can prove this for himself by tracing the area 6000 miles from the periphery of the United States on a globe map.

Already German bombers take a heavy toll of British commerce in the Atlantic more than a thousand miles beyond the coastlines of Europe. Already by the spring of 1941, an ocean convoy sailing toward England had to count on the hazards of aerial raids during the last third of its journey, and the zone of overhead danger was being widened with every month. In the first year of the war the world was startled to find Nazi bombers infesting the skies a hundred miles to the west of Ireland; soon it became accustomed to find them stalking prey five or eight hundred and even more than a thousand miles from their bases.

In truth there was no real cause for astonishment. Clipper ships of the air had been spanning ocean distances for years. Nonstop flights of thousands of miles had become familiar front-page news items. Regular airlines from Africa to South America had operated continuously as a routine matter. Soviet Russian airplanes had reached the American continent across the North Pole. British planes had jumped 7000 miles from one point of their empire to another. Germany's Condor had easily crossed from Berlin to New York. The marvel is not that aviation has achieved transoceanic range; the marvel is that our own country and other nations have failed to construct air power of such range.

Why have the principal nations refused to build air power capable of delivering blows at targets thousands of miles away? Primarily because the principal aeronautic nations did not consider such air power necessary for their immediate

tasks. Most Americans are familiar with the main facts about
the new Douglas B-19 and the Glenn Martin flying boat,
with their range of nearly 8000 miles and their ability to
carry a bomb load of eighteen tons. During the launching
of the giant flying boat, Mr. Glenn Martin stated that he is
already at work on a plane nearly twice as large as the present—a plane which will weigh approximately 250,000 pounds
and will be able to carry twenty tons of explosive to any
part of Europe and return nonstop; subsequently he even
doubled his estimate of the potential bomb load.

The present Douglas and Martin superbombers have neither the speed, the armor, nor the armament to make them
true dreadnaughts of the skies, capable of fighting their way
through to an appointed target, dropping their explosives,
and fighting their way back. They were conceived some time
ago, as purely aerodynamic experiments, without planned
relation to practical employment in warfare. Consequently
they are little more than "blown-up" versions of the so-called
"flying fortress," embodying on a larger scale all the tactical
limitations of that misnamed "fortress." The true air bomber
will have much greater speed, superb armor, and imposing
fire power.

But as a preview of the great ranges now possible and the
greater ones still to come, the B-19 serves its purpose. Obviously such a plane could leave New York, bomb an objective anywhere in Europe, and return to its base; no less obviously, the reverse is true: a group of such planes could take
off from Berlin or Paris, wreck the Pittsburgh or Detroit area,
and return home. The eighteen-ton hitting strength of this
plane equals the hitting strength of thirty-six German Stuka
dive-bombers, which carry only 1000 pounds of explosive
each.

Five thousand bombers of such size, with an adequate pursuit escort, in the possession of any country—a striking power equal to 180,000 Stuka bombers!—would make it the military master of any other country within a radius of 3500 miles. An intervening ocean would offer no protection. Unless the chosen victim possessed an equal or stronger air force, it would be as helpless against the threat as were Czechoslovakia and Denmark against the air might of Hitler's Germany. And the B-19, or even the projected 250,000-pound Martin, is only the beginning of a process of range extension which has the ultimate circumglobular distance as its appointed climax. It is no secret that a number of other bombers, with vast range and great load-carrying capacity, are being developed, though unfortunately on a timid experimental basis.

Extraordinary advances are being made in aeronautical materials, more efficient fuels and fuel-consumption processes and general aerodynamic refinements, all of which will be translated, among other things, into aviation "reach." Neither am I disclosing secrets in asserting that research is proceeding successfully on airplane engines that develop as much as 8000 horsepower! Imagine a bomber equipped with six such engines, as against the present 2000-horsepower engines: a total of 48,000 horsepower—as much as some battleships in active service with our fleet possess!—instead of the present 8000, together with other vital aerodynamic advances already available. Imagine that and you grasp the emerging revolutionary possibility of ranges circling the entire globe, with plenty of margin for tactical operations.

Under these circumstances rhetoric about "our impregnable ocean ramparts" is reduced to dangerous gibberish. It attests the stubbornness of the human mind that such delusions of physical isolation can persist under the impact of everyday facts spread out for all to see. Like the yokel who

saw a giraffe for the first time, our military monitors look at
long-range airplanes, fly in them, exclaim over them, but
insist all the same that "there ain't no such animal." The psychological comfort of two oceans to cushion us against danger is so pleasant that we cannot easily relinquish it.

The word "isolation" became, after the outbreak of World
War II, a kind of political football in America. Some were *for*
it, others *against* it. But the airman cannot face the issue in
political terms. For those entrusted with the physical defense of our country isolation is a geographical and tactical
problem rather than a matter of policy. The issue, for them,
was not whether isolation for the United States is desirable
but whether it was possible. I for one was deeply convinced,
on the basis of sheer mechanical realities, that isolation no
longer exists outside demagogic vocabularies. Delusions of
defensive invulnerability are fairy tales carried over from an
earlier period in our history, just as grownups carry over
consoling fairy tales from their sheltered childhood.

Those who advocate continued reliance on "impregnable
ramparts" concede that bombing of American targets from
overseas is already possible. But they do not follow the implications of this concession to its logical conclusion. They
have failed to catch up with the realities of a changing physical world, a world made narrower with every advance of
science.

As a designer and pilot of aircraft who has devoted his
mature life to the study of the science of war, I thought of
isolation not in terms of national political slogans but in
terms of *space relations*. With continents and oceans traversed
in a few hours, it no longer made sense to measure distances
in miles. They had to be measured in the units of time needed
to bridge them. Aviators are especially impressed with this

PICTURE PARADE, PHILADELPHIA INQUIRER

The 82-ton Douglas B–19 bomber; range, 7800 miles; bomb load, 18 tons.

AVIATION

The Glenn Martin Flying Boat; performance approximately the same as the B–19.

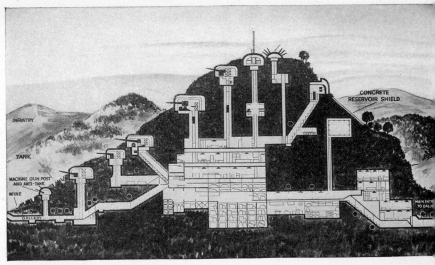

Cross section of a Maginot Line fortress, trench warfare de luxe.

An entrance to a sector of the Maginot fortification.

MONUMENTS TO OUTMODED STRATEGY. The advent of mode
air power makes some recent surface military concepts seem as ancient
the Egyptian pyramids.

elementary truth. In 1938 I covered the interval between New York and Los Angeles in ten hours, establishing a new record; inevitably, in my inner mind, the continent shrank to a degree that the average nonflying American cannot appreciate. Similarly, the "ferry" pilot who flies an American bomber across the North Atlantic in seven or eight hours is conscious of how close the Old and the New Worlds are and not how far apart.

Considered solely from the tactical and geographical viewpoint, many government and military leaders who, before we entered the war, excoriated the "isolationists" were in actuality hidebound isolationists themselves. Emotionally and verbally they were opposed to the false and dangerous isolationist philosophy, but in their military ideas they remained as isolationist as any America Firster. They accepted uncritically the *military* premises on which the isolationist ideology rested, and evolved defense programs on the bankrupt assumption that by enlarging and improving the "ocean ramparts," the "outer defenses" of naval strength, they could frustrate any threat to our country. They are still, at this writing, busily constructing two-ocean navies with the same innocent self-assurance that the French leaders once built an "impregnable" Maginot Line along their frontiers. They prepare armies and navies for the traditional A.E.F.—for a mile-by-mile struggle for territorial occupation, as though nothing had happened to revolutionize the nature of warfare. They resemble the Indians who sharpened their arrows and tuned up their bows to meet conquistadors armed with guns and girded with armor.

It is my contention that the "isolationists" were dismally and dangerously wrong—because the military notions on which they relied are no longer tenable. Insofar as those notions are still accepted and acted upon, the procedure is truly isolationist, even if it is done by vociferous opponents of the isolationist philosophy.

Every advance in the science of human communication—the railroad, the automobile, radio, aeronautics—has made the world smaller. Each of these developments has reduced sharply the scale of continents and oceans. And every such advance has ended somebody's cherished isolation. The Indians were isolated in the Western Hemisphere until sailing ships and gunpowder overtook them and obliterated their isolation. The interior of Africa was isolated until railroads and automobiles and finally airplanes ended that isolation. By this time the process of shrinkage of our planet has proceeded so far that only small margins of physical isolation remain in any part of the globe; and those margins, too, are crumbling at their edges with every extension of the "reach" of aviation. It is only a matter of time before there will not be even a sliver of it left anywhere.

Long before the extreme circumglobular range of aviation is achieved, the shielding distances of oceans will have evaporated. We had better discount them in our thinking and planning now, while acknowledging their temporary and restricted immediate validity. We had better do so before that illusory sense of safety which they engender in American minds puts a brake on real, daring, creative planning for victory.

Forget military flying for a moment. Certainly civilian, commercial aviation will in the near future bind every nation of the planet in an immense network of aerial transportation. The United States, lying between the two great oceans, is marked out by fate to be the crossroads of this gigantic traffic: this country will become the "four corners" of air routes not only over the Atlantic and Pacific but over

the North and South Poles. Like the residents of some isolated prairie town suddenly yanked into the big wide world
by a new railroad junction, we shall find ourselves in the
very midst of a planetary air traffic, some of it not even pausing to refuel or reload in America as it makes express jumps
between continents.

Our minds accept this coming peacetime aviation without
too much resistance. They balk at accepting the same facts
in relation to war movements, since they cut athwart established military "laws" and patterns of thought. However, we
must in the nature of the case be as completely open for destructive attack as for commerce. In fact, air commerce will
of necessity be as thoroughly guarded by air power as in the
immediate past sea commerce has been guarded by sea power.

We can head off disaster only by recognizing its looming
shape and by beginning now to prepare to meet any challenge.

---

4

---

THE NAZI *Blitzkrieg* took the world by surprise. Actually,
however, every element of the new strategy had been revealed in cold print and demonstrated in German maneuvers. The *Blitz* method remained "secret" only in the sense
that general staffs and orthodox military writers closed their
minds against it. They shouted down "heretics" who dared
suggest that the new war would be anything more than a
larger and more mechanized version of 1914–18. What were
their Maginot Lines but bigger and more luxurious embodi-
ments of trench warfare? What were their navies, super-
dreadnaughts and all, but preparation for a more modernized repetition of regulation sea conflicts?

Even after the *Blitz* technique had been displayed in all

its grim efficiency on the plains of Poland, the High Command and public opinion in France refused to be disturbed. They continued to nestle snugly and smugly in the shadows of their Maginot Line. France could not summon the will power and the mental strength to break through habit, tradition, routine, when confronted with a new revolutionary type of military action. The French political leaders, no matter how brilliant they may have been in their own domain, were wholly at the mercy of military experts in the domain of strategy.

On the American side of the ocean the smugness, it must be admitted, was no less profound. Insofar as we had been preparing at all, it was on the assumption that nothing new had come to pass since Argonne-Meuse in 1918. Even after the fall of Poland, orthodoxy continued to rule the military roost. The Hitler strategy did not fit neatly into Army and Navy routines, and hence was properly snubbed. When finally we did begin to bestir ourselves, after the collapse of France, our near-panic took two directions:

(1) We hastened to enlarge and improve existing weapons, without troubling to inquire whether they were still fully effective. We undertook the construction of supernavies as the American equivalent of France's "supertrench," and soon thereafter the training of ground forces along the old lines. (2) We hastened to copy the Nazi *Blitzkrieg* machine, determined to produce the makings of a bigger and better *Blitz* than any which Germany might muster. Since aircraft had served brilliantly as a component of surface task forces in the conquest of Europe, our highest military authorities were confirmed in their prejudices against releasing air power for its own strategic destiny over and above its co-operative functions.

In short, we aped the past and aped the triumphant Germans—but failed utterly to strike out for ourselves in new directions. The few who saw—in the Battle of Britain, Crete, and other episodes—portents of aerial strategies beyond the *Blitz* technique were silenced or ignored. Our responsible military leaders have advertised their new parachute units, their new task formations, their improved aircraft types. But these things represent merely a process of catching up with the enemy.

Now America is in the war all the way. As the strongest of the democracies it had been regarded by the Axis from the start as the central and ultimate enemy. Nazi propaganda, often speaking through the mouths of honest but tragically confused Americans, had harped on our immunity to attack—on our "impregnable" ocean ramparts and our defensive naval strength. Unwittingly those who put their reliance on surface forces and ridiculed the "aviation crackpots" played into the hands of Goebbels and Göring.

The encouragement of blind faith in the Maginot Line in France had been one of the great achievements of the Fifth Column. It was an achievement in which many patriotic Frenchmen co-operated with the highest motives. Hitler even went to the length of constructing a line of his own, the Siegfried Wall, to strengthen the Maginot illusions on the other side. Encouragement of blind faith in our Navy—and in the great armies which a supernavy would ultimately transport across the oceans—had the same function in America. It is no accident that Nazi propaganda sheets in our midst invariably stressed the defensive security of America, ringed by its naval wall. Many patriotic Americans, frequently in high military posts, have argued passionately against air power. This should not blind us to the fact that every restraint put on development of the new weapon has been a major victory for the Axis.

If this book succeeds in its purpose, it will demonstrate that only through supreme air power can America attain the supreme victory. I undertake the task fully aware that it implies serious criticism of the established military order. But I count on the common sense of the American people to realize that the emergency is too great for double-talk.

If our basic strategy is mistaken, the sooner it is revised the better. There is no virtue in mere perseverance. The man who finds himself on the wrong train moving in the wrong direction cannot do better than climb down at the first stop and get going in the right direction. If, as I am deeply convinced, we entered the war with outmoded strategic concepts, the sooner we abandon them the better. We must understand the Axis methods without repeating them automatically.

In essence we are committed, at this writing, to the creation of a super-*Blitz* mechanism. Reflecting the military ideas percolating down from the top, the average American visualizes a super-A.E.F. carried across the oceans by supernavies for old-fashioned campaigns to seize territory, mile by mile. In those campaigns, of course, the navies and the expeditionary troops would have the benefit of all the modern gadgets, from huge tanks to aviation support.

I submit that such a procedure, under certain circumstances, may succeed, but at best it would be disastrously costly in resources and man power. Why need we adhere to the ancient pattern of warfare when air power offers a simpler and more effective strategy, and one in which America's potential—in resources, personnel, and productive genius—is so clearly superior to the enemy's that it guarantees complete victory?

Assume that we succeed in deploying immense American ground forces in a series of great invasions of Axis-held territory. The assumption under modern conditions implies the possession of correspondingly vast and powerful aerial forces; even naval spokesmen by this time concede that navies cannot approach hostile shores which are defended by superior aviation. The successful transport of these huge expeditions to many parts of the globe implies, likewise, control of the skies above the sea lanes; after the experience of the initial weeks of the war in the Pacific Ocean no one will again claim seriously that navies can venture into areas dominated by enemy air power, even if the enemy is entirely lacking in naval force.

The maintenance of the vast armies, moreover, would call for continuous lines of communication with the American mainland across thousands of miles of land and sea. The mechanized armies of this day and age move on their fuel pipe lines, so to speak; they must also be fed uninterruptedly with armaments, supplies, replacement, reinforcements in men and machines. The whole enterprise is not even thinkable except on the basis of a great network of conduits. Now every mile of these connecting lines, whether on dry land or on water, would have to be shielded by American aviation. The most modern dreadnaughts are impotent against overhead attacks: airplanes can attack ships but ships cannot attack airplanes: only air power can effectively overcome air power. Except in limited stretches of ocean as yet beyond the reach of land-based aviation, ship-borne aircraft is a most hazardous substitute for true air power: first, because it is inferior to the enemy's land-based planes, and second, because the carriers themselves are perfect targets for enemy aviation, being among the most vulnerable ships afloat.

Thus the picture of super-A.E.F.'s transported and supplied by supernavies resolves, from any angle that it is viewed, into a struggle for domination of the skies. Without

mastery of the air over the expeditions and over their thousands of miles of communication, the whole undertaking
turns into gibberish. Having recognized that much, any layman can understand the unwieldiness of such a strategy.
Obvious questions will come to his mind:

If we do develop the equipment and the tactics to achieve
such widespread mastery of the air, why bother to send those
colossal expeditions? What chance do enemy sea and land
forces have to operate with any hope of success under skies
held firmly by our air power? Why should we match soldier
for soldier against the teeming hordes of Europe and Asia
in a duel of mutual slaughter when American industrial and
inventive genius, translated into genuine air power, can make
the short cut of all-out aerial assault on the enemy? Why
seek to smother the Axis with American bodies, why crush
the enemy by the sheer weight of material, when we can
bring into play our brain power and our inventive genius?

The details will fall into place, I trust, in the following
chapters, but here is the crux of the matter: *We cannot and
must not dream of conquering the enemy without first cap-
turing dominance in the air—but once we have clear-cut
dominance in the air, all else becomes a secondary subordinate, auxiliary operation.*

The vision I have evoked of a full-fledged long-distance
attack on the American continent through the skies contains
nothing more extreme than the picture of *Blitzkrieg* presented to a complacent unbelieving world before it actually
occurred. It will be put into effect first by the side which
first throws off the weight of military orthodoxy—the side
which has the imaginative daring to visualize such a campaign and the technical resources to implement it with
equipment.

Americans are the natural masters of the new aerial

weapon, if only they become conscious of the fact and act without delay. What enemies can do to us across the oceans, we can do to them even more thoroughly and more decisively, because we have more of what it takes in materials, inventive skills, and the natural technological psychology of our people. Given the appropriate equipment, and aerial organization freed from restraint by the older services, we can impose a suffocating tridimensional aerial blockade on the enemy. After defeating his air forces, we can smash his economic conduits on the high seas, and at the same time sever the arteries of his life inside his own frontiers.

This does not mean that we must cast aside older weapons. America is rich enough to duplicate weapons in the transition period, and we shall always need surface forces on land and sea for auxiliary purposes, for supporting actions and for the final tactics of occupation and policing. It does mean that we have not a moment to lose in undertaking the planning and construction of a striking air power which utilizes the last ounce of potentiality of twentieth-century third-dimensional warfare. It is apparent now that only air power can carry an offensive war to the enemy, and only the offensive can win the war. The main investment of our American wealth and energies must therefore be put into aviation. We can assume a defensive strategy on the sea, hold our land forces in abeyance for the issue, while air power takes the initiative and batters through to a victorious decision.

I for one have no doubt that the native intelligence of our great nation will assert itself before it is too late. It will realize that America has within its grasp—

*Victory through air power!*

# CHAPTER II

# SKAGERRAK AND DUNKIRK

## 1

ALTHOUGH THE airplane was first employed as a military weapon in the Balkan war of 1912–13, it did not assume a conspicuous role until the World War of 1914–18. And there has been an unfortunate tendency to minimize its performance in that conflict. The truth is that the air power of the future was demonstrated in miniature in that war, despite technical shortcomings due to the novelty of the weapon. Tactical principles were evolved which were destined to remain applicable for the future. Unfortunately, the high moguls of orthodox military science either did not grasp those principles or else they promptly discounted and forgot them. Only a few bolder, more imaginative spirits in all countries were able to visualize the potentialities of the fully developed air power on the basis of its crude beginnings—in America General William ("Billy") E. Mitchell holds first place among these men of exceptional practical foresight and military intuition.

Aerodynamically and structurally the planes we flew in that war were primitive. In such essentials as speed, load-carrying capacity, and striking power their performance was low. To the physical hazards involved in piloting those early machines must be added the mental strain induced by the awareness that we had no parachutes and that we had no chance of escape from a burning or crippled plane. Yet the meager scope permitted by that stage of aviation was utilized to the limit. By the time the war ended, four-engined bombers were in the air, and pursuit planes were equipped in some instances with two and three fixed machine guns firing forward and even with a cannon. The significance of this must be gauged by the fact that twenty-one years later, at the time of the outbreak of World War II, some of our American pursuits had even less armament than those of World War I.

Because of the limited performance elements, however, airplanes in the First World War remained little more than an extension of existing weapons. For the Army they were chiefly valuable as a more expeditious form of reconnaissance, photography, and control of artillery fire. For the Navy they became "the eyes of the battle fleet." As a direct striking force, operating "on its own," the usefulness of aviation was exceedingly limited.

Flying the planes over the battle areas, we sensed the possibilities of the weapon. We were conscious of the brakes on performance and of what we could do once those brakes were removed. I served for three years as an active pilot in the Baltic Sea for the Russian Navy, operating both against German land forces and the German fleet in the Gulf of Riga and the Baltic Sea. I still recall vividly my own dismay and frustration when attacking coastal fortifications and German battleships with small bombs—scoring direct hits with apparently no effect, and thinking, "if only these were 2000-pounders!" I recall no less vividly the combat and diving attacks on enemy aircraft, when the fear of losing wings was far more disconcerting than the hail of machine-gun bullets. It took no exceptional powers of divination to foresee what would happen when airplanes acquired great speeds, could bring real explosive loads to their targets, and were amply protected by armor and defensive fire power. Active fliers on all the fronts of World War I inevitably were impressed with the unexplored horizons of military aviation. Years later, in discussing strategic problems with General Mitchell and others, we invariably drew on our war experience to indicate the inherent but undeveloped possibilities in the new weapon.

That World War was decided overwhelmingly on land. The collapse of Germany was clearly hastened, also, by the strangulating blockade by the British Navy. Victorious military and naval men, in the enthusiasm of their triumphs, gave scarcely a thought to their young progeny, air power—to the crude air machines which, for all their melodramatic exploits, did not bulk large in the final victory. Aviation was brushed aside. If it was included at all among the elements of war, in the calculations of admirals and generals, it figured as an adjunct, and a most unreliable one at that. Those who insisted on evoking startling pictures of strategy to come, based on the employment of aviation to come, seemed impractical and rather annoying dreamers. When they insisted on fighting for their dreams, as General Mitchell did, they were treated as so many nuisances to be exposed and liquidated.

The potentialities of aviation as an independent weapon became a little more obvious to a greater number of students of strategy in the 1930's during the conflicts in China and Spain. For the "dreamers" these offered substantiation of their early conviction that air power, having opened up a new sphere for conquest, would inevitably develop as a major factor acting on its own strategic principles. Not until World War II was unleashed in September, 1939, however, did the full import of the new weapon become generally apparent.

By this time even the most casual observer has become

aware of the crucial part played by Nazi aviation in clear-
ing ground for Germany's mechanized forces to accomplish
the amazingly swift and thorough conquests of Poland, Norway, the Low Countries, France, Yugoslavia, Greece, and
Crete. The ease with which formidable ground fortifications
like the Maginot Line were cracked and virtually *ignored* has
registered on the world's imagination. The Maginot Line, a
true marvel of mechanical ingenuity, offered an almost perfect defense against invasion in its old preaviation forms.
The fall of that Line was therefore tantamount to the fall of
a whole epoch in the history of warmaking.

The world recalls, too, the high hopes attached in advance
to the dykes and canals of the Low Countries. Twenty-four
hours after the new Nazi war machine began to roll across
Belgium and Holland—along paths cleared by air power—
these barriers of water were quite forgotten. The collapse of
the Maginot Line was thus underscored by the contemptuous dismissal of the obstacles in the Low Countries. It all
added up to a fateful blow to the old automatic *reliance on
surface barriers* which had sufficed to block the advance of
invaders in the past.

The bankruptcy of that form of defense marked the end
of two-dimensional warfare. Human conflict had been lifted
suddenly from the surface of the earth into the third dimension, nullifying all fixed two-dimensional defenses, whether
dykes, fortified walls, or other impediments to surface movements. It nullified also the obstacles represented by oceans
and by navies—although that phase of the revolution in
strategy is not yet fully understood. Certainly it has not been
grasped by untrained minds, or by minds too well schooled
in the outlived tactical notions of an obsolescent era.

On a gigantic and tragic scale the new war demonstrated
that a fence which can imprison a raging tiger cannot, be it

ever so thick and tall, confine a soaring eagle. Only an impregnable roof can do that. Poland had none. As for Belgium, Holland, France, Greece, their aviation roofs were too flimsy and full of holes for the Nazi eagle of air power.

-------------------------------- 2 --------------------------------

THE HISTORIC seventeen-day campaign in Poland that opened on September 1, 1939, gave the first shocking demonstration of the German *Blitzkrieg* technique which Hitler's High Command followed in essence in all its other drives. Its principal features are now familiar to every newspaper reader. The static trench warfare was a thing of the past, and with it the "front" of former wars. In its place came the dynamic, highly mechanized war of movement and penetration.

Observers could no longer follow the progress of battles with colored pins on maps. Neither, for that matter, could generals. Nazi knives of mechanized strength—heavy motorized columns pushing forward at top speed ahead of the main forces, under the shield of air power—cut through the lines of defense; then they joined to surround and annihilate the segments. The trapped sections of armies unprepared for this type of action found themselves attacked from the rear and from above, cut off from their main forces, disrupted and demoralized.

The obvious defense against such a procedure would be a counteroffensive of an analogous character, poking mechanized fingers into the invader's flesh, pinching off the enemy's motorized columns at their base, where they join the main attacking forces. But that defense called for equipment at least equal to the attacker's, and particularly for aviation fully capable of neutralizing the enemy's aerial forces.

This Poland did not possess. Compared to the huge German *Luftwaffe,* Poland had practically no aerial defenses at all. Besides, as the first victim of the *Blitz* technique it was caught completely off guard; Polish aviation, designed to fight in the air, was thus destroyed on the ground. The public opinion of the world owes an apology to the Poles for the first harsh judgments of their fighting quality. Certainly France, Belgium, Holland, and Britain, having seen the *Blitz* method spread under their eyes as in a laboratory, bear a heavier blame. Their failure to read and understand the lessons attests the stubbornness of human habits of thought.

Two episodes of the first year of the war merit particularly close study for what they have to reveal of the new strategic realities. I refer to the invasion of Norway in defiance of Great Britain's overwhelming naval might, and the evacuation of Allied troops from Flanders by way of Dunkirk notwithstanding Germany's powerful ground forces. The two events can and should be examined together. They reveal, as we stop to analyze them, the two sides of the same medal of air power.

After the first shock of Germany's seizure of Denmark and intrusion in Norway on April 9, 1940, friends of the democracies went through a period of fevered optimism. There were those who publicly hailed the whole undertaking as "Hitler's big mistake," and among them were a good many military experts of established reputation. The landing of an English expeditionary force on the coast of Norway seemed a portent of victory. The optimism, of course, rested on Britain's unquestioned superiority on the seas and the routine assumptions about the functions and tactical scope of sea power.

It seemed as though the Nazi High Command, in selecting a theater of war which, under past conditions, would have been perfect for the operations of a vastly superior

fleet, had invited disaster. Here was the Scandinavian peninsula, within easy access of warships on two sides and, should
Sweden be drawn in as a battleground, also on the third
side. Here was an invasion that must sustain itself across a
sixty-mile water gap, importing its fuel, food, mechanized
units, and man-power reinforcements. Old-line military commentators looked over this picture and glibly estimated that
Hitler's forces, having entered by a surprise sally, had in fact
entered a trap. The peninsula would now be isolated by the
British fleet, and Hitler could only sacrifice his limited sea
units in a futile tussle with the British Navy, in a hopeless
attempt to keep open communications with his forces in
Norway.

Winston Churchill, then First Lord of the Admiralty,
summed up the illusions when he declared: "I consider
that Hitler's action in invading Norway and Scandinavia is
as great a strategic and political error as that committed by
Napoleon when he invaded Spain. . . . He will now have to
fight, if necessary, during the whole summer against powers
possessing vastly superior naval forces and able to transport
them to scenes of action more easily than he can."

And, indeed, there followed a series of seeming "victories"
to bolster such forecasts. In initial skirmishes the British fleet
did penetrate deeply into the Skagerrak and Kattegat channels, inflicting notable damage on Germany's small navy.
British sea power did reach across the North Sea to land
additional expeditionary troops on Norwegian coastal points
from Narvik to Stavanger. Momentarily Hitler seemed
bogged. By all the old rules he should have remained bogged.

Unfortunately those old rules had been invalidated by the
new element of air power. The British naval forces were
obliged to withdraw in haste from the Kattegat and then
from the Skagerrak, to escape brutal punishment from the

The author in a Farman–4 after his first solo flight at the School of
Military Aviation in Sevastopol, spring, 1915.

"Anyone looking at the photographs of the re-embarkation, showing the masses of troops assembled on the beaches, affording an ideal target for hours at a time, must realize that this embarkation would not have been possible unless the enemy had resigned all hope of air superiority at that point." —*Winston Churchill on the Dunkirk evacuation.*

Typical scene at an improvised airdrome in the conquest of Norway, showing arrival of a transport plane with troops and supplies.

skies by the Nazi air arm. Hitler, it became apparent, dominated the skies over these channels. The German air force soon turned them into Nazi corridors, through which men and supplies could flow by air and by sea almost without hindrance.

The British might continue to harass Nazi transport in night raids by naval units under cover of darkness. The bomber planes of the British Royal Air Force might make night visitations. But British fighter planes—the superb Spitfires and Hurricanes of the RAF—could not participate. The battle area lay much too far outside their range. Without the protection of fighters, bombers could not cut through Nazi air strength in the daytime, at the crucial spots.

Germany, therefore, had the right of way over the Skagerrak. By virtue of its aeronautical superiority at that place it enjoyed complete and practically uninterrupted communications with the invaded area across water despite its lack of sea power. Britain's ship-borne aircraft attempted to dispute this, but gave up the job as hopeless, after sacrificing planes and carriers. Students of aerial warfare saw in practice what they had foretold in the abstract: that the carrier-based planes would be like so many clay pigeons for land-based air power. Of necessity encumbered with special takeoff and landing paraphernalia for operation from their "floating bases," the carrier aircraft are no match in performance, type for type, against land-based aviation. Moreover, the carriers themselves offer a tempting expanse of deck as target for hostile aviation, and even if they are not sunk, successful hits can disrupt the elaborate deck machinery, trapping the planes on board and depriving those in the air of a base to return to.

Thus the world's largest, most experienced, and most courageous navy, even with the help of its own aviation arm,

failed utterly to block a hostile force in a narrow water area
—this against an enemy practically devoid of naval strength.
Here was something startlingly new in the history of naval
warfare, something that Admiral Mahan could not have
foreseen and fitted into his pattern of sea power.

The British "victories" in Narvik, Stavanger, and other
points likewise proved empty. They lasted only until Germany was able to bring its air power within striking distance
of the areas occupied by the British. In the past, since they
were all coastal points, they would have been adequately
shielded by their naval support. Now the Navy was ruled out
by the enemy's aerial fire. At the beginning of May the British evacuated Aandalsnes, Namsos, Trondheim, thus abandoning southern Norway to the Nazis. At the end of May
the last British foothold, Narvik in the far north, was evacuated; it had required that much additional time for Germany
to move its air bases close enough to make Narvik untenable
to surface forces on land and on sea.

In brief, the British withdrew in the very midst of the alleged "victories." They withdrew so suddenly that to the
uninitiated it looked like undue and inexplicable haste, raising bitter and pointed questions in the House of Commons.
Even before Narvik put a period to the whole enterprise, Sir
Samuel Hoare, then Secretary of State for Air, had explained
that British inferiority in the air over Norway was the crux
of the matter. Having failed, like most of his confreres, to
understand the full import of aviation, he had not foreseen
what he now fumblingly tried to explain.

"German air power is not invincible," he said. "Air power—
German or any other—is only invincible when there is not
sufficient counter-air power against it." This elementary truism marks England's awkward first steps toward an under-

standing of the principle that mastery of the skies is primary
under the new conditions of warfare.

"In this case," Sir Samuel Hoare went on, "we had no
fighter force to cope with the German bombers. . . . These
operations show that a strong air power must be met by a
stronger air power." The British were thus beginning to
sense that perhaps sea power is not a cure-all.

From point after point on the Norwegian coast, the British
had to withdraw to evade the scourge of the skies. Here, as
in the Skagerrak region, British bombers were ineffective because, without the protection of pursuit fighters, they could
not undertake bold daylight operations. A desperate experiment in massed daytime bombing without fighter convoys
proved futile and costly, with the attacking armada nearly
wiped out. Airplane carriers, here as at the Skagerrak,
showed themselves unequal to the duel with land-based airplanes and beat a retreat, after having paid a heavy toll for
the daring undertaking.

Many and complex factors entered into the clean-cut German triumph in Norway. But the basic factor was air supremacy. That, in turn, was decided by geographical distances. From the start, Hitler's Messerschmitts and Heinkels
and other fighters were able to cover the Skagerrak, which
the British Hurricanes and Spitfires, lacking the required
range, could not reach.

This does not imply that the Germans had been any better prepared in the matter of range. On the contrary, they
were as limited as all other nations in this respect and we
shall see how this lack of strategic vision imposed upon the
Nazis many failures and disruption of war timetables. But in
the Norwegian action Hitler simply had the geographical
advantage in that he could throw his air power into Norway

directly from Denmark. Once on Scandinavian soil, he unavoidably paused long enough to acquire the necessary bases
for carrying that air power farther. Through a chain of steppingstone bases—as a compensation for the lack of sustained
range—he brought his aviation to the rim of the North Sea.
As Nazi aviation came within striking distance, no alternative remained for the Allied troops but evacuation, usually
carried out with terrific losses in men and ships under the
hammering of overhead bombers. The sinking of British,
Norwegian, and French destroyers marked the withdrawal
from Namsos. British naval trawlers and other units were
sacrificed to air attacks in the evacuation of Trondheim.

Then the Germans extended their chain of air bases northward, toward the only town still held by the British: Narvik.
On May 4, dispatches from London were highly optimistic
about the chances of holding that extreme northern outpost.
Not only did Narvik seem far away from Hitler's *Luftwaffe,*
but, as one dispatch put it, "British sea power was holding a
dominant position." When this bubble, too, burst, the British in desperation risked important naval strength to achieve
a costly evacuation.

On May 31, the 4290-ton antiaircraft cruiser *Curlew* was
sunk in the first big clash between air and sea forces off Narvik. Eight days later, in the final evacuation, the 22,500-ton
aircraft carrier *Glorious* was lost, as well as the destroyers
*Acasta* and *Ardent,* a transport, tanker, and other craft. The
British Admiralty, it must be said, was not caught unawares
at Narvik. It deliberately jeopardized the *Glorious* and its
complement of planes to cover the evacuation, by opening
the flimsy umbrella of ship-borne fighters, well aware that
the vessel was highly vulnerable.

In the Norwegian campaign the British thus had the
first disillusioning taste of the superiority of aviation when

matched against naval surface forces. Eyewitnesses of some of the sinkings have reported the incredulous consternation with which seasoned naval men watched specks in the sky— German bombers—as they waited, almost helplessly, for the blows to descend. One plane, one bomb—and a destroyer costing several million dollars collapses and is swallowed up!

One cannot help pausing to speculate how differently the war might have gone if the British pursuits had possessed an effective radius of 600 miles, sufficient to bring them to the Norwegian arenas of action. Such a range, of course, was technically entirely possible.

From the day of the Norwegian invasion until now, the peninsula has been controlled by the Nazis, its every approach by water policed by German aviation. Except for surprise attacks on the hit-and-run principle, it has been inaccessible to British sea power notwithstanding its proximity to British naval bases and notwithstanding the virtual absence of German sea power.

---

### 3

THE HANDICAP of inadequate fighter-plane range cost Britain control of the Skagerrak. But this handicap vanished as soon as the struggle was transferred, in the spring of 1940, to the English Channel. Here the Spitfires and Hurricanes could function. Because of their qualitative edge, in fact, they could dispute and conquer the air over the Channel as well as a segment of Flanders against the numerically superior German aircraft. (There is, of course, a point at which overwhelming quantitative advantage will smother aviation with a strong advantage in performance; but the Nazis at the time did not have the necessary bases in the region to make their numerical superiority felt.) The "miracle of Dunkirk"

was essentially a miracle of modern aviation. Having thrown
a powerful canopy of air power across the Channel, the
British were enabled to withdraw hundreds of thousands of
troops from the European mainland.

There have been curious attempts to credit the dramatic
evacuation to the British Navy. Neither responsible Admiralty leaders nor British statesmen have made any such
claims, but muddled American "experts," more intent upon
saving face for sea power than facing facts for America, have
tried it. I have no intention of underestimating the British
Navy. But facts are facts. In the English Channel as in the
Skagerrak, the determining element was air control. The
Skagerrak belonged to the Germans and the Channel belonged to the English, by virtue of different air potentials.
That was why British surface ships could operate in the
Channel, though they had failed to do so in the Skagerrak.

True, the actual physical transfer of troops from shore to
shore was made in surface vessels like freighters, barges,
rowboats, and naval craft. In all, according to official accounts, 887 vessels took part during three to four days, res-
cuing 335,000 men. But to interpret this as an achievement
of sea power is to do violence to logic. Only one quarter of
the gathered transports, 222 vessels, were ships of the Royal
Navy, and the whole undertaking was in no sense an orderly
and planned naval operation. It was, rather, a random exo-
dus, in which naval ships had no essential advantage over
other vessels in the common task of providing bottoms for
ferrying troops across the Channel.

Photographs of the Dunkirk drama indicate clearly that
the retreat was, unavoidably, improvised, as evidenced by
the masses of humanity grouped haphazardly on the shore
lines. These troop masses and the bevy of miscellaneous vessels in the shallow waters would have made perfect targets

for German planes—the evacuation, that is to say, would
have been transformed into a shambles before it started—if
the air above had not been effectively held and patrolled
by the RAF.

The operation was made possible solely because a solid
and impregnable roof of air dominance was established by
the British and maintained during four epoch-making days.
Under that shield the action could proceed successfully despite its random character, despite the improvised transport
service. A tactical victory had been won exclusively by aviation, and was exploited below on the surface of land and
water.

When this significant contrast between the Skagerrak and
the English Channel was first made, early in June, 1940, in
an analysis which I prepared for the United Press, it was
met skeptically by orthodox military experts. The deductions
went against the grain of their accustomed ideas on the subject. Besides, Nazi air power then enjoyed such prestige that
any reference to British aerial superiority, even if limited
to a local area, sounded farfetched if not deliberately sensational.

Yet two weeks later a British naval man bold enough to
concede the obvious, and less hidebound than most American military writers, substantially confirmed that analysis. I
refer to Prime Minister Churchill, who had shared the illusions of his countrymen on the efficacy of sea power, as indicated in the passage from an earlier speech quoted above.
Now he declared that in the Dunkirk evacuation the primary
role was played by aviation. In effect he drew the same contrast between events in the Skagerrak and the Channel
which I have drawn in this chapter. Speaking on June 18,
1940, Mr. Churchill said:

"In the Skagerrak, because of the distance, we could give

SCOTLAND

150 MI.

STRIKING-COMBAT
RADIUS OF BRITISH
FIGHTERS

North

IRELAND

ENGLAND

STRIKING-COMBAT
RADIUS OF BRITISH
FIGHTERS

150 MI.

LONDON

Channel

DUNKIRK

English

EVACUATION OF
DUNKIRK UNDER
CANOPY OF
BRITISH FIGHTERS

FRANCE

BATTLE OF DUNKIRK

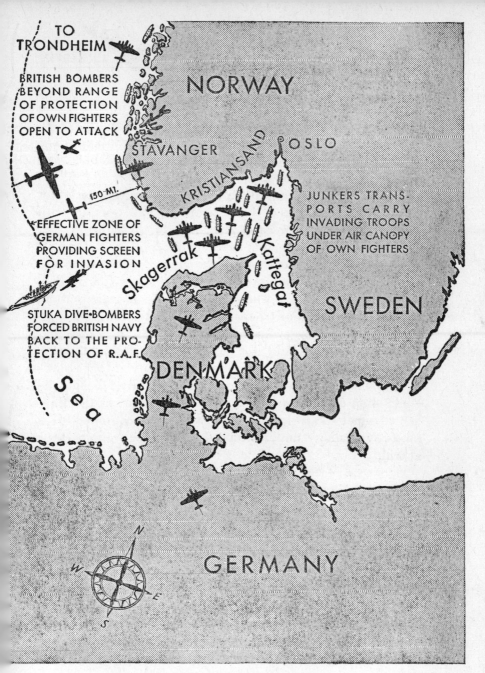

TO
TRONDHEIM

BRITISH BOMBERS
BEYOND RANGE
OF PROTECTION
OF OWN FIGHTERS
OPEN TO ATTACK

NORWAY

STAVANGER    KRISTIANSAND    OSLO

150 MI.

EFFECTIVE ZONE OF
GERMAN FIGHTERS
PROVIDING SCREEN
FOR INVASION

JUNKERS TRANS-
PORTS CARRY
INVADING TROOPS
UNDER AIR CANOPY
OF OWN FIGHTERS

Skagerrak

Kattegat

SWEDEN

STUKA DIVE-BOMBERS
FORCED BRITISH NAVY
BACK TO THE PRO-
TECTION OF R.A.F.

Sea

DENMARK

N

W        E

S

GERMANY

BATTLE OF SKAGERRAK

no air support to our surface ships and consequently, lying as we did close to the enemy's main air power in Norwegian waters, we were compelled to use only our submarines. We could not enforce a decisive blockade or interruption of the enemy's surface vessels. Our vessels took heavy toll but could not prevent the invasion.

"But in the Channel and in the North Sea, on the other hand, our forces, aided by submarines, will operate with close and effective air assistance. . . . In the fighting over Dunkirk, which was a sort of no-man's land, we undoubtedly gained a local mastery of the air and inflicted on the German air force losses on the scale of three or four to one. Anyone looking at the photographs of the re-embarkation, showing the masses of troops assembled on the beaches, affording an ideal target for hours at a time, must realize that this embarkation would not have been possible unless the enemy had resigned all hope of air superiority at that point."

Thus in the Skagerrak—"no air support" and hence the elimination of the Navy as a decisive element; in the English Channel—"local mastery of the air" and consequently a protective canopy under which surface vessels could move at will.

# CHAPTER III

# THE BATTLE OF BRITAIN

1

THE JUNKERS 87, better known as the Stuka dive-bomber, has registered on the popular imagination more deeply than any other airplane thus far exhibited in combat. Its swooping, plunging flight has a melodramatic quality that terrifies and sows panic. It suggests ominously the image of an eagle pouncing on its prey. With characteristic thoroughness the Germans equipped the plane with weirdly wailing sirens to heighten its capacity to inspire fear. Moreover, the Stuka revealed itself to the world, first in Poland and then in Western Europe, as the most conspicuous element in the fearsome *Blitzkrieg*, in a setting of demoralized armies, terrorized refugee populations, and swift collapse of nations.

All this tended to surround the Stuka with an aura of invincibility, of power far beyond the limited functions for which it had been specifically designed. Even some military experts were too dazzled by the achievements of the Stuka in its appropriate place—as a supporting type for surface forces—to recognize its shortcomings when removed from that place. It was hard for them to realize that the very airplane which made the largest contribution to the Nazi conquest of Europe proved worthless in the attempt to invade the British Isles. It is a fact nonetheless that unwarranted reliance on this and similar types of aircraft was one of the principal contributing causes of Germany's defeat in the Battle of Britain.

As the basic ingredient in Hitler's *Luftwaffe,* indeed, the
Stuka stands as a symbol of the essential lopsidedness of that
service in Germany. It refutes the puerile assumption in some
American circles that Germany is somehow "a natural air-
power nation" with a divine mandate to rule the world in
this air-power age.

The Stuka is an all-metal, low-wing monoplane of cantilever construction, with a top speed of 242 miles an hour—
130 miles slower, that is, than its destined nemesis, the British Spitfire fighter. Its entire armament consisted of two fixed
machine guns in the wings and one flexible machine gun in
the rear cockpit, but it was entirely unprotected by machine-
gun defensive fire power from underneath. When attacked
from the rear, the Stuka had only one light-caliber machine
gun to ward off the eight machine guns of the standard Royal
Air Force pursuits; attacked from below, it was wholly defenseless. Its striking radius was no more than 200 miles and
it usually carried one bomb of 1100 pounds and four of 100
pounds each.

Not until the Battle of Britain put this airplane to a genuine test were its limitations uncovered in action. The Stukas
performed brilliantly on the European continent; first, because in that theater of war they were able to exploit fully
the element of surprise and hence did not meet a real modern pursuit force in reasonably effective strength; and second, because there they did not operate as an air-power
weapon but essentially as an auxiliary of the army.

What is true of the Stuka is true, with exceptions, of German aviation as a whole. The chief task of Hitler's air arm in
the Low Countries and in France, as in Poland before that,
was to co-operate with the mechanized and motorized forces.
In the European campaigns Nazi aviation acted as a vital
member of a team. Naturally, it also cleared the skies of

hostile aircraft—pursuits engaging enemy planes in the air and dive-bombers destroying them on the ground through devastating blows on airdromes, fuel concentrations, aviation factories. Meeting little opposition in the air, however, its primary job was to clear the ground for armored columns and motorized troops, helping to cut the enemy armies into ribbons for piecemeal annihilation, demoralizing armed forces and civilian populations behind the main fronts, and cutting interior lines of communication.

The Nazi air arm was basically conceived to deliver short, swift, relatively light blows—the kind that stagger the adversary and leave him helpless against the immediate follow-up by plunging mechanized divisions and an avalanche of motorized infantry behind them. German military aviation, in other words, in the main had been planned and built for simultaneous, co-ordinated action with surface forces.

The *Luftwaffe* is a distinctly separate and autonomous military service, on a basis of full equality with the German Army and Navy. The Panzer divisions and other ground units do not have any aviation units attached to them permanently. Air support is given at places and in quantities found necessary by the High Command, and any of the available air strength is flexibly at the disposal of any commander of a local land, sea, or air action. Yet, because the main Nazi strategic conception rested on land operations, the German air power was primarily geared to answer the tactical demands of such operations. The strategy called for mechanized surface warfare, with the armies crossing only narrow water gaps, which could be readily done under the protection of the co-operating air force. That pattern dominated the creative minds entrusted with the designing of air equipment.

This, in the final analysis, resulted in a certain bias. While

the *Luftwaffe* was separate and entirely autonomous, the
emphasis on land operations affected the equipment in a
way that showed up unfavorably in all-out air action. The
kind of blows the *Luftwaffe* was capable of delivering, its
restricted effective range of operation, its inadequacies in
speed and fire power and protective armor, made it almost
useless when there were no land forces present *to exploit the
initial demoralization*—that is to say, in an unadulterated
aerial assault against an enemy air force and vast ground
targets. In short, German vision and audacity failed to go far
enough.

The invasion of Holland, Belgium, Luxembourg, and
France was undertaken almost simultaneously on May 10,
1940. Four days later the Dutch armies gave up resistance.
On May 16, Germany broke through the Maginot Line at
Sedan. By May 21, Hitler's war machine reached the English Channel at Abbeville; a week thereafter King Leopold
of Belgium surrendered.

There was a pause in the German onward sweep at the
Somme River, when the Nazi High Command seemed, to
most observers, to be debating whether to pursue the advantage southward toward Paris or to swing northward to
attack England. The British Isles squared themselves for the
latter contingency, in definite expectation of an attempted
invasion at that time. The people of the islands were sum-
moned to prepare to receive the enemy with pitchforks and
shotguns and improvised tank traps if necessary.

The pendulum of public sentiment swings hysterically
from extreme optimism to extreme pessimism and back again.
When Hitler launched the Norwegian campaign, observers
on the whole were sure that he was slated for disaster,
though it should have been obvious that no naval force could
block the German invasion of that country. Now, as the

Germans stopped for breath behind the Somme, the same observers, reflecting the unreasoned popular feelings, were no less sure that Hitler could go on into England. They were wrong again. Before the Nazis could dream of diverting their campaign from France into England, they had to reduce the Royal Air Force to impotence. And to accomplish that they had to bring the *Luftwaffe* within striking distance by building and equipping a string of air bases. They had to organize an uninterrupted line of supplies, fuel, spare parts, and all this under the continual harassment of British airplanes. Also, they had to provide the necessary transport for moving expeditionary forces across the Channel. Without such preparations the German machine could not keep rolling across the water gap.

Ignoring these elementary considerations, the prophets of doom, official and civilian, held the floor.

-------------------------- 2 --------------------------

ONLY THOSE equipped with a comprehension of the functions of aviation, uninhibited by traditional ideas on the subject of invasion, remained aloof from the general orgy of pessimism. Neither did they rest their hope of defeating the invasion, if it should be undertaken, upon the fragile reliance on surface impediments; the memory of Maginot and the Dutch dykes was too fresh in their minds. Those events on the mainland were not mysterious accidents, as old-fashioned experts reared on Marathon, Mahan, and the Marne assumed. To the aviation-minded they were corroborative evidence of totally new principles of conducting war—principles conditioned by the injection of a new weapon and, through that weapon, the opening of a vast new sphere for conquest.

No special merit attached to those who grasped the stra-

tegic picture while the orthodox strategists fumbled and
fussed over the "impending invasion." Men with a key de-
serve no special credit for opening locked doors which do
not yield to pushing. *Air power happens to have become the
key to modern strategy.*

I draw on my own files to illustrate the effectiveness of
that key. I do so without self-consciousness because I happen to know that my own record is typical of the thinking of
any number of other aviation men who have cleared the
cobwebs of traditional military ideas out of the chambers of
their minds.

In a press interview published on June 1, 1940—the moment when the Germans were supposedly considering the
variant of an immediate move against England, and when
military analysts and the public alike expected an invasion
—I was quoted as saying:

"There can be no immediate invasion of England, because, while Germany has complete mastery of the air over
Scandinavia, she does not have it over England by a long
shot. Defensively, Britain is greatly superior. Her Spitfire,
which I flew last summer, is a superior plane to any which
the Germans have in great numbers. Therefore, no invasion
of England is possible, until that superiority of the air over
England is achieved."

Hitler's troops marched into Paris on June 13. The Battle
of Britain did not begin until August 8. In the interval of
nearly two months, the Germans organized their intended
invasion of the British Isles. The process was unconcealed.
"Secret" invasions are the stuff of fiction: undertakings of
that magnitude cannot be successfully camouflaged.

When the terrifying Nazi engine of war rolled to the brim
of northern Denmark, it had no real trouble, as we have
seen, in making the sixty-mile jump across a water gap to

Norway. After the conquest of Western Europe it was confidently poised on the northwestern edge of the continent
for a jump into the British Isles. This time the water barrier
amounted to only twenty-odd miles; the impetus behind the
engine was infinitely more powerful; the stakes were vastly
higher; the German readiness to pay an exorbitant price for
victory was clearly unlimited. The fateful jump now seemed
even easier than at the Skagerrak.

Small wonder that things looked dark and ominous for
England. Outwardly, Hitler's boastful optimism on the eve
of his supreme undertaking, and the corresponding fears in
Britain and America, seemed fully justified. An invasion of
England was everywhere assumed inevitable. The desperate hope of defeating the invasion rested upon the inadequate coastal fortifications, hastily improvised local barriers,
and deployments of half-trained and untrained man power
around the periphery of the island. Chancellor Hitler had
made his "last-chance" speech demanding a negotiated peace
—or else! There were demonstrative preparations for the
move into England all along the European "invasion coast."
Yet on July 22 I found it possible to write:

"I remain convinced that there will be no such invasion—
unless Germany possesses a huge secret armada of new types
of fighting aircraft about which the outside world has as yet
no inkling."

I added:

"The effective invasion of the British Isles is impossible as
long as its defenders retain mastery of the skies over the
island and over the English Channel. The transporting and
landing of large numbers of troops are unthinkable without
the shield of a solid ceiling of air protection."

At the time the aerial battle for England got under way,
the British themselves were at bottom unconvinced of their

own defensive might in the skies. They had celebrated the "miracle" of Dunkirk without quite comprehending its significance in terms of principles of aerial warfare. The likelihood of a successful invasion was accepted by military spokesmen no less than by the civilian public. The most exalted military circles both in Britain and in the United States entertained no serious doubts that the bombardment of harbors, airdromes, and factories would be followed quickly by an actual invasion; that the damage inflicted on southeastern England would provide a bridgehead for invasion and that a traditional mile-by-mile struggle for territory would follow. By all the familiar rules of the war game as played in the past, such was the natural and predictable course.

But those rules had been made obsolete by the new weapon. Again air power provided the key to the strategic riddle. Interpreting the tragic event with the aid of "aeronautic orientation," I was able to write, on August 15:

"Those who have failed to adjust their tactical thinking to the realities of 1940 take it for granted that the old pattern of battle will be followed. Wherefore, they assume that the stage is now merely being set for the regulation war of mile-by-mile conquest.

"But soon it should become apparent that something new and unique is transpiring. The classic all-air battle foreseen by a few of the more imaginative tacticians, aware of the potentialities of the new weapon, has become a fact.

"When the question of mastery of the skies over the British Isles and their sea approaches is definitely answered by the course of the present 'aerial Trafalgar,' the other questions still remaining to be answered with the aid of armies and navies will be minor by contrast, from the strategic point of view."

Because of the general expectation of a quick decision I added that "this air engagement . . . may not be decided for weeks and even months." I might have been bolder and said "years."

In short, from the vantage point of air power the attack did not seem, as it did when viewed from the ground, a "prelude" to some grand offensive, even though that was the German intention. The aerial onslaught was not, I wrote, "a preliminary match," but "the main bout." Being acquainted with the aerial forces involved and their relative military characteristics, it seemed clear to me that regardless of the invaders' intentions, the engagement must resolve into a pure air struggle. In retrospect it has become more and more certain that the German High Command made approximately the same error as most old-style experts in judging the looming action. The Nazis, too, were viewing the undertaking as part of an army strategy. For a full month, from the opening attack on Channel shipping to the first big attack on London, the Germans themselves clung to the notion that they were fighting a preliminary engagement, until cumulative losses and frustrations convinced them that it was the main show. I shall examine the process of their enlightenment farther on.

By the end of 1940 a new panic of invasion fears spread through England. It is not unlikely that the panic was stimulated by Nazi propaganda and skillfully supported by military "feinting." It was taken seriously on this side of the Atlantic. As a matter of fact, a number of aviation spokesmen, lacking sufficient military background and failing to appreciate the qualitative advantage of the RAF, pictured the *Luftwaffe* as invincible and expressed their conviction that Hitler would establish the necessary bridgeheads across the Channel. Having learned in actual combat to respect speed and fire power, and being conscious of British superiority in these respects, I was able to write in a United Press analysis on January 2, 1941:

"The minimum precondition for an invasion is new German air equipment capable of brushing aside the Royal Air Force in open daylight combat, with the same ease that the British are brushing aside Italian aviation in the Mediterranean. Until we see convincing evidence that Hitler has developed such equipment, the invasion threat may be regarded as a psychological rather than a physical reality."

The invasion, of course, did not take place. Adolf Hitler's aerial *Blitzkrieg* against the British Isles came to naught. The damage visited on dozens of cities and towns, on harbors and communications, was tragic enough. But it did not suffice to knock out the sturdy Islanders or to make them really groggy.

-------------------- 3 --------------------

IT IS IMPORTANT to try to understand why Hitler met his first and most significant setback, because it has a lot to teach us about German aviation in particular and about air warfare in general. Let us, therefore, first look at the aerial weapons with which Britain and Germany confronted each other across the English Channel in the nerve-racked summer of 1940.

The Germans had a formidable numerical preponderance. Accurate figures cannot be ascertained, but an estimate of 3000 Nazi pursuit fighters against 1200 British fighters seems reasonable from the available information. Both sides, of course, possessed more, but these were roughly the units thrown into the battle over southeastern England. In bombers the Nazis' quantitative advantage was even greater. As

the attacker, moreover, Hitler had the advantages that ac-
crue to the initiator of an action.

We have considered at the beginning of this chapter the
Junkers 87 or Stuka, the basic element in Germany's aerial
equipment. The Nazis also used a twin-engined dive-bomber,
the Junkers 88, with a speed of 300 miles, a crew of four,
and a striking range somewhat more extended than the Stuka's 200 miles. It was equipped with three machine guns:
one flexible machine gun firing forward, operated by a gun-
ner in front of the pilot, and the other two in the rear, one
above and another below the fuselage. Slower by some
twenty-five miles, but otherwise very similar to the Junkers
88, with the same disposition of armament and crew, was the
horizontal bomber, the Heinkel III Mark V, also a twin-
engined, low-wing monoplane. There were in addition variants of the Dornier 17, or so-called "flying pencil," in the
array of level bombers.

The general military characteristics of all these twin-
engined bombers were similar. They were fast for their
time, but the speed had been bought at a serious cost in
fighting ability. The Germans had chiseled on range, load-
carrying capacity, armor, and armament for the sake of additional miles per hour. The effective radius with a full explosive load was only about 600 miles—about half of the British
range. The bomb capacity, varying with the range of operation, averaged one ton.

Aside from the limited orbit of operations with large loads
of explosives, the most serious handicap of the German
bombers was insufficient defensive fire power. In most instances they could meet an eight-gun assault from a British
pursuit with only one gun, making a hopeless ratio of eight
to one. Had Hitler's bombardment aviation carried adequate
protection, they might have succeeded in fighting their way

through to appointed targets, destroying the British air forces not only aloft but by destruction of ground facilities; thus, a reversal of the whole battle might have resulted.

The amazing shortsightedness of the Germans in respect to aircraft armament may be judged by the fact that even in the First World War bombers were often better armed than those on which Hitler relied for his conquest of England. Twenty years before the Nazis built their flocks of Stukas and Heinkels with only one gun against pursuing planes, twin machine guns were employed for protection against stern attacks. Since the extensive armament of British planes was public knowledge, exemplars having been exhibited at aviation shows, the vast German investment on virtually defenseless bombers betrays a basic lack of understanding of the tactical realities of pure aerial warfare and a stubborn faith in the efficacy of mere numbers.

The Third Reich, in brief, had built bombers which were beautiful flying machines, incorporating the latest aerodynamic knowledge. They were excellently constructed, of fine workmanship, and very well fitted out for the pilot's efficiency. But they failed to embody the reach, the necessary bomb wallop, armor, or gunfire, to assure the delivery of explosives to targets under true conditions of aerial conflict.

In the fighter class, the Messerschmitt 109, equipped with the Daimler Benz engines, developing 850 horsepower at the start of the war and gradually boosted to the present 2000 horsepower, was the standard type. The great mass of Messerschmitts at the beginning of the war did not have more than 330 miles an hour of speed, though the later models, with the improved power plant, could do better than 350 miles. The Messerschmitt 109 had six machine guns—four in the wings and two in the fuselage, firing through the propeller, with a consequent lowering of the rate of fire; a can-

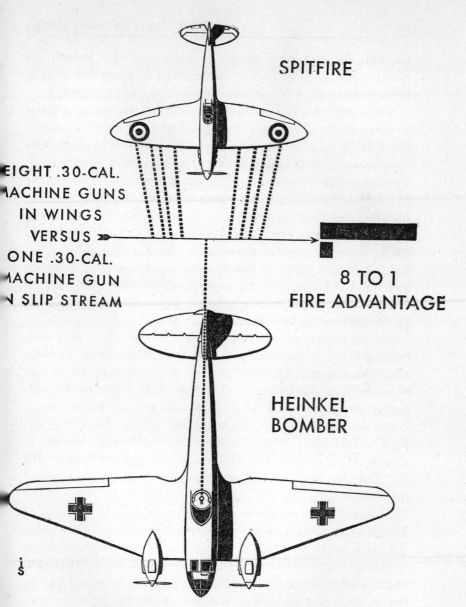

SPITFIRE

EIGHT .30-CAL.
MACHINE GUNS
IN WINGS
VERSUS
ONE .30-CAL.
MACHINE GUN
IN SLIP STREAM

8 TO 1
FIRE ADVANTAGE

HEINKEL
BOMBER

FIRE POWER OF RAF VERSUS *LUFTWAFFE*

non firing through the propeller shaft was installed later. The plane was all-metal and of low-wing cantilever construction.

The Messerschmitt 110 was a two-seater fighter, powered with two Daimler Benz engines. It had two fixed cannons in the fuselage and four fixed machine guns, all firing forward through the nose. Like all twin-engined planes, it could not maneuver as easily or as rapidly as the single-engined Messerschmitt 109. Furthermore, in addition to the fuselage it had two propeller disks and two engine nacelles; the damaging of any of these elements put the plane out of action, so that it presented a greater area of vulnerability. Occasionally the Nazi fighter force also employed the Heinkel 113, which had a good margin over the Messerschmitts in performance. The Germans claimed 380 miles per hour for this fighter. Theoretically it was the one fighter which might have come up to the Spitfire, but apparently because of some defect it never appeared in quantity. It should be noted that because these pursuits could shoot only or chiefly forward, they were handicapped for their important function in convoying bombers. Convoy fighters call for entirely different disposition of armament, and different military characteristics.

To the aviation specialist even such a brief summation of the German equipment discloses that the Nazi aerial armada was built principally for action against ground targets. He deduces that the Germans, counting on their great numerical advantage, planned to ignore and circumvent the enemy's air power. Contemptuous of the decisive value of quality, they assumed they could proceed directly at their goal, which was the demolition of surface objectives—the blasting of obstacles to the progress of surface troops, tanks, motorized equipment. The general trend of Marshal Göring's aviation, it thus appears, was to become a co-ordinated element for supporting surface operations. Adequate for such undertakings, his air force revealed its fundamental weakness when called upon to tackle pure aerial operations in the face of a powerful aerial foe. Nazi aviation simply was not geared for battling its way through hostile aircraft, carrying out its job over a target, and battling its way back again. Yet this is precisely the fighting quality it needed for the conquest of the skies over Britain. It had evidently counted on destroying the enemy's aviation on the ground—as in Poland and France—rather than on grappling with it in the skies.

British aviation, while numerically weak, had come closer to achieving the military characteristics of true air power. In scale these qualities may have been primitive, but the underlying conceptions were correct. British bombers sacrificed speed for defensive armament, range, and bomb load, which is a justifiable exchange. Since bombers cannot get away from fighters anyhow, speed becomes a secondary consideration. RAF bombers were equipped with rear turrets, housing two and four machine guns, and were able to fire them backwards through an unobstructed arc of 180 degrees. This wide coverage was attained by installing the turret in the extreme end of the fuselage. The front turret likewise had two or four machine guns, firing forward. The Wellington bomber, for instance, had an effective radius of 1200 miles with a substantial cargo of bombs, and was protected by both rear and front power-operated turrets. In general it is fair to say that the British bombardment aircraft, possessing better range, armament, and bomb load than the German, were therefore superior. This more than made up for an average inferiority of about fifty miles an hour in speed. These aircraft did not figure in the early stages of the Battle of Britain. In time, however, the British

realized that the battle for England must be fought over
Germany, and bombing planes intensified their counteroffensive on the enemy's home grounds.

The backbone of the British fighter command was the
Spitfire, which was and remains the most effective single-
engined fighter in the world. It had a speed of 370 miles
which has since then been raised to over 400 miles. Its eight
machine guns, installed in the wings, were free-firing. In
speed, armor, fire power, and disposition of guns, it had the
edge on the Messerschmitts. The Hurricane, second in importance in the fighter command, was a somewhat larger
plane, with a top speed of only 335 miles, but very maneuverable. (The present Hurricane is powered with a Napier
engine, has a speed of 400 m.p.h. and carries four 20-mm.
cannon or twelve machine guns.) In the beginning the British defenders also used the Boulton-Paul Defiant, a two-
seater pursuit fighter with a speed of about 300 miles, but
the Germans soon discovered its deficiency in protective
armament from below and forced the RAF to restrict its use
to night fighting. Throughout, it can be seen, the British Air
Force possessed greater fire power than its adversary.

A fair qualitative ratio of Nazi and British fighting aircraft in the Battle of Britain is provided by the Spitfire and
the Messerschmitt, and the advantage in the confrontation
indisputably favored the British. The Spitfire had a margin
of twenty-five miles an hour in speed. Though it did not at
that time have a cannon, it had two more machine guns—
none of them handicapped by synchronization through the
propeller—and hence possessing a greater volume of fire.
Flying qualities were approximately the same, with a slight
edge for the British, since the Spitfire was better than the
Messerschmitt at stalling speeds and maneuvering.

The amazement and terror evoked by the *Blitzkrieg* tri-

umphs in Europe fortified the myth of German aviation
supremacy. The less discriminating the observer—even if he
happened to be an aviator himself—the more shrill he became in glorifying the alleged genius of the Nazis in the
science of military aeronautics. In a few instances this un-
restrained and uncritical admiration for German aviation
served to warp the whole outlook of Americans on the world
we live in. Certain in their own minds and nerves that Hitler's *Luftwaffe* was invincible, they yearned to make terms
with the inevitable and the preordained; they could not and
would not concede even the possibility of a defeat of Germany.

The Battle of Britain, however, cannot be explained unless
and until we acknowledge the qualitative superiority of British air power for the specific task of seizing and holding the
skies.

------------------------------ 4 ------------------------------

THE BATTLE OF BRITAIN, a pamphlet summing up the official
British Air Ministry record covering the period of August 8
to October 31, 1940, distinguishes four phases in that epochal
struggle:

The first, from August 8 to August 18, was marked by a
concentrated all-out attack on Channel convoys, the southeastern coastline and harbors of England and the airdromes
located in that area.

In the second, from August 19 to September 5, the aerial
fire of Germany was directed against inland fighter airdromes.

The third phase, from September 6 to October 5, compassed the mighty attack on London, seat of the government and heart of the British Empire.

Finally, in the fourth phase, which the Air Ministry dates

as October 6–31 but which has really continued since then, the *Luftwaffe* has been attacking the entire country in night flights in a diversified action against all vital objectives.

Behind this matter-of-fact recapitulation of the campaign lies a clear record, for those who can discern it, of Nazi aerial failure. The Air Ministry account at several points indicates frank bafflement at the shifting of the Nazi strategy in these various stages. Without apparent or sufficient cause, the conflict kept entering a new phase of operation without having brought the preceding phase to a conclusion. But by now we have enough detailed information from official and unofficial sources to permit a consistent analysis of what happened.

I am convinced that the failure of the first all-out effort to capture the southeast segment of English sky astonished and shocked the Germans. Whatever misgivings they may have entertained on the further developments, they gambled optimistically on that initial success. The startling loss of this gamble, throwing doubt on their fundamental strategic ideas, left the Nazis as bewildered as the French had been by the crumbling of their defensive Maginot Line strategy. The bewilderment was merely deepened by the miscarrying of the second stage of the undertaking. Far from adhering to a rigid program or schedule, as some have supposed, the German High Command was forced to improvise in an almost panicky spirit as it went along.

Curiously, it may well have been the British success at Dunkirk which encouraged Hitler and his associates in their self-assured expectation of easy access to England. It had been possible for the Royal Air Force, under exceedingly unfavorable conditions, to achieve a local if temporary air mastery over a corridor of Channel stretching from Dunkirk to England. The Nazis consequently estimated that they could do the same, and even more easily.

The bridgehead which they sought on the British side of the water barrier lay within easy reach of their new and well-supplied chain of French, Belgian, and Dutch bases. They had overwhelming numerical strength in the air and were keyed up to a pitch of exceptional self-confidence by their remarkable record of easy conquests. As for the one setback at Dunkirk, they preferred to credit that to extraneous circumstances—such as their lack of prepared bases and the resultant inability to send into combat a sufficient number of aircraft—rather than to the intrinsic superiority of British air equipment.

The *Luftwaffe* attacked the coast from Weymouth to the Thames Estuary, pounding Portland, the Isle of Wight, Portsmouth, Dover, Norwich, and striking at the fighter airdromes in the area—at Dover, Hawkinge, Middle Wallop, Biggin Hill, even as far as Croydon. The tactical objective was to seize local air domination and under its cover to land a great expeditionary force.

Göring threw his Stukas, Dorniers, Junkers, Heinkels, and Messerschmitts into the enterprise unsparingly. The fact that he lost at least 697 aircraft in the first ten days is a measure of the fury and profligacy of the onslaught. He was willing to pay any price for that invasion bridgehead and counted on overwhelming numbers to make up the differential in aviation performance. His calculations proved wrong. It is true that the British pilots, because of their numerical weakness, were overworked, being obliged to fly and fight from dawn to dusk and beyond. But in the end it became apparent that numbers without adequate quality are well-nigh worthless against a determined opponent properly equipped.

Notwithstanding initial failure, the *Luftwaffe* continued to fight an advance action for the ground forces waiting on the other side of the Channel. When Messerschmitts showed themselves unable to eliminate the British Spitfires and Hurricanes in the air, the attackers evidently decided to eliminate them on the ground, in their airdromes. They assumed—mistakenly, as they soon learned—that the RAF fighter command, being chiefly concerned with the defense of the coastline, would not only be concentrated within easy reach, but that as a result the airdromes would be packed tight with aircraft.

But the RAF had profited from the experience of the Polish and the French airmen. Instead of bunching their planes at known spots where the enemy could attack them by surprise, the British wisely dispersed them in the environs of the bases, singly and often under camouflage.

Some airdromes were, in fact, quickly put out of action in the second phase of the battle. But the birds had flown these nests. Before long the RAF was locating and intercepting the invading aircraft and cutting heavily into its strength. The German bombers were like so many clay pigeons for British aerial gunners, and few of them ever reached their targets. In this second phase the Nazis lost at least 562 aircraft at a cost of only 119 to the British.

Failure to defeat the British fighter command meant failure to accomplish the preliminary objective: the capture of aerial control as a prelude to invasion by mechanized forces. It meant that the German invasion program was doomed. Hitler's High Command had planned a combined land, sea, and air lightning stroke against the island, analogous to the stroke against Norway and thereafter broadened into a campaign analogous to those on the mainland. This did not materialize. Instead the Germans unexpectedly faced a prolonged all-air struggle, for which they were neither equipped physically nor prepared psychologically. An all-air struggle it has remained throughout, with the armies and navies on both sides, rather to their own surprise and chagrin, reduced to the role of impotent spectators.

The huge German mechanized forces were immobilized on the continental side of the Channel, the British troops on the island remained virtually idle, and the naval contingents on both sides played an accessory role in this particular drama. The stage was the air, and ground services of necessity had to remain in the wings. Had the land and sea forces on both sides been ten times bigger—or only one tenth as big—it would have had no effect on the duel for mastery of the skies, fought exclusively in the skies.

The German engine of war could not leap over the narrow waterway for the same reason that it could not prevent the evacuation from Dunkirk: the Royal Air Force was superior. That one fact tripped up Nazi plans and, for all we know, changed the course of human history. There have been confusing claims and counterclaims. But no one can successfully dispute the elementary and now obvious fact that Britain's qualitative aviation advantage headed off the invasion. That advantage in quality, small as it may appear in relation to the huge size of the German air armadas, nevertheless canceled out Hitler's numerical superiority.

"Never in the field of human conflict," in Churchill's immortal phrase, "was so much owed by so many to so few." It underscores a point to which I shall have occasion to return in later pages: the critical importance of quality in air equipment and, by the same logic, the danger of obsession with numbers in planning for American security.

As the shortcomings of these aircraft became manifest, almost from the first day, the Germans kept shifting their formations, increasing and rearranging their pursuit convoys, desperately seeking to convert their numerical strength into tactical values. The obvious lack of clarity and sureness in the tactics during these critical days and in the subsequent phases of the battle may justly be taken as proof that the Germans were as backward in their air strategy as in their air equipment; the two things go together as a matter of course. But no matter how the invading planes jockeyed, the faster, deadlier British craft beat them to the punch. The Germans lacked the appropriate equipment and the attempt to use makeshift equipment proved costly and useless.

The failure of the second phase of the battle underlined the bankruptcy of Germany's aerial conceptions. For the first time, perhaps, the High Command was obliged to concede that there was some logic to the contentions of aeronautical "visionaries" who had foreseen and foretold an all-air war in which the other services would be supernumeraries. At that point, it may be surmised, the mirage of a simultaneous land, sea, and air campaign began to evaporate. The realization probably dawned in Germany's army minds that joint movement on two levels, the surface and the air above it, is impossible when the upper level is in hostile hands—that mastery of the air *must come first*. The air component must establish its authority, or at least neutralize the opposing air force, before the surface components can come into full play. The Germans must have grasped this principle in its particularly clear application to a water area.

In any case, it is apparent that Germany's air force was finally released, at that point in the Battle of Britain, to fight on its own, simply and solely as air power. It was given a free hand to act as a genuine and independent strategic arm, not merely as an advance agent of the army.

Marshal Göring's *Luftwaffe* began its new phase of activity with an attempt to destroy London. This harked back to textbook strategy of the army type, which had always regarded the capture of the enemy's capital as a first goal.

# ONE REASON WHY THE *LUFTWAFFE* FAILED OVER BRITAIN.
Inadequate fire power of its bombers was a major contributing factor.

ACME

Stuka dive-bomber. Its only defense against stern attack is a single .30-caliber machine gun on top of the fuselage.

ACME

Heinkel bomber accompanied by Messerschmitt. Inadequate fire power of the Heinkel is apparent; note the .30-caliber machine guns—one protruding behind the windshield on top of the fuselage, another below the fuselage, and the third in the nose, firing forward.

INTERNATIONAL NEWS PHOTO

French plane in World War I. Twin machine guns used for rear protection indicates early recognition of fire power—a lesson the Germans failed to learn.

BRITISH COMBINE

British armament. Typical four-gun power-driven turret, forming major defense of British bombers; installed to enable unobstructed fire rearward.

# THE ATTACKERS

ACME

**Messerschmitt 109 Fighter**

ASSOCIATED PRESS

**Germany's Dornier D–215 Bomber**

The Hurricane Fighter

The Spitfire Fighter

These are the fighters that denied the skies of England to the Nazis.
Note the emplacements for eight machine guns in the leading edge of
the Spitfire.

Typical scene of bombing damage in the city of London. The war prove
that such haphazard morale bombing is ineffective.

Under modern conditions, of course, the capital is not as vital an objective as in the past; modern communications and other technical advances now enable a government to function from almost any place. The attack also fitted into General Douhet's aerial doctrine, prescribing an attack on an important and sentimental or emotional target with a view to coaxing the entire defensive aviation into action and forcing it to accept combat. London was certainly that sort of target. But the Douhet doctrine holds good only when the attacker has sufficient integrated combat power. Hitler's aviation decidedly did not possess this.

And so inevitably the assault on London resulted in a wholesale slaughter of the attacking German aircraft.

There are certain psychological phenomena connected with the use of vast numerical superiority in any military sphere which now showed up for the first time in the sphere of air conflict. The attacker, depending on sheer weight of his man power or equipment, is naturally prepared to sacrifice a lot of it to attain his objective. Yet, when his losses in life and material begin to assume huge proportions, with a decision seemingly as far off as ever, his morale begins to crack. The panicky feeling grows upon him that his forces are melting away while the objective remains invincible. Frequently in the past this psychological factor has stampeded generals and admirals into calling off an offensive on the very threshold of a likely victory.

There is reason to suspect that this element of panic came into play on the German side as the attack on London proceeded. In addition, the Germans were up against another psychological factor. While keenly and desperately aware of their own huge losses, they had no way of knowing the extent of British losses or their effect on British stamina. The RAF seemed unbeatable. Many battles in the past were affected by the commander's inability to learn the magnitude of the damage imposed on the enemy in comparison with his own losses.

For a while the Nazis tried to maintain their morale by concealing the magnitude of their losses from the *Luftwaffe* personnel. For instance, they ordered pilots to land at airdromes other than those from which they had taken off, so that they would be unable to check up on the casualties. But the mounting total of destruction to their own forces finally undermined the self-confidence of the leaders and the attack on London was called off.

There is strong reason to suppose that the all-out assault on the British capital, if it had been kept up a few weeks longer, might finally have succeeded. In the long run overwhelming mass and continuity of action have their effect. The RAF pilots were brave and skilled, but relatively few and overworked beyond human endurance. It is possible that they might not have held out another thirty days' unrelieved bombardment. But Marshal Göring saw his aerial armada and his men being whittled down almost to the point of elimination, while he had no way of estimating the seriousness of the situation on the enemy's side. It is not at all out of the question that he stopped the offensive just in time to nullify his whole investment.

Having learned the tragic effect of the inferiority of their aviation the hard way, the Nazis refrained from further bold bombardment of predetermined targets protected by concentrated aerial forces. Instead they decided to exploit the element of surprise. They began to scatter their strength by attacking a great variety of targets over a huge area. Their efforts resolved into a haphazard attempt at aerial blockade of the British Isles. In this they again disclosed their confusion. They should have known in advance that successful blockade—whether on the surface or in the air—cannot be enforced until the opposing force is neutralized or eliminated. They could do neither to the RAF.

Shortness of range automatically safeguarded important industrial objectives farther north and counted out the Stukas except in the southeast of the island. A few experiments in daylight bombing ended disastrously for the Germans. Hitler's planes did not possess the combat power for bold daylight operations or the bomb capacity to make them decisive.

Thus the Germans were restricted to the comparatively ineffectual night hours. The destruction accomplished in night raids from the very high altitudes may be enormous; surely there is no call to minimize the total death and property destruction and dislocation of everyday existence achieved by this method. But in raiding under the veil of darkness the aim is necessarily haphazard, and the type of methodical, planned annihilation of specific military and morale targets essential for victory is made difficult if not impossible. The hope of cracking British morale by means of such hit-and-miss tactics soon faded.

In desperation Marshal Göring resorted to a trick which we had used back in the First World War. In 1917 the German Navy was pressing its entry into the Gulf of Riga. The Germans brought in so many pursuits that our bombers were easily intercepted and destroyed. Under these circumstances the tasks of the bombers reverted to the pursuits. Equipped with extra gas tanks and bomb racks, we attacked shore fortifications and the German Navy, only to find that we lacked the striking power to do real damage. Twenty-three years later the Germans, at this stage in the Battle of Britain, similarly converted their pursuits into bombers.

They were no more successful than we had been. The improvised bombers could deliver only weak explosive loads, which are useful in co-operative action with land forces, but were inadequate for strategic demolition. Approaching in daylight, they were soon forced into combat, whereupon they had to unload their bombs willy-nilly and revert into pursuits. Outclassed, they were doomed as soon as overtaken. The expedient was abandoned and nothing remained to the Germans but more night raids—an operation which has become increasingly hazardous as countermeasures such as radio detection of night fighters have progressed.

From August 8 to October 31, the Germans lost 2375 aircraft in England in daylight. The Air Ministry figure, clearly on the modest side, does not include planes destroyed in night fighting, aircraft damaged, and the large number which unquestionably succumbed over the Channel and beyond it on their retreat from England. In a single day, on September 15, the *Luftwaffe* left 185 of its planes in England. This immense investment had killed some thousands of Englishmen, wrecked a vast amount of British property, destroyed some RAF planes and pilots. But strategically it had got Hitler nothing.

Seven years of Nazi concentration on aerial preparedness thus ended in fiasco. Only the impressiveness of the preceding European victories blurred this fact. A *Luftwaffe* which proved well suited to act with the Army and the Navy showed up as helpless in unadulterated air combat.

The Nazis, it is quite true, were far ahead of the rest of the world in visualizing the possibilities of military aeronautics. Their imaginative daring in this branch of modern warfare, more than any other single factor, gave them the jump on the rest of Europe. But everything is relative. They fell short of the wholly self-sufficient air power needed for the conquest of the skies. German vision and daring did not go far enough. It took the Battle of Britain to prove that Hitler, Göring, and their associates, too, had not carried their thinking on military aviation to its logical conclusions.

In the democracies the full growth of air power had been retarded by the inertia and the mental timidity of old-line naval and army leaders with whom the final decisions rested. It was an aspect, one might say, of general social conservatism.

These brakes on air development did not exist in Germany, where the revolutionary Nazi mentality broke through traditional restraints. The terms of the Versailles Treaty, in forbidding the expansion of armed forces, and the circumstance that Germany had no real navy, almost automatically turned the German mind toward the new weapon and its potentialities. It is often overlooked that the development of military aeronautics in Germany predates the ascension of Hitler to power. The Germans have always been successful in taking over the inventions of other nations and utilizing them to an extent outdistancing the inventors' imagination. This was true of the submarine in the First World War and it was even more true of the airplane in the long period of the incubation of the Second World War.

The Nazis, kicking over all traditional notions, new to political power and hence with less *to unlearn,* broke through traditional barriers. Broke through—but stopped far short of an air power as fully self-contained in its actions in the air as navies used to be in their actions on the seas. The claims of Germany's supreme aerial destiny—even if reiterated endlessly by an aviation hero—are nonsensical. In fact, an excellent case could be made for the opposite claim—that Germany is too deeply bound in an army psychology ever to become the world's leading air-power nation. The mere fact that the Germans have a separate air force—the *Luftwaffe—*

does not mean that the leaders of that air force necessarily have grasped the full implications of the military instrument in their hands.

However that may be, this much is certain: Germany has made as many aviation blunders as other countries. Only the circumstance that it began to build military aircraft sooner —partly through necessity rather than by choice—and did so on a larger scale than other countries gave it a temporary semblance of aviation leadership.

---

5

---

ON THE basis of the Battle of Britain, a good many military students in America jumped to the rash conclusion that air power alone cannot achieve a definitive victory over an enemy. This is not only erroneous but, to the extent that it may influence our American aviation ideas and war strategies, also mischievous.

The fact that the Germans failed to knock out England from the air decidedly does not mean that knockouts from the air are impossible. It means only that Germany was not properly prepared to do it. One might as reasonably argue that because some armies have failed to do so, armies in general cannot score a decision. In claiming that air power can, under certain circumstances, win a battle or a war, we necessarily assume that the appropriate strategy, tactics, and weapons for that purpose are available.

German failure over England was not a failure of air power but of German vision—a failure to exploit fully potentialities of the new weapon already in existence. As I have indicated sketchily in the first chapter, aviation is already technically capable of concentrated destruction to force a decision, even though not one of the belligerents has as yet used those capabilities to the full.

I have referred to the German four-engined Condor in discussing the expanding horizons of aviation range. In flying from Berlin to New York nonstop, the Condor had to carry about 20,000 pounds of gas. The same type of plane, in a flight from the French coast to London and back, would need only about 5000 pounds of fuel. The difference of some 15,000 pounds in that Condor designed as a short-range bomber might have been used to provide adequate defensive fire power, with enough margin to spare for a load of explosives that might have worked as much havoc with a single salvo as is now accomplished by ten Stuka dive-bombers or five mediumweight horizontal bombers of the sort commonly used in the Battle of Britain. Hitler, had he foreseen the need, could have possessed an armada of such bombers. If, in addition, these bombers had been suitably protected by defensive armament, the whole story would have been quite different.

As a matter of fact, all the belligerents have fallen far short of utilizing the full possibilities of destruction from the skies. Germany has failed in this as completely as other nations, and the failure to conquer the British Isles with the *Luftwaffe* is the irrefutable proof.

We may fairly say that for more than a year Germany was stabbing at the British lion with a penknife, hoping to bleed it to death. Of course, even a penknife sometimes can finish off a lion if it happens by lucky accident to sever the jugular vein. The Nazis, that is to say, might conceivably have landed a few lucky blows that would have prostrated aviation or cut some other vital artery. But that does not alter the fundamental fact that the *Luftwaffe* was unsuited for the all-air job—and did not know this until too late.

Just as the scientist learns from an unsuccessful experiment how to achieve success in the next try, so the Battle of Britain has given aerial strategists proof that nations can be wrecked and forced to surrender from the air alone. In the very shortcomings of Nazi equipment for such an enterprise they can see clear indications of the future development of equipment to match the tactical task. The student of aerial warfare can discern the nature of the German errors and, therefore, how they can be avoided and how to score a decision through air power. Those errors are as follows:

1. *The attempted strategic bombardment of a nation without sufficient combat power to eliminate or neutralize the opposing air power.* If German bombers, instead of carrying three single machine guns, had been equipped with turrets like the British bombers, each housing four machine guns, Hitler would have been spared his four-to-one ratio of losses. A great many more British planes would have been shot down, and this drain on the RAF might easily have given Germany mastery of the English skies.

2. *A mistaken choice of the vital target.* Those thousands of planes and pilots invested in striking at London might have been expended more intelligently against key industrial centers; against production units of the aviation industry, especially those related to the fighter command, such as the Rolls-Royce engine plants as well as Spitfire and Hurricane plants; and, in general, against the ground potentials of the air force. That would have amounted to a double-barreled attack on the opposing air power, eliminating it simultaneously in the air and on the ground.

3. *Inadequate bombing power, in relation to the load-carrying capacity of aircraft at that time.*

4. *Lack of continuity of action.* The bombing procedure, as we have seen, was frequently interrupted due to the lack

of a clear strategic picture and requisite tactical preparations. The interruptions obviously gave the British air forces and people invaluable breathing spells for repairing damage, replenishing energies, and utilizing the experience for more efficient resistance in the next stage.

In fine, the Germans used the wrong kind of air force, in the wrong way, in the wrong place.

We must assume that lessons of the Battle of Britain have not been lost upon the Germans and that they are putting all their skills and energies behind a far-reaching revision of their *Luftwaffe* to make it a real instrument of air power. Moreover, that revision, we must assume, compasses also the possibilities of transoceanic air struggle with the United States. After all, the Battle of the U.S.A., if and when it comes, will in general follow the experience of the Battle of Britain, since the difference is only one of scale.

# CHAPTER IV

# THE MEDITERRANEAN AND THE *BISMARCK*

1

WITH THE Battle of Britain stalemated by the qualitative advantage of the Royal Air Force, the center of gravity of the conflict shifted to the Mediterranean Sea. Here lay the life line of the British Empire and the chief arena over which British sea power had for generations exercised domination.

Hitler had not succeeded in crushing England, the head of the enemy, though he had left it aching and bloody. He had little alternative but to turn against the most vital portion of the enemy's body, the Mediterranean area. Possessing no navy that he could set into motion against the British Navy—and sufficiently convinced that Italian military prowess was no match for the Britons—his aim, inevitably, was to obtain air control in the Mediterranean basin, thus making it untenable for the British Navy.

The role of aviation in the Mediterranean theater of war was obscured at the outset by the dismal inferiority of Italy's air power. For many months the British Mediterranean fleet could lord it over that great body of water, practically ignoring Benito Mussolini's aircraft. The fact alone that Italian battleships hugged their bases, seeking the protection of coastal guns, amounted to an admission of aerial impotence. Had Italy possessed a genuine air force, its fleet units could have operated under a roof of air power at least in sectors of the Mediterranean beyond the reach of land-based RAF

74

fighters. But even Britain's naval aviation, its "portable umbrella" of ship-based airplanes, usually sufficed to cancel out Italy's air force.

During the Ethiopian crisis of 1935, Italy, ironically enough, had forced Britain to withdraw its massed naval might in the Mediterranean by merely brandishing its air arm. Now it developed that the gesture might have been bluff, perhaps an unconscious bluff, since the Italians probably were unaware of their inability to carry out the threat. In any case, the first real encounter disclosed that Italian air power had no punch.

Italian aviation was in large part constructed with inferior basic materials, deficient in speed, and inadequate in striking force. But along with obsolescent types, it also counted some fairly modern all-metal craft which might have been expected to make a good showing. Thus, while its aircraft was on the whole inferior to Britain's, the trouble with Fascist air power was not limited to the quality factor. It apparently extended to the personnel, to the fighting morale of Italian airmen, and to their aerial strategy. Technical deficiencies would have explained disproportionate losses in combat. They could not explain the more serious fact that Mussolini's aviation did not show up at all at points where it could logically be expected to challenge the enemy. At times—particularly in the Albanian campaign against the Greeks—it was almost as if Italian air power had gone on a "sit-down strike." All of this attested basic disorganization.

Whatever the story behind Italy's impotence in aviation, it gave some overeager experts of an older tactical vintage, in America and other neutral countries, the illusion that sea power could afford to ignore air power. In November, 1940, they saw British battleships, in defiance of Fascist aircraft, enter the Gulf of Taranto and, with the aid of torpedo-carry-

ing naval planes, sink and cripple an array of Italian battleships. A month later they saw Vice-Admiral Cunningham's
fleet attack coastal points in the Strait of Otranto, again
scorning the threat of Fascist air power. Above all, they saw
British naval might interrupting the flow of Italian materials
and men to Africa, leaving General Graziani's forces bogged
down there.

This growing illusion that at last a naval force had counted
out an air force was deepened by the important part which
the British fleet played in supporting General Wavell's sensational drive from western Egypt to a point well beyond
Benghazi. The entire action took place along the North African coast, wholly within range of naval guns. This fact was
exploited in the fullest measure. Naval units helped to clear
the road for Wavell's army and provided a continuing shield
of fire. In effect we had an old-style tactical undertaking, in
which fleet and ground forces were co-ordinated for a slow,
steady, inexorable advance. The naval units operated under
the protection of ship-borne aircraft, which in most cases
served well enough to counter Italy's aviation.

But the entry of German air power on the scene demolished the illusion of sea power triumphant. In January, 1941,
Hitler's aviation struck unexpectedly from Sicily. In a few
days it inflicted more damage on Malta and on the British
fleet than the Italian force had inflicted in half a year.

Sympathy for the British in that encounter in the Strait
of Sicily blinded many observers to the fact that in the first
genuine encounter between air and sea forces in the Mediterranean Hitler's *Luftwaffe* won out. The behavior of the
men of the British fleet under the severe air attack was magnificent. No one can conceivably attribute the result to any
fault of the Navy. Nevertheless, the battle off Sicily, on January 10, 1941, gave the world a practical demonstration of the

effectiveness of a well-organized air force with the best equipment and first-rate morale at its disposal, when pitted against even the best and the bravest naval adversary.

The cruiser *Southampton* was sent to the bottom. The destroyer *Gallant* and the aircraft carrier *Illustrious* were badly crippled. The *Illustrious* was able to limp to Malta under the protection of pursuits based on that island. But Malta, once a redoubtable fortress, now could not offer sanctuary to the wounded ship, which was spirited away to Alexandria. It had suffered such damage that it had to be removed for major repairs beyond the reach of the enemy and finally showed up at Norfolk, Virginia, U. S. A.

Only a handful of German planes, using bombs of no more than 1100 pounds, were used in the Sicilian encounter, yet they visited a considerable total of damage on the British vessels. Had the Germans been able to mass larger aerial strength, with heavier bombs, few of those vessels could have survived. Though the cumulative physical losses were comparatively modest, the engagement, all the same, marked a critical stage in the Mediterranean conflict. It shook, if it did not end, the myth of British control of that sea. At the time and in the teeming war books since then, the Sicilian action has been reported, if at all, as a minor incident. In a sense, nevertheless, it may be counted as one of the most significant encounters of the Mediterranean campaign. That was where the aircraft carriers of the British Navy in the Mediterranean first grew bomb shy in relation to enemy aviation—a shyness which manifested itself in the African campaign thereafter and at Crete four months later. There again the Germans tested their aerial advantage and found it valid. The sensational Axis comeback in Libya soon afterward and the German campaign in Greece were both affected by the small but meaningful Sicilian battle.

No matter how that engagement is viewed, the fundamental fact emerges that a comparatively small land-based
aerial force had outclassed a comparatively important naval
force; this despite the fact that the naval units were protected by their most modern accessory: the fleet air arm.

-------------------------------- 2 --------------------------------

ONE OF the most dramatic naval engagements in the Mediterranean occurred off Cape Matapan in the Ionian Sea, on
March 28, 1941. British naval squadrons cornered and virtually annihilated a large part of the Italian fleet; five Italian
warships were sunk and several others were unaccounted for.
The fleet air arm and the RAF played an important part in
the proceedings; they scored hits on the battleships, thereby
wiping out the speed edge of the Italians and forcing them
to accept combat under disadvantageous conditions. Nevertheless, it was a naval battle and the exciting rout of the
Fascists was rightly described in the press as "the greatest
naval engagement since Jutland." Enthusiastic experts spoke,
a little hastily, about the Mediterranean having been converted into a "British lake" through this humbling of Mussolini's sea forces. In the following months, however, the practical importance of the impressive triumph dwindled and
soon the victory was all but forgotten.

Considered purely as exercises in naval skill, the British
victories over Italian ships were indubitably splendid. As
"shots in the arm" for British morale they had a certain value.
But in relation to the general strategic picture the importance of the spectacular battle—and of other British naval
triumphs at the expense of the Italian Navy—turned out to
be exceedingly limited. Far from turning the Mediterranean
into a "British lake," events quickly disclosed the helpless-

. ness of John Bull's fleet in the face of superior air strength.
After all, control of the sea is an empty phrase unless it con-
notes the denial of sea communications to the enemy.

No champion of air power contends that naval power is
not an effective weapon against other naval power; he merely
rounds out the picture realistically by adding that the surface struggle is tactically futile when the new element, aviation, is in a position to make itself felt. Only when the air
overhead is beyond the range of aviation—or when it is eliminated by an aerial stalemate between evenly matched air
forces—does the surface contest begin to have real meaning.

In any case, the trouncing of Italy's Navy seemed an empty
satisfaction when General Wavell's forces of occupation in
Libya began their hurried retreat under Axis pressure. The
reversal of the North African campaign revealed that the
Germans had managed to transport and supply a considerable mechanized force to North Africa despite the undoubted
and almost monopolistic British naval superiority.

The exact size of the Italo-German forces was not known,
but they were large enough and well enough equipped to
retrieve nearly 500 miles of coastline in about three weeks.
The Axis man power was backed by trucks, tanks, armored
cars, and other heavy equipment. The plain fact is that all
of this had been transported safely across a 300-mile stretch
of the Mediterranean, between Sicily and the African coast.
The force was large enough to oblige the British to withdraw under its pressure. Moreover, we must assume that the
Axis command would not have dared to undertake the offensive unless it felt confident that lines of communication between the two continents across the Mediterranean could be
kept open.

How did the troops and heavy equipment get to North
Africa, ignoring the overwhelming British naval forces, in an

area close to Malta and therefore presumably under continuous and effective surveillance?

There were suggestions at the time that the Germans had merely "slipped" through the British sea control; that they had, as it were, "sneaked" across. But such secret and uncertain transport is unthinkable because the doors through which reinforcement and supplies might come could be closed tightly at any moment. Given the German capacity for careful planning, it makes no sense. Hit-and-miss blockade running must be logically counted out as a factor. The distance between Sicily and the nearest nonneutral point on the African shore is 275 miles. Over such distances ships cannot "steal bases" under cover of darkness. The journey takes a full day or more, in a region carefully patrolled from Malta. Even if the shorter gap between Sicily and Tunis had been used, it would still mean a trip of ten or twelve hours by water, consequently exposed to daylight detection.

The fact is that after the victory over the British Navy in the Strait of Sicily, the Axis confidently concentrated sufficient aerial strength at this neck of the Mediterranean to build a canopy of sky control, under which Axis ships moved back and forth with relative impunity. The fastest units of the British Navy did sink a number of the Axis convoys, but not enough to affect the total undertaking. Here, as in the Norwegian campaign, aviation successfully defied huge naval aggregations of great power.

Too inhibited by their training to recognize this rather obvious strategic layout, many analysts treated the sudden discovery of an Axis expeditionary force in North Africa as a "mystery." They preferred to believe that thirty-ton tanks had been smuggled in by air, rather than concede that Axis surface ships had done the job under a roof of local air control. One commentator, I recall, said he could account for the thirty-ton tanks, but he could not for the life of him figure out how the Nazis got their sixty-ton tanks over; perhaps he suspected a tunnel under the Mediterranean. . . . Actually there was no more mystery about the successful invasion of Libya from Europe than there had been about the successful invasion of the Scandinavian peninsula across the Skagerrak. In both instances hostile air power held vastly superior British sea strength at arm's length.

In the Axis drive eastward across Libya to Egypt, the frustration of sea power was particularly in evidence—for those, at least, willing to accept the "new strategic order." The same British warships which had operated so effectively a few months earlier in taking the African shore line should logically have been no less effective in resisting the Nazi-Fascist counteraction along the same coast. Every town, fort, and road was no less vulnerable to naval fire than previously. Yet there was almost no sign of naval participation in this critically important campaign during the three weeks when the Axis forged ahead from beyond Benghazi to Solum.

Where was the fleet, so recently and melodramatically victorious over the Italians? Why did it do nothing to stem the tide of the Axis force rolling toward its Suez life lines?

Certain amateurs offered the explanation that British naval strength was too deeply engaged at the moment in the Greek campaign. The explanation does not stand up under analysis. The units needed for co-operation with the land forces on the African coastal stretch were capital ships, and these were not primarily involved in the transport of expeditionary troops to Greece. That transport had the benefit of cruisers, destroyers, and other vessels, as well as aviation conveniently located for the purpose on Crete and Egyptian bases.

Some capital ships could readily have been spared for the purpose of aiding the hard-pressed African occupation. It

would have been elementary good sense to do so, considering the tactical and moral significance of the Libyan conquest. If it was not done, the explanation is simply that those
ships did not dare to approach within striking distance of
German aircraft. They had functioned freely in General
Wavell's campaign several months earlier against Italian
aviation, but they could not carry on under the deadly barrage of Hitler's aviation. British carrier-based planes were
equal to Mussolini's challenge, but not to the attacks of Hitler's *Luftwaffe*.

When the counteraction in North Africa started, it was
possible to foretell approximately where it would come to a
halt; namely, at some point inside the Egyptian frontier,
where the Royal Air Force, taking off from Egyptian bases,
could contest the control of the skies. It was no less possible
to indicate the same point as marking the renewed activities
of the British fleet. Under an umbrella of RAF protection
British warships, held at bay farther west, could swing into
action again. And this, indeed, is precisely what happened
at the end of the three-week drive.

In the autumn of 1941, the British, having accumulated
sufficient equipment and man power to risk another attempt,
undertook a Libyan counteroffensive. The scale was larger
than the Nazis had estimated, and it therefore succeeded in
reaching points beyond the previous advance. But again the
Germans ignored enemy naval power and quickly replen-
ished their Libyan forces, pushing the British back. At this
writing the campaign is still under way. That campaign,
however, does not offer serious guidance on major strategy,
because both sides evidently consider it a secondary front to
which inferior, untried, and even obsolete equipment has
been assigned. The one certainty is that there can be no final
decision in North Africa until a clean-cut mastery of the air

is obtained by one side or the other. Meanwhile, increased air activity on both sides further dims the role of sea power in that arena.

—————————————— 3 ——————————————

THE BRITISH and Imperial Army of the Nile opened its offensive against the Italians in Egypt on December 9, 1940. It occupied the most westward point in that drive, Benghazi, on February 6, 1941. Axis forces initiated the counteroffensive with the recapture of Benghazi on April 4, 1941. Germany invaded Yugoslavia and Greece two days later, on April 6. These dates of the African and the Balkan campaigns—the two arms of what was evidently envisioned by the Nazi High Command as a pincers aimed at the Suez region —are significant. The fact that the drive from Benghazi eastward and from Yugoslavia southward were almost simultaneous disclosed the German intention of splitting the limited British land and air forces in the Mediterranean area.

Britain had held all or part of the Libyan coast for nearly four months. The most important result of that conquest, from a purely tactical standpoint, is that it opened up far-reaching possibilities for the revision of the aviation map of the eastern half of the Mediterranean. "With the coastline all the way from Egypt to Tripoli in their hands," I wrote on February 13, 1941, "the British will be in a position to establish a series of bases dominating the waters to the north of them. . . . We may assume that construction of suitable bases is already under way."

It was the natural assumption for any student of aerial warfare. After the demonstration of Axis aviation ascendancy in the battle of the Sicilian Strait had opened such ominous vistas, it seemed simple good sense to bring land-based aviation closer to that neck of the great sea. The opportunity cried out for the establishment of appropriately spaced bases to serve as "anchors" for a canopy of British air power shielding the southern portions of the Mediterranean in that region. Under such a canopy, naval and merchant vessels could have plied in relative safety. The fleet would have been able to help beat back any such counteroffensive in Libya as, in fact, developed in April.

The planting of such a chain of bases, moreover, would have been valuable from another, broader standpoint. Germany held (and at this writing still holds) a strategic advantage as against the British Isles, in that it had air bases surrounding the Islands in a semicircle from Narvik to the Bay of Biscay. Charles A. Lindbergh and others who argued that Britain's position was hopeless have used that encirclement as their main argument. Their fallacy has been that they failed to visualize the broader possibility: a Nazified Europe ringed by British and Allied aviation. Except in the matter of scale, the position of Europe surrounded by the British Empire and associated territories is not unlike the position of the British Isles surrounded by Europe.

As a step toward such encirclement of Hitler's domain, the British seizure of the African coast was obviously vital. Here was another reason why aviation-minded strategic thinkers assumed that the conquerors would proceed energetically to convert the African coast into a bastion of anti-Axis air power. From that area they would hold a position in relation to Nazified Europe not unlike Germany's position on the northwestern edge of Europe in relation to the British Isles.

But we made these assumptions without counting on the deep-rooted conservatism of the naval-minded leadership of Mediterranean strategy. The German counteroffensive, as we have seen, found the skies unprotected, the fleet eliminated as a factor, and the road in effect cleared as far as the line where the land-based RAF could function again from their primary bases in the Suez region.

Another major error of the same caliber, likewise mirroring stubborn reliance on old-fashioned naval strategy, was being made by the British in the northern part of the east Mediterranean. I refer to their failure to prepare Crete for an all-out aerial defense. From an aviation standpoint that was elementary and indispensable. As early as November 11, 1940, many months before the Battle of Crete, I wrote:

"In the past any discussion of the control of the Mediterranean revolved around Gibraltar, Malta, Haifa, and Alexandria. But air power once again, in the unfolding campaign of this crucial area, will recast the old and accepted strategic maps of the world. Little mention, for instance, was made of Crete in the past. Yet today that island to the southeast of Greece seems destined to be the pivotal point in the great struggle for Mediterranean mastery. That is where the decisive air battles of the campaign are shaping up. One look at the map discloses how Crete, heretofore an insignificant island, viewed through the glasses of air power becomes the logical commanding center of the entire eastern half of the Mediterranean."

It was clear that the Axis must bid for the possession of Crete. Any nation well based on this island can maintain an impregnable cover of air power, denying passage to enemy ships underneath, over a region of immense tactical value.

At least from October 28, 1940, forward, which is to say from the time the Italians attacked Greece, the British had access to Crete. They thus had more than six months in which to entrench their aircraft there—time enough despite

the difficult terrain. Again aerial strategists assumed that this
was being done, and again they were mistaken. Still under
the hypnotic spell of their routine reliance on naval forces,
the British made little if any use of their chance to build an
aviation citadel at a point commanding both southern Greece
and an important area of the Mediterranean. After all,
couldn't this small island be completely covered by the
mighty guns of the British Navy? This error, flowing from
an automatic and tragically mistaken overconfidence in naval
might, proved disastrous in the Greek and Crete campaigns
during the spring of 1941.

The Nazi attack on Yugoslavia and Greece was in line with
the evident plan of the Germans to bring their aviation down
to the Mediterranean to challenge British naval overlord-
ship. Hitler's military moves in Rumania and Bulgaria, as
well as his political blackjacking of Yugoslavia, left no margin for doubt on that score. And as the Nazi military power
drew closer and closer to the frontiers of the menaced Balkan countries, Britain faced a racking decision: whether or
not to withdraw part of its restricted land and air strength
from Africa for the unpromising if not hopeless gesture of
defending Greece.

The decision to defend Greece may have been unavoidable for political reasons, and no outsider has any right to
criticize it. But viewed simply from the angle of abstract
military science, it was a tactical blunder. It did not save
Greece; instead it meant the loss of the north shore of Africa
and loss of the possibility of "sandwiching" Germany between two air forces.

There was, at the time, a great deal of public enthusiasm
in pro-British circles over the alleged formation of a "second
front." That was little more than a self-consoling fairy tale.
If Greece and Yugoslavia represented a "second front" for

the Nazis, then where was the first front? So far as the German armies were concerned, the Balkans and the Near East were the only fronts, and at that involved relatively small numbers. In Western Europe the war was being carried on solely in the air.

Instinctively everyone felt the necessity for splitting German strength. But it was the Nazi *Luftwaffe* rather than the Nazi armies which, at that point, had to be divided if Hitler's stranglehold was to be broken. The Balkan campaign did not accomplish this. On the contrary, in forming a Greek front, the British divided their own very limited air power, without affecting Nazi air power to any serious extent.

They did draw off some German aviation. But the type of aircraft chiefly used in that Balkan drive by the Nazis was the Army co-operation aviation. Except for occasional participation in raids on the English Channel and the south coast of England, this force had been "on ice." In drawing it toward the Balkans, therefore, the German air potential against the British Isles was not basically weakened.

From the vantage point of aerial warfare, it would have been more desirable to constitute a real "second front"—one that would split Hitler's *Luftwaffe*. North Africa offered that opportunity, but it was sacrificed either on the altar of political necessity or through deficient understanding of the role of air power.

----

4

----

THE GERMAN conquest of Greece was a typical Nazi *Blitzkrieg* with a typical denouement. As in nearly every other *Blitzkrieg*, there were intervals of Allied optimism stimulated by pauses in the German forward drive. As on former occasions, these stops turned out to be periods of consolidation

during which the invaders built advanced air bases and
brought up necessary supplies. They were neither more nor
less than delays to compensate for the shortness of the *Luftwaffe's* range.

The last British expeditionary troops were evacuated from
the Greek mainland at the end of April, 1941. After more
than a fortnight of inactivity—during which the Germans unquestionably were fortifying their positions for the aerial attack on the elongated island to the south—the Crete campaign was launched. It began with an exploratory assault on
airdromes on May 16, during which the RAF shot down a
batch of Messerschmitts. Four days later came the news of
parachute- and glider-troop landings. Day after day these
forces poured into the island by air, despite a heavy concentration of defending naval units around the island.

Almost at once control of the air was surrendered to the
Nazis. The London accounts disclosed that what few fighter
planes there were on the island had been withdrawn and
that fleet forces were being seriously menaced by the enemy's aerial fire. Mr. Churchill, with characteristic honesty,
put the matter frankly. "Our side," he said, "has no air force
because they have no airdromes." But there was the presence of a great British naval force, providing as clean-cut a
confrontation of sea versus air power as anyone could have
conceived for a scientific test of the subject.

Again I cite from my own files a few examples of strategic
judgments made in the light of an understanding of military aviation. While a false optimism was still being whipped
up in America, I wrote on May 27:

"Long-range aviation from Alexandria and heavy sacrifice
by the British and Greek troops on Crete may delay the
Nazi conquest. But the hope that the British fleet will make
up for the loss of the air is doomed to disappointment.

"Possession of superior naval strength provides important additional power when the adversaries are evenly balanced in aerial strength, but a fleet obliged to operate virtually without protection from the hammering of strong hostile air power invites disaster."

Naval-minded commentators on the Crete campaign were not merely wrong, they practically went haywire, in their bewildered attempts to follow the developments. Events moved in directions strictly prohibited by the rules of outmoded strategic thinking. One radio analyst went so far, I recall, as to assert that since Germany controlled the air and Britain controlled the sea, the two nations were "evenly matched"—which is like saying that two men are evenly matched when one has a baseball bat and the other a rifle of approximately the same weight. This analyst overlooked the minor matter that naval units without sufficient aerial protection are helpless targets for enemy aircraft. While the battle was in progress, the Australian Army Minister said: "There is no doubt in my mind that if Germany had not enjoyed the advantage in the air, the issue would have been decided long ago." Which was an admission that not even a monopoly of sea power in the battle area could make up for the adversary's advantage in the air.

By June 1 the British conceded that lack of aerial defense necessitated the abandonment of the island. The Germans, it was estimated, had used 1000 planes, including troop carriers, and about 200 of them had been shot down. The *Daily Mail* raised a question then in many minds: "Why has it been repeated in Crete? We have been in the island since November. What was done in those seven months which failed to prevent another evacuation after a twelve days' stand?"

The answers are not far to seek. The elimination of the

British air forces and the consequent loss of Crete were telltale items revealing the sad state of British strategic thinking. The same defects disclosed by the Battle of Crete run
through practically the whole record of British retreat before Axis offensives. They add up, in simplest terms, to smug
old-fashioned reliance on naval might in situations where it
is certain to be checkmated by the enemy's aviation.

No other hypothesis can explain the failure to make Crete
an aviation stronghold. The alibis advanced, such as the
mountainous terrain, are unsatisfactory in view of the extreme value of the island for the outcome of the whole east
Mediterranean struggle. Even if landing fields had to be
hewed out of solid rock, it was worth doing, and there was
ample time and man power to do it. We have the Prime
Minister's testimony that it was in the first place shortage of
airdromes which gave Hitler immediate air dominance. The
laborious apologies for the British in this situation collapse
in view of the fact that the Germans, once in Greece and
Crete, succeeded very well in establishing strategic air bases
where the British had failed to do so. The difference is not
in the technical skill—it lies in the psychology of the two
High Commands.

The fact that the island was allowed to remain defenseless
against aerial onslaught bespeaks either fantastic military
astigmatism or criminal negligence. The qualitative advantage of British aircraft in defensive work against the German
aircraft had been demonstrated beyond doubt in the Battle
of Britain. A few hundred Spitfires and Hurricanes might
have held off many times their number of Nazi airplanes
and made Crete as inaccessible as England. They could
readily have been spared from the British Isles.

Naval thinking and naval leadership would seem to be at
the bottom of the sad story of Crete. If the spectacular vic-

tories over the Italian fleet tended to make the British leaders cockily overconfident in their reliance on sea power, the naval triumphs in the Ionian Sea and Taranto and the Strait of Otranto were really important victories for Hitler and Mussolini. In any event, habit had prevailed over realistic analysis in leaving the critical strategic point called Crete without aerial protection.

At least three cruisers, one antiaircraft cruiser, and six destroyers were sunk, while two other cruisers, two battleships, and some destroyers were badly damaged. Over a quarter of a billion dollars' worth of naval force was lost or damaged—the economic equivalent of about 5000 airplanes! The fact that only one Axis warship, an Italian destroyer, was lost in the engagement indicates that Axis naval forces were practically not involved in the action. In the history of modern warfare Crete will remain a milestone of all-air invasion. Not only troops but supplies, fuel, ammunition, reinforcements, everything was brought by the air routes and the whole area was covered by air power.

Let us pause and survey the implications of this picture. It is entirely reasonable to regard Crete as the prototype of a method of warfare applicable to vastly larger areas. Except for a change in scale, we have seen in Crete a preview of total aerial warfare which could apply to the British Isles or to an entire continent, given the appropriate aircraft. Having taken control of the skies over Crete and its water approaches, Hitler had the island conquered. Because he wished to possess it, as a base for further activities, he proceeded to wrest it from the forces on the island. Had he merely wished to eliminate it, he could have exercised his air monopoly to bomb the island systematically into one vast ruin.

A significant feature of the Crete story, almost unanimously overlooked, is that British aircraft carriers apparently did not figure in the engagement. Here was the British fleet called on to do a difficult job, yet it did not bring its most modern auxiliary, its air arm, into action. The omission is the more remarkable in view of what we know about the desperate British need for aviation support; even bombers were refitted as pursuits and flown from Egypt in a desperate hope of offering a little protection. It would seem at first glance that carrier-based pursuit planes might have intercepted the German troop planes and gliders, and that carrier-based dive-bombers might have given the defending troops the same support the Stukas were giving the German invaders. Lacking land bases, the next best thing would seem to be the use of these "floating bases" to the maximum extent.

But they were not used. Why? Because experience in the North Sea and, even more so, the experience of the *Illustrious* in the Strait of Sicily had driven home the lesson that ship-based planes are committing suicide if they fight a duel with land-based planes, and that the carriers themselves are exposed to disaster if brought within range of land-based enemy air power. In the epoch of aviation the British Navy could not use its aviation adjunct. Neither will the American Navy ever be able to use its aviation adjunct—except in regions out of touch with the enemy's powerful land-based air force.

The German success in Crete was widely and erroneously heralded as a test or rehearsal of an invasion of the British Isles. Much nonsense was written on that theme. Actually, the Nazis learned in Crete only what every aviation man knew all along—namely, that elimination of the defending air forces is the first condition for a successful invasion across water. The German Ministry of Propaganda took advantage of popular innocence in strategic matters to claim Crete as a "proof" that the same would soon be done to England. It stimulated a new wave of invasion fears in England, which was useful in bottling up ground and air forces and supplies which might have been diverted to other theaters of war.

It is certain that German military leaders did not share the confidence pretended by Dr. Goebbels' department. If anything, the German victory in the Mediterranean had once again proved that command of the skies is the first step in an invasion across a water gap. Crete must have disabused any remaining skeptics in Hitler's High Command who still hoped to skip this first step. Germany could overpower the Greek island despite the opposition of a great British fleet because Germany could assume air mastery. That is precisely what it had been attempting to do, without avail, in England. Once such mastery is solidified, the method of reducing into submission is at the discretion of the captor of the skies.

Had the British and the Greeks possessed a semblance of air defense for use in Crete, the Nazis would undoubtedly have been stopped. The naval concentrations would then have furnished an additional leverage. Without such aerial protection, the battle was lost from the start. If the Admiralty had been able to bring every ship it possessed into the action, the outcome would not have been any different.

To earthbound military minds the entire Crete action was incomprehensible. It involved new relationships beyond their mental range, and their bewilderment was attested by farfetched explanations and complaints. The confusion has been particularly in evidence in the United States, where officially inspired naval propaganda went to the length of blaming Britain's separate air force for the Crete defeat.

The gist of their charges—intended to discredit the idea of a separate American air force—was that the RAF failed to give effective aerial support because it was not "co-ordinated" with the naval forces.

Flawless co-ordination between air and surface forces could not have altered the mechanical fact that the limited number of fighter planes available in the Near East, based in Africa, lacked the range to take part in a theater of combat 300 or more miles distant. Besides, the talk of lack of co-ordination contradicts the unambiguous picture of the situation presented by Mr. Churchill himself to the House of Commons at the time:

"Co-operation and co-ordination between services," he declared, "is carried to a high pitch. The chief air officer lives in the same house in Cairo as the commander in chief . . . The idea that any one of these problems would be studied by one without close association with the other is illusory."

Then he added:

"The decision to hold Crete and to fight was taken with full knowledge of the fact that air support would be at a minimum. I take the fullest responsibility for that decision."

The attempt by American naval spokesmen to distort these facts into an argument against a separate air force is utterly nonsensical and indicates the extremes to which "loyalty" to an older service can be carried by well-meaning men. After all, it didn't matter who controlled the shortage of airdromes and equipment. The naval propaganda missed the core of the Battle of Crete: the bankruptcy of naval strategy in areas within reach of genuine air power.

To us airmen Crete stands as a classic battle. It established the validity of the new military order. Together with the Battle of Britain, it disclosed the fundamentals of aviation strategy. That strategy may be expanded and intensified by better equipment, but the basic pattern and principles are likely to remain unaltered. They prove the reality of pure air strategy as the basic component for conquest and victory in our epoch. Crete showed air power not only as a direct striking force, but as a self-contained military force—the only one able to operate alone, as well as to give powerful support to surface forces and to provide the most expeditious transport of man power and the implements of war.

--------------------- 5 ---------------------

THE LESSONS of Crete were reinforced by the brief life and sudden death, on May 27, 1941, of the German superdreadnaught *Bismarck*. Had the strategic moral of these events been understood, the disasters for Anglo-American sea forces which marked the opening of the war with Japan in the Pacific might have been avoided. In the drama of the *Bismarck*, Britain and Germany presented, at a cost of perhaps a quarter of a billion dollars in equipment and thousands of lives, what was almost a laboratory case study in ocean warfare of the new aviation age.

That air power played a leading part on both sides of the action has been generally acknowledged, but the significance of that participation has not been sufficiently emphasized. To begin with, it should be recalled that the departure of the *Bismarck* from its nest in Bergen was discovered by the RAF. This enabled the British to deploy their naval forces in the attempt to corner the Nazi battleship. Had it not been for long-range aerial observation the *Bismarck* might easily have sunk hundreds of thousands of tons of British shipping before it could be located and overtaken; or it might ultimately have bobbed up as a potent addition to the Japanese Navy.

The actual engagement started in the Straits of Denmark, where the action ended in the destruction of the British warship *Hood*. The battle there was typically an old-style naval engagement faithful to all the glorious traditions of sea power. Guns were guns, armor was armor, and lucky shots were lucky shots. A lucky shot sunk the *Hood* just as similar lucky shots finished off battleships at Jutland and other classic sea battles.

Immediately after news of the *Hood* disaster became known, diehard exponents of sea power underlined the fact that here, at last, was a regulation ocean battle according to the familiar rules of naval textbooks. But they spoke too soon.

Having sunk the *Hood*, the *Bismarck* disappeared. Because of its edge in speed it normally would have eluded the enemy, retrieved safety, and lived to pick off shipping convoys. But long-ranged RAF planes of the coastal patrol—incidentally, American-built planes—intercepted the German dreadnaught and thereafter directed its hunt from the skies. The RAF overtook the *Bismarck* about 550 miles westward of Brest and the vessel rests on the floor of the Atlantic about 400 miles from Brest. For 150 miles, therefore, the *Bismarck* was hammered by airplanes until it was reduced to a helpless derelict. At that point a British warship moved in for the kill. However, had there been no fleet within hailing distance, a squadron of aerial bombers and torpedo planes could have finished the job. Once a battleship is disabled, the manner of its final disposition is of relatively minor importance.

In this decisive battle which eliminated the *Bismarck*, the British sea forces played an auxiliary role in helping dispose of a ship made derelict by aviation. On the German side, the only important retaliation inflicted in this final engagement

INTERNATIONAL NEWS PHOTO

Gliders like this one, and even larger, were used in the invasion of Crete.

BRITISH PRESS SERVICE

Maleme Airdrome, Crete, after the German invasion with air-borne troops.

Four-motored Focke-Wulf Courier used by the Germans in their aerial blockade of Great Britain, operating over the Atlantic hundreds of miles west of Ireland.

These trimotored Caproni bombers and the Savoia Marchetti bomber comprised the bulk of Italian bombardment aviation.

Morane-Saulnier 405, French single-seater fighter. This plane, although greatly inferior to foreign models, was stubbornly built in ever-larger numbers for bureaucratic reasons.

was the destruction of the *Mashona* from the air. The Germans, for reasons of distance and the suddenness of the whole episode, had only meager aviation forces on hand to take advantage of the unprecedentedly large British fleet concentration.

It was the air arm of the fleet, in the shape of carrier-based aviation, that did the major part of the work. This fact has been made the basis for superficial assertions that modernized sea power, in the sense of navies carrying their own aircraft, has been demonstrated as the best solution of the problem of sea warfare. Such a deduction collapses when it is realized that there is nothing which carrier-based aviation can do *that cannot be done more effectively by land-based planes*. Obviously torpedo planes taking off from land could carry bigger and more deadly torpedo loads than aircraft encumbered with all the prerequisites for operation from ship decks. Indeed, had the airplanes which discovered the *Bismarck* been equipped with torpedoes they could have struck at the Nazi warship there and then. It is only the lack of adequate range which necessitates "floating bases" in the form of airplane carriers.

After the *Bismarck* had been subjected to bombardment (the British Navy, after all, had not had much chance in this war to practice on a live target) it was finished off by the cruiser *Dorsetshire* with two torpedoes fired at close range. Those torpedoes might just as easily have been fired by airplanes from a carrier or RAF coastal patrol. The *coup de grâce* was left to the Navy as a matter of jurisdiction and did not imply an inability of aircraft to get the same results. It was a "Navy show" and the RAF kept politely aloof.

It should be noted that the British Navy frivolously sacrificed a providential opportunity to ascertain whether air bombardment was capable of sinking the most modern type

of battleship, as claimed by "air-power enthusiasts." When
the *Bismarck* had been reduced to a derelict condition from
the air, it offered a perfect test target to help settle a much-
disputed question, the answer to which was of extreme importance to the further conduct of the war.

The chance was thrown away. The enemy dreadnaught
was disposed of in the routine and traditional fashion—almost as if to perpetuate the legend of the invincibility of
battleships to the blows of air power. Unfortunately the
demolition of that legend was left to Japan, at the cost of
the British battleships *Prince of Wales* and *Repulse*, not to
mention American victims.

All the efforts of aviation men to bring the facts of the
Crete and *Bismarck* events home to the American people
were of little avail. These men had only knowledge to pit
against the age and prestige and vested authority of old-
line strategists. It is not yet clear, indeed, whether even the
tragedies in the Pacific have finally forced a breach in the
walls of complacent conservatism.

# CHAPTER V

# POSSESSION OR ELIMINATION

—————— 1 ——————

FOR SEVERAL centuries the procedures in warmaking remained fairly stabilized, reflecting the relative stabilization of the instruments of warmaking. The scale and intensity of the enterprise were constantly enlarged, it was made more and more destructive, but the basic patterns of action did not change. There was always a war "front": a line where the contending forces met in a deadly pushing match for possession of territory; and there was the supporting strategy of siege, including the blockade of entire nations, to starve out and break the moral resistance of the enemy.

These procedures had become so familiar that they seemed eternal. The nations of the world, after 1918, prepared for the next installment on the assumption that the plot would be fundamentally the same. Witness the millions of dollars in concrete and steel poured into "walls" and "lines" and other gigantic fences between countries. Witness the undiminished reliance on the floating fences on the high seas: the navies. Witness the failure even of the aviation-minded Nazis to equip themselves for anything beyond the routine war of mile-by-mile conquest, though all the technical conditions for the new type of war were already at hand.

Yet students of the history of war science know that the methods and objectives of conflict have changed through the ages. Primitive man could overcome his enemy only by grappling with him. Then came crude clubs and knives which

ended the need for hand-to-hand combat; later the killing
of adversaries at a distance without direct physical contact
was made possible by slings and bows and arrows; finally
firearms lengthened the intervening distances beyond the
range of human vision.

At one stage the foe was killed and his head or scalp exhibited as a trophy; at another he was taken alive and carried off as a slave. Conquered nations have been turned into
serfs or merely disarmed and obliged to pay heavy tribute
to the victors. In modern times, except where the siege of
blockade sufficed to subjugate a country, there was always
the need for taking over territory, from the frontiers inward,
and destroying the opposing armies in the process; invasion
by land or sea, followed by occupation of the invaded region. It was, in a sense, hand-to-hand grappling between nations—until aviation, able to strike the foe from above in any
portion of his anatomy, broke through the two-dimensional
restraints.

The crucial fact about the advent of air power is that it
has widened the choice of methods for the enforcement of a
nation's will on an adversary. At one end, modern aviation
reinforces the old patterns of warfare, in that it facilitates
invasion and occupation. At the other, it can strike at an
enemy nation *as a totality,* reducing that nation to helplessness without the time-honored preliminaries of invasion and
mile-by-mile conquest. Within this range of possibilities, of
course, there are any number of in-between variants. In the
final analysis, the aim in armed conflict is to disarm the enemy. Until the advent of air power, this could be done only
by armies. Navies merely provided the transportation. Air
power revolutionized human conflict in that it provided the
means to disarm an enemy directly—by knocking the weap-

ons out of its hands, so to speak, through the destruction of its entire war potential.

As the full potentialities of air power are unfolded—and we have seen only the crude beginnings—the first question in relation to a war, or to any specific campaign, will be: *Does the attacker aim at the possession of the enemy country or at its elimination as an economic and political factor?* The conduct of war will be determined by whether the purpose is to destroy the enemy or to capture him, whether the prey must be killed or trapped alive.

Once control of the air over hostile territory is assumed, the further disposition of that area is normally at the will of the conqueror. On the one hand, he may find the elimination of the country as a world factor more desirable, or more expeditious, than its actual subjugation. On the other hand, he may find the acquisition of an area intact, for its resources or industry or other economic values, more desirable than its destruction.

The deeper the civilization and the national pride of a people, the more likely it is to be subjected to the method of extermination, since such a people cannot be reconciled to living the life of the vanquished. More backward people, accustomed to the rule of force and less ardent in their national or racial awareness, can more readily be made docile and co-operative. Because they represent a constant source of danger to the conqueror, through the threat of a "comeback," advanced peoples must, if possible, be reduced to impotence beyond easy recovery, through the annihilation of the industrial foundations of their life.

Industrialized nations, in addition, are more vulnerable to the war of total destruction, as we have noted in another context. At least part of the secret of China's continued resistance to the Japanese war from the air is that its primitive economic existence cannot be destroyed as easily as a complex machine-age society would be. China's life does not depend, as the life of the United States does, on a few colossal aggregates of electric power and industrial machinery. China lives on the earth, every locality more or less sufficient to itself. Possible targets of bombardment are scattered throughout a huge country and not concentrated, as in England or Germany or America, in a few places. Total war from the air against an undeveloped country or region is well-nigh futile; it is one of the curious features of the most modern weapon that it is especially effective against the most modern types of civilization. The very ease with which a machine-age country can be blasted into chaos from on high is an invitation to the war of annihilation.

Thus the United States, as the world's most industrialized area, is also the most vulnerable to aerial attack. Our great territorial expanses may give us the illusion that overhead attack would be spotty and ineffective; but the fact is that our essential targets are concentrated at a few spots. To put the human body out of commission it is not necessary to riddle all of it with bullets; by piercing vital organs and nerve centers the entire mechanism can be paralyzed. In this sense, our industrial and power aggregates are vital organs of the national body; their annihilation would incapacitate the entire nation. For instance, the destruction of Detroit would paralyze our automotive strength and hence help to stall our mechanized forces. In addition, the destruction of a few cities like Hartford, Paterson, Indianapolis, and Columbus, Ohio, would at one blow ground our air power, since practically our whole output of airplane engines is concentrated in those cities. I should not be surprised if the future aerial strategy of our enemies is predicated on the elimination of such key economic points, even at enormous cost to themselves. Industrial concentration is essential to modern civilization, but unfortunately it runs counter to national security in the light of air power. Industrial dispersement must be undertaken in the interests of security. As we stand today, America represents a perfect target for bombing from the skies; here an enemy can hope to achieve more devastation per ton of explosive than in almost any other part of the world.

Though these considerations may sound abstract, and have been wholly ignored by our established military writers, they represent a concrete and practical aspect of the current world struggle. In the conflict between Great Britain and Germany, we see essentially a war of physical elimination. Despite their wealth of industries and communications, Hitler is more interested in destroying the British Isles than in acquiring them. He would rather wipe out the British economic setup than capture it. He cannot hope to enslave it and exploit it as he might some African colony or some small European country. He must therefore seek to enfeeble it for as long a period as possible by demolishing its entire industrial structure.

By the same token, British aims must be to wreck German economy rather than to take it over; the memory of how a beaten and debilitated Germany quickly recovered because it had the nucleus of a machine civilization and national pride is too fresh to be ignored.

The Nazis tried to capture England in line with the old pattern only because they had not yet realized the possibility of destroying it and consequently had not prepared for the task. Without doubt they now recognize that with the appropriate weapons they might have obliterated the British Isles. What they did to Rotterdam and Coventry and Belgrade, they will try to do—unless stopped in time—to the islands as a totality.

When the skies over a nation are captured, everything below lies at the mercy of the enemy's air weapons. There is no reason why the job of annihilation should at that point be turned over to the mechanized infantry, when it can be carried out more efficiently and without opposition from overhead. Indeed, the kind of large-scale demolition which would be looked upon as horrifying vandalism when undertaken by soldiers on the ground can be passed off as a technical preparation or "softening" when carried out by aerial bombing. The technique of three-dimensional blockade—cutting off exterior contacts and continuously demolishing internal communications and economic life—can be applied for a protracted period. Only when the master of the skies wishes to conserve the property and the man power below for his own use or for some other reason will he, normally, need to take possession of the surface through employment of armies brought by land, sea, or air.

---

2

---

THE GERMAN conquest of Norway, Holland, Belgium, France, and the Balkans was dictated in the first place by the tactical necessity of acquiring bases for military action against the chief enemy, Great Britain, and its life lines in the Mediterranean. The industrial and raw-material resources of those countries are useful for Germany, but an improved tactical position was the main objective. As a result, the Germans could be ruthless in visiting destruction on those areas. They needed physical possession of the terrain for advanced air bases, and were not much worried about the extent of the damage they inflicted.

Russia, however, presented quite another problem. Various political and moral objectives were involved. It is likely, for instance, that Hitler wished to overthrow the Stalin government in order to pose as the "savior" of the world from Bolshevism. Yet the primary aim was to take control of Russia's natural resources and of its large industrial setup. The Nazis needed the minerals, the petroleum, and other raw materials, and the food-producing facilities of Russia for the further conduct of the war. Hitler and his associates probably believed that in German hands the huge Soviet industries would produce far beyond their output under Russian management.

Therefore, the Germans needed to trap the Russian bear alive and put him to work. The fine pelt of a dead bear might be worth displaying for admirers, but the living animal was infinitely more useful. The obvious procedure was to conquer Russia with as little economic destruction as possible. The Germans figured that they would have to rebuild every bridge, every railroad, every factory which they bombed. While sparing no explosive in blasting Stalin's armed forces, the invaders pulled the punches of their aerial bombardment when harbors, factories, and other useful targets were in question. That, we must assume, was why the port facilities of Odessa in the South and Leningrad in the North were pocketed and for a long time spared the ordeal of all-out aerial attack. Only as a last resort, less destructive techniques having failed, did the Nazis undertake frontal attacks of annihilation against such objectives. In short, general strategic bombardment of the nation as a whole was withheld, only tactical obstacles immediately in the path of action were demolished from overhead. In the nature of the case Hitler wished not merely to knock out Russia but to take its riches as nearly intact as possible, ready for immediate and intensive exploitation.

In such a war the hitting strength of air power is deliberately held back, which explains why the German *Luftwaffe* played a lesser role than had generally been foreseen.

The obvious Soviet answer was the policy of the "scorched earth" announced by the Moscow dictator soon after hostilities began. This sort of response comes almost automatically to Russians. Elsewhere the strategic axiom has been that the best defense is the most vigorous offense, but the Russians through their whole history have tended to depend on vigorous self-destruction as a defensive strategy. It was thus in 1812, when they wiped out city after city in Napoleon Bonaparte's path, ending with the burning of Moscow. A national mentality thus conditioned naturally countered the Nazi assault with an attempt to deprive the invader of the economic fruits of his advance.

Hitler's countermeasure—one that helps explain phases of Nazi strategy in Russia which have puzzled military analysts —has been to encircle vital areas in great sweeping movements. A frontal assault leaves the enemy full possibility for escape. The retreating forces can scorch the abandoned area; the local population can pack its belongings and flee before the attackers. But when retreat is cut off, extreme demolition is impossible. The trapped troops cannot destroy the area into which they are penned without, in effect, destroying themselves. The civilian population, unable to flee, will resist the annihilation of their homes and goods.

The Nazis launched head-on offensives against Smolensk and other cities. These cities possessed comparatively minor industrial and strategic importance, or else the strategy of encirclement could not be used against them. In nearly all other cases the Germans preferred to take objectives by surrounding them, in the hope of thereby outflanking scorched-earth tactics. That is why there was repeatedly a time lag between the German announcement of the taking of towns and cities and the Russian admission of their fall. Having surrounded a city, the Nazis considered the task accomplished, while the Russians understandably did not concede the conquest until it was physically completed.

The attack on England serves as an example of the war of elimination—though negatively, since it failed on account of the shortsightedness of German preparations. Russia represents the war for possession. The distinction between the two types has not generally been recognized by old-line military specialists. In my view it is a distinction which will gain in force as this war progresses and which must affect profoundly the development of aerial equipment in the immediate future.

The country whose defense leaders shy away from such novel concepts, and from the implications in terms of weapons and strategy, is handicapped in advance in any test of strength with a nation thinking along modern lines. The war of possession calls for ground forces, for aviation co-ordinated with those forces, for air power on a tight leash in order to avoid unnecessary destruction. The whole technique changes when it is a war of elimination. Air power then assumes the leading and sometimes the exclusive role, utilizing its great range, striking force, and combat power.

Obviously the war of possession is more difficult, more costly in man power, more hazardous for the nation undertaking it. The hardships increase enormously with increase in the size of the invaded country and the distance of the theater of operations from friendly primary bases. Hitler's troubles multiplied as his armies plowed more deeply into enemy territory, thus extending lines of communication to an unwieldy

length. Incidentally, that is a consideration which should
not be overlooked by those of our strategists who think only
in terms of wars of possession—that is to say, great invasions
of enemy-held regions all over the world by American man
power. Such undertakings, sprawled through many parts of
the globe, would be dependent on supply channels much
longer and much more difficult to defend than Germany's
lines into the interior of Russia. For America, the war of
elimination, by means of direct long-range air power, is by
contrast a simple and economical procedure. It is, moreover,
a procedure more likely to succeed because it is linked more
intimately with America's native mechanical and production genius.

At this writing the Germans are already in possession of
the major portion of Russia's economic life. Even if they fail
to achieve total possession, they hope to hold on to enough to
justify the military investment. What is more, insofar as they
may be obliged to disgorge the seized areas, they are likely to
leave little of it in condition to do the Russians much good.
What they cannot possess—by holding the territory or by
transporting physically to German soil—they will destroy.
Strategic retreats that are not panicky routs are like tidal
waves in recession, uprooting everything valuable in their
path. Since possession is already a fact at that point, there
is no need to employ aircraft for purposes of demolition—
the retreating ground forces carry out that task.

The distinction between wars of possession and elimination naturally disappears when the tide of battle turns
against the invader. The Germans, in their retreat after they
lost Rostov and were driven off in the central Moscow area,
demolished as much Soviet economic property as possible.
The war of possession, in other words, automatically changes

into a war of elimination when the attackers are forced to retrace their steps.

-------------------- 3 --------------------

THE SCALE of the campaign in Russia presented the Nazi High Command with tactical problems which did not arise in the narrow arenas of conflict in other countries. The layman supposes that the enlargement of a theater of operations calls simply for the multiplication of the same tactics used in smaller areas. This is not so. It may and usually does call for the application of entirely different tactical principles. Certainly the application of the *Blitzkrieg* technique to a region as huge as European Russia revealed "bugs" in the German war machine that had gone unnoticed in more restricted regions.

It is clear that the Germans, in tackling the Red Army and Red aviation forces, counted on swift victory. This expectation was based in part on the dismal Soviet showing in the Russo-Finnish war in the winter of 1939–40. Although Stalin's forces in time won the conflict, it was a humiliating victory considering the relative size of the two contenders. It was a victory attained at a fantastic cost in life and equipment—and also at the cost of a public display of military shortcomings. In a sense the Nazi invasion of Russia, having been encouraged by the fiasco in Finland, may be looked on as Russia's dividend on its investment in the Finnish war.

Yet the Finnish struggle revealed another factor which the Nazis would have been wiser to observe and to ponder. That was the fighting quality of the ordinary Russian soldier, and his will to fight. With a kind of fatalistic abandon, the Red troops went to their deaths obediently, division

after division, until the Finns were almost smothered by
Russian corpses. The muzzles of Finnish guns were hot and
worn out with killing Soviet soldiers, but still the flood of
men poured over them and finally overwhelmed the defenders.

That type of resistance, utterly heedless of cost in life and
equipment, served to slow up the German machines even
where the Nazis were technically superior. The job of plow-
ing through a solid millionfold mass of humanity and acres
of equipment cannot be underestimated. In addition, the
Germans found in Russia little of the fuel and other supplies they needed. Belgium and France, on the other hand,
had well-developed automotive traffic. Thus the invaders
found their broad highways dotted with garages, gas stations, repair facilities. All of this facilitated the movement
of mechanized forces. In Russia, such aids to invasion did
not exist. Partly because of the scorched-earth policy, partly
because of the technical backwardness of the country in regard to motorized transport, the invaders had to haul along
with them every gallon of gasoline, all the spare parts, repair shops, and everything else which they had been able in
some measure to confiscate locally in other countries.

Nazi optimism, as the eastern war started, also rested on
the indubitable fact that Germany had a distinct edge over
Russia in the matter of military aviation. While Soviet aircraft were numerically strong, possibly as strong as Germany's, the Nazi planes in the main possessed greater speed,
better tactical balance of types of planes, and far superior
behind-the-lines organization. Soviet aviation had sheer
bulk, being largely equipped with horizontal bombers capable of carrying substantial loads of explosive. Such bombers, however, are practically useless in action against fast-
moving mechanized invasion of the sort faced by Stalin. His

defense required speedy, highly maneuverable fighter craft and dive-bombers, and in these items the Russians were below the Germans in performance.

Moscow's main aviation difficulty has concerned airplane engines, and behind that difficulty lies the familiar Soviet industrial inexperience. Engine models were acquired by the U.S.S.R. in the United States and other places, but by the time they were put into practical production, they had been superseded in the countries of their origin. Engine inferiority does not so much affect the value of heavy bombers, since total horsepower can be increased by installing additional engines; Russian bombers, for instance, carry six engines where similar aircraft in other countries usually carry only four. A reduction in the speed of a bomber, in any event, does not materially affect its tactical quality, since maximum speed in that type of aircraft is not the paramount consideration. It is load-carrying capacity of fuel and bombs and defensive fire power that count. But in pursuits, where single-engined types are most effective tactically, engine deficiency shows up as a terrific handicap. Of course, it became known that the Russians possessed some advanced aircraft types, such as the MIG-3 fighter. This machine, with its 1300-horsepower engine and powerful armament, compared favorably even with the British Spitfire. But due to the scarcity of such equipment, it did not affect materially the general balance of the air forces.

The Nazi aerial advantage, utilized in co-ordination with ground forces on the same general plan as in Poland, accounts for the rapid progress of the invasion of Russia in its first stages. That advantage, it should be noted, holds good only as long as the struggle remains dynamic, in a war of swift movement. As soon as the war is stalled and turns static, the aerial edge is canceled out. This is what happened in Russia at certain points, in consequence of the vast distances.

In general the *Blitzkrieg* operates as follows: the initiative is taken by the air arm, which assumes control of the skies. This it accomplishes by the use of pursuit airplanes to annihilate opposing aircraft in the air, and by dive-bombers and horizontal bombers, under protection of pursuits, to annihilate opposing aircraft on the ground. Mastery of the air having been taken over, the mechanized forces roll forward along paths cleared for them by dive-bombers; the ground forces thus exploit the initial advantage scored by aviation. Then the motorized infantry moves in for the final mopping up and policing of the conquered region.

But it should be borne in mind that control of the skies is limited, in geographical extent, by the effective range of the conquering aviation. The reach of an air force, like the reach of a boxer's fist, can extend so far and no farther, depending on the range of the equipment. Germany's horizontal bombers have a long range, as has been demonstrated in the battle of the Atlantic. But the section of the *Luftwaffe* created for co-ordinated action with the ground troops, the fighter planes and dive-bombers, at present average an effective striking reach of not more than 200 miles.

Thus the Nazi domination of the air ends about 200 miles from the last dependable line of German air bases. In all the theaters of this war, observers have noted the same phenomenon: a lull in the *Blitzkrieg* at roughly 200-mile intervals. Much of the misunderstanding and wishful thinking concerning the *Blitzkrieg* methods may be traced to this limitation on the German offensive in any one effort. Since the tanks and other ground forces can operate only under the shield of aviation, the range of the *Luftwaffe* fixes the depth of the offensive movement in any one action. At the

extreme range, the action unavoidably stalls. That explains
the periods of lull after every major *Blitzkrieg* undertaking
—the pauses when hopes have flourished in the anti-Axis
camp.

Having taken a stretch of territory within the compass of
its army-co-ordinated aviation, the attacker must halt to establish a new line of bases, with all that this implies in new
airdromes, communications, repair shops, fuel, ammunition,
and the rest. Only when that is accomplished is the attacker
ready for another "bite." *Blitz* or lightning offensive does not
roll in a continuous stream, as generally supposed, but works
in spurts. It does not progress continuously but in a series of
jumps, in a pulsating movement. Every pause temporarily
transforms the dynamic war into a static engagement, providing intervals during which a determined adversary can
make himself felt.

From the first day of the war, Germany has been obliged
to compensate for range deficiency by pauses during which
it moved its bases forward for the next advance. In Norway
the British were able to take control of coastal areas beyond
the reach of the *Luftwaffe,* but these "victories" lasted only
for the weeks that it took Hitler to carry his aviation close
enough to those coastal areas. A series of steppingstone air
bases covered more and more of the country and finally ex-
pelled the British even from Narvik in the extreme north.

In France, similarly, the Nazi push halted at the Somme.
What was accepted by wishful thinkers as the arrest of the
action was merely a lull preparatory to the next pulsation.
The maneuvering in the Balkans was likewise conditioned
to a large extent by inadequate range of German air power.
Had the Nazis been able to strike at the British life lines in
the Mediterranean directly from their home grounds, they
could have "skipped" a few of the nations lying in between.

Yugoslavia, let us say, might conceivably have remained an island of neutrality like Switzerland.

But the need for steppingstone air bases necessitated conquest by arms or by diplomacy. Sometimes, in fact, diplomatic efforts camouflaged the furious building of bases and concentration of forces for the next move: the preparation of new lines for new jumps. The time that elapsed between the conquest of Greece and the invasion of Crete was neither more nor less than the invaders needed to construct an adequate chain of bases on the southern shores of Greece.

Because of the short distances in Europe, the pulsating motion of the *Blitzkrieg* was not always apparent. One or two bites of 200 miles sufficed to swallow an entire country. Moreover, good roads, good local airdromes, and local availability of some supplies frequently reduced the duration of the interval.

The great expanse of Russia, on the contrary, resembled a huge canvas on which the *Blitzkrieg* jumps and halts were clearly discernible. A *Luftwaffe* "bite" which swallowed a Belgium or Holland merely took a small chunk out of the Russian bear. Because of primitive local conditions, moreover, the task of establishing a new line of bases, mobilizing supplies for the next spurt, extending the permanent lines of communication, was extremely difficult and time consuming.

The shortcomings of the *Blitzkrieg*, due to the inadequate range of operations, thus became manifest in Russia. At the point where German air control ended, the dynamic war changed into a static engagement and Germany's advantages temporarily ceased. A strategy that had been deadly in a narrow field of action proved defective in the vast spaces of a country like Russia. A determined defending force, such as the Russians created, could utilize the static periods to launch counteroffensives and to harass the efforts to form a new jumping-off "platform" for the next stage of the *Blitz*. The Nazis were forced to fight an old-fashioned battle in place, at some points even on a trench-warfare basis reminiscent of the First World War.

Aviation protection at those points loses much of its normal effectiveness, because the aircraft are operating at their extreme range, far from their bases and fuel supplies. Having reached their utmost range, their available fuel has dwindled and operations are limited in time by the need to return for replenishment. The fuel element also stalls the tanks and other mechanized elements far from established bases—and stationary tanks make easy targets for artillery and air bombing. In general, control of the skies at the extreme reach of the pursuit defense tends to become blurred and uncertain.

The *Blitzkrieg*, as defined for us in Poland and Western Europe, is a method adapted to the war for possession of territory. It becomes uneconomical and unnecessary in the war of total destruction. In the latter the initial stage of the undertaking, seizure of the skies, tells the whole story. Under conditions where the attacker is so weak on the ground as to be unable to exploit the initial victory in the air, the campaign automatically turns into a war of annihilation. Both the success and the failures of the *Blitzkrieg* in the West and in the East are replete with significant tactical and strategic lessons. These are bound to be translated by the world into more effective methods of aviation procedure.

———————————— 4 ————————————

SHOULD GERMANY begin to seize bridgeheads to the south of us in the New World, or to take over Latin American areas through internal Fifth Column methods, we may conceivably be confronted with the job of neutralizing the intrusion militarily. The method of occupation may then have to be used, and the co-ordinated action of all three elements of modern warfare—land, sea, and air forces—would be brought into play. Naturally our aim would be to keep destructive tactics down to a minimum, taking temporary possession with the least possible damage to our neighbors.

I cite this as a possible typical contingency for which the present American strategy seems well suited. But that contingency is secondary, in relation to our larger war problems. The same strategy, when an attempt is made to apply it on a world scale, becomes so cumbersome and costly in life and substance that it tends to become impractical if not self-defeating.

The mischief of it is that the mainstays of our national defense, while good enough for the secondary probable tasks, are unrealistic for the primary and actual tasks of this war. It assumes expeditionary undertakings to solve problems which—had we possessed the appropriate long-distance air power—could be solved more cheaply and more surely without A.E.F.s. It assumes an automatic unreasoning reliance on the war of occupation in relation to problems that should be solved through a strategy of elimination. In the prevailing strategic conception the method of expeditionary forces— involving huge investment of American lives—is an unconscious but real form of compensation for lack of true long-ranged air power.

Let us apply this line of thought specifically to the situation in the Pacific Ocean:

Japan's war against the Allies is clearly in its main phases a war of possession. In China the Nipponese have sought to take over territory and potential resources "for keeps." The Island Empire is seeking conquest of the sources of oil and rubber and other essentials—as well as toeholds in the form of bases—in the East Indies and the British and American possessions.

At our end, on the contrary, that war should be of an entirely different character. There is nothing on the Mikado's islands that we wish to possess and to use; we entertain no dreams of conquest. We are concerned simply with the elimination of a menace. So that it is a war of elimination that we should have planned for and built for. In the measure that our fundamental strategy is still stuck in the mire of superexpeditions and faith in dreadnaughts, it is at present unrealistic and risky.

Basically, in relation to Japan, we have the advantage from the outset because of the fact that we propose to eliminate rather than to take over Japan. Whether that advantage will be translated into victory depends on how quickly we can implement it with the instruments of air power. The great danger is that we may be catapulted into extreme schemes for colossal trans-Pacific A.E.F.'s dependent on old-fashioned "control of the seas" based on the obsolescent battleship.

Events in the initial weeks of the Pacific war quickly opened the eyes of some to the fallacy of our basic strategy in that theater of conflict. Even laymen soon began to sense the tragic absurdity of matching man for man and ship for ship in the huge expanses of the Pacific world, instead of relying on our obvious technological advantages. In that game of matching, the Japanese have an edge on us because of their shorter interior lines.

It is clear as day that had our strategy been based on dominant air power, we would have answered Japanese aggression with immediate all-out aerial bombardment of the

Japanese islands and their surrounding waters. Alaska, on our mainland, would have been set up as an aviation stronghold. Alaska, being on our continent, with only friendly Canada intervening, can be considered a primary base, with direct access to all the resources and manpower for self-contained air power. Japan would thus have been under the terrifying threat of direct onslaught from a main base of well-nigh inexhaustible air power.

As far back as 1929 General Mitchell wrote that "Alaska is really the key point to the whole Pacific." Alaska, he pointed out, "is within striking distance of any place we want to approach in Asia, either commercially or in a military way." I often discussed the details of the strategy involved with General Mitchell personally. His vision and intuition have been completely vindicated by history. The picture as he saw it in relation to the backward aviation of 1929 is infinitely more impressive today in relation to current technical possibilities. But even then General Mitchell concluded an article with these prophetic words:

"In summation, we can make the statement, without fear of being gainsaid, that air power is the deciding factor in our defense of the Pacific. Without it, any attempt to hold our possessions or protect our own country against an enemy will be fruitless."

Most likely it will become apparent fairly soon that the opposing navies in the Pacific are supernumeraries in this war. The chances are that both forces will be reduced almost to the vanishing point by mutual extermination, from the air and on the surface, unless the fleets avoid one another. Intermediary bases within bombing distance of enemy air power from primary bases will be counted out one after the other; naval protection is now useless and in the nature of the case an intermediary base cannot normally be equipped and supplied in sufficient strength to hold out against a main aerial force from its home bases.

Assuming that the most optimistic naval hopes are realized and the Japanese Navy is entirely destroyed, the war would by no means be ended. In the past, our battleships under those circumstances could have steamed up to the enemy shores and taken over. Now they will be kept at arm's length by hostile aviation. In the past the triumphant navy would have cut off Japan's contact with the Asiatic continent by taking charge of the narrow intervening waters. Now it will no more venture into those waters, protected as they are by Japanese land-based aviation, than the British Navy ventures into similar waters dominated by Hitler's *Luftwaffe*.

We could impose a partial external blockade; it would mean relatively little, as Japan had been deprived of imports from sources under American and Allied control even before it started this war. But we could not with our naval force interrupt either the coastwise communications or the internal lines of transport and economic centers on the Japanese islands. The position of a navyless Japan would be more or less like that of Germany, which likewise has no real sea power, yet controls the coastlines and maintains its interior lines of communication in Europe.

For a definitive victory over Japan we must be able to impose a tridimensional blockade, through air power. Our aviation must wrest the dominance in the air in the narrow waters separating Japan from the mainland. A strategy based on air power is unquestionably indicated for us in the Pacific. That in turn calls for aircraft, organization and leadership thoroughly cured of inherited naval obsessions. As a concession to public opinion and to obvious day-to-day events, we have been improving our aircraft, making them more efficient, longer in range, better armed. But in relation to our tactical needs in the Pacific, we remain unprepared and backward—more unprepared and backward than were the Germans for their war of elimination against the British Isles. At least the Germans were able to reach their objective, although their equipment was inadequate. In our case, not only is our equipment inadequate for the job, but it is ill-conceived to the extent that our land-based aviation cannot even reach the vital strategic centers of our enemy.

On the whole, because we have no imperial purposes, but in every case want only to remove a threat to the normal life of the world, American strategy must be geared for the war of elimination—which is as good as saying war predicated on superior air power. Fundamental American policies can be implemented most expeditiously by a properly designed, equipped, and organized air force. That will assure us complete control of the skies, making the attainment of freedom of the seas and dominance on land relatively simple tasks.

# CHAPTER VI

# AIR-POWER LESSONS FOR AMERICA

THROUGHOUT HISTORY, new weapons have imposed new tactical principles upon the science of warmaking. Throughout history, too, some nations have been quicker than others to recognize and apply those principles. In this, as in every other field of human endeavor, new ideas have had to contend with the inertias of habit and enshrined precedent. The very military leaders who should be most keenly alert to detect and utilize new instrumentalities are often musclebound by traditional thinking. Only that can account for the stubborn reluctance of our own higher authorities to revise their standardized attitudes radically in line with the experience of the war to date, not to mention their inability to project their thinking into the future, beyond current events.

We have summarized the recent experience in the preceding pages. In telling the story of the conflict from the vantage point of aviation, even as briefly as we have, certain basic truths about the new military relationships have become apparent. The lessons of air power are implicit both in the things aviation has done and the things aviation, because it was not geared for them, failed to do. The least we Americans can do is to isolate those lessons, learn them thoroughly, and make the fullest use of them.

Since September, 1939, we have had front-row seats, so to speak, to watch the tragic spectacle—on land, on sea, and in the air. We have seen new weapons, new strategies, and new tactics. More than that, for those who are able to dis-

cern the shape of the future in the facts of today, the experience has provided a chart for the warfare still to come.

"If any man will be a great general," Napoleon Bonaparte
once said, "let him study history. Study the campaigns of the
great generals—Alexander, Hannibal, Caesar, as well as those
of Turenne, Frederick, and myself, Napoleon." As a great
strategic innovator, he certainly did not mean that the past
was to be blindly copied. The task of each generation is to
interpret accumulated experience and to adapt it to new
conditions. The past and the present are useless to us unless
they enable us to see boldly into the future.

The lessons of this war must be grasped, but chiefly as
basic starting points for strategic planning beyond the present experience. The success of Hitler in the first two years
of this war derived in the first place from the intellectual
surprises that he sprang on the world. Six years before its
advent he began to study his war. In 1933 he began to plan
a strategy and tactics based upon the weapons that could be
expected to emerge by 1939. Unhappily there are no signs
that our own military leaders have grasped the moral of that
fact.

Other nations have had legitimate excuses for their humiliating defeats. They were taken unawares by the new
German methods and equipment. We in the United States
no longer have any such alibis. The lessons of this war have
been demonstrated for us as in a gigantic laboratory. On
the basis of trial and error, at enormous cost in life and substance, the belligerents, before our own entry into the war,
established a series of strategic axioms for air power. There
is no reason why we should retrace the same step-by-step
process in the development of our own ideas and equipment.
We are in the advantageous position of being able to leap
over intermediary stages, to skip in-between transitional

types of planes, to attain points far in advance of all other nations.

The first requisite for that, of course, is a clear understanding of the new principles demonstrated by the war. Here, in the most elementary and fundamental terms, without excessive technical embellishments, are the most significant lessons of modern air power:

1. *No land or sea operations are possible without first assuming control of the air above.*

This is a principle of warfare so thoroughly demonstrated and so widely acknowledged that it has become the fundamental axiom of the new strategy. Against an adversary possessing effective air power, the capture and control of the skies overhead are now the first condition for operations on the surface. The principle holds equally true over large or small areas, in carrying war across rivers, lakes, or oceans. The enforcement of one nation's will over another can no longer be achieved on the surface of our globe unless ascendancy is already established and maintained in the air overhead.

In the preceding chapters we have seen how German control of the skies over Denmark, the Skagerrak, and Norway prevented Britain from using its preponderant sea power. The magnificent French Army never had a chance to show its mettle; having captured dominance in the skies, the Nazis were able to defeat the ground forces before these could go into action. Dunkirk showed the same picture in reverse: operations across the English Channel could be carried out successfully because the air was in British hands. Similarly, the only reason the Nazi warships *Scharnhorst, Gneisenau,* and *Prinz Eugen* were able to escape from the harbor of Brest in February, 1942, and pass through the

Straits of Dover, was that the Germans threw a powerful
canopy of land-based air power over the whole operation.
Because of the surprise element and weather conditions, the
time interval was too short for the Fighter Command of the
RAF to break that canopy. Without the elimination of German air superiority at that place, direct attack on the ships
was futile.

The original British operations in Libya, with the co-operation of the British Navy, were successful because the RAF
and ship-based aircraft had command of the air against
Italy's inferior aviation. When this aerial potential changed
in favor of the Axis by reason of the arrival of German aircraft in that theater of war, the British had to withdraw to
Egypt, where they enjoyed safety under the shielding wings
of the RAF operating from primary bases. The British comeback in Libya at the end of 1941 again occurred under a
reinforced aerial roof.

In the Battle of the Atlantic, long-range German aircraft
threatened the vital ocean routes on which the British Isles
are so dependent. The threat was averted when Britain and
America, having established bases in Greenland and Iceland, were able to contest the skies over the Atlantic sea-
ways; fighter planes on catapults were installed on merchantmen and every other device for neutralizing the
Germans in the air was exploited. An oceanic conflict conditioned by a contest in the air—there we have the summation of the principle.

The Pacific struggle presents the same general picture. In
every instance—from the attack on Pearl Harbor and the
sinking of the *Prince of Wales* and the *Repulse* through the
conquest of Hong Kong, Malaya, the East Indies, as well as
in the plight of our heroic forces in the Philippines—the
first arena of combat has been the "air ocean." Whether

ships and tanks and infantry could operate at all depended, in the first place, upon whether they had friendly or at least neutralized skies above them.

An umbrella of adequate air power is the minimal condition today for surface warfare anywhere within striking distance of enemy aviation. Those who do not understand this or still cavil about it—those who dare send battleships or land units into action under skies controlled by the foe—cannot be trusted with authority in modern war or in the preparations for modern war. Since weapons of air power can now be constructed to cross the oceans and to reach any objective on land or sea by air, the axiom applies to practically any area of military operations. Control of the skies has become the paramount condition for strategic jurisdiction on any land or water surface of the earth. National dominance in war or in peace must now be measured with the yardstick of air power.

## 2. Navies have lost their function of strategic offensive.

No less obvious is another tactical reality, namely, that navies have lost their former function of strategic offensive. Air power has taken that over.

In the past, battleships carried war to the shores of the enemy nation. Today, if the enemy possesses anything resembling real air power, that can no longer be done. Defensive aircraft can make it impossible for warships to approach or to land armies on hostile shores. Navies still exercise important defensive strength, in the ever-narrower area beyond the reach of aviation, but they have definitely lost their former *initiative* in the matter of offensive action.

A good many military experts, including high ranking officials, refuse to acknowledge this, either through misguided "loyalty" to the past or through mental "blind spots." The

fiction that navies are still our "outer defense" is maintained
through sheer habit. Thus the annual report of the Secretary
of War for 1941 describes the Army air force exclusively in
defensive terms, as a weapon for intercepting invading or
attacking navies. The job of striking at the enemy on his
home grounds across the waters is thus, by implication, re-
served to our Navy. All of which is pure make-believe, the
maintenance of an illusion, since no naval force can any
longer approach hostile shores, even if the enemy is wholly
devoid of naval protection.

The fact that Britain, with its vastly superior naval
strength, has been unable to tackle the shores of the European continent, ringed with Axis air power, tells the story.
At an earlier stage the British Navy landed expeditionary
forces at several points in Norway only because Axis aviation was not yet close enough to interfere. As soon as the
Germans advanced their air bases sufficiently to take those
occupied points into their orbit of striking power, the British were forced to withdraw.

Hereafter the strategic offensive rests with aviation. Only
after air power has established control can fleets attempt to
follow it up with any hope of success. Surprise raids and
landings do not alter this picture. Without air mastery, landings accomplished on a surprise basis expose themselves to
overhead annihilation. Those who urge premature invasion
of the European continent should ponder this fact. In Europe, as in Britain, the question of who owns the air must
be answered *first*. There are no short cuts.

The attempt of the *Prince of Wales* and the *Repulse* to
attack Japanese expeditionary forces protected by Japanese
air power proved disastrous. An equivalent attempt by the
Japanese warship *Haruna* to support an invasion of the
Philippines cost that ship its life. It became a target for the

American air force. The inadequacy of that air force—in other words, Japanese superiority in the skies—explains the subsequent landings on those islands. On Wake Island, too, the enemy needed to cancel out our air potential before it could achieve control.

It is now the task of air power to destroy harbors, docks, shore-line fortifications—all of which were naval objectives in the past. The primary job of the fleet was to keep the sea lanes open to its own country and to deny them to the enemy. The latter half of this job was accomplished either by destroying enemy shipping on the high seas or by destroying the terminal facilities of the enemy's navy and shipping. In view of the fact that the fleet now cannot approach those terminals, that phase of the enterprise has become the exclusive function of military aviation.

The immense coastline of Western Europe, from Narvik to the Bay of Biscay, with its array of important harbors, submarine bases, drydocks, warehouses, and industrial plants, is virtually devoid of naval defenses. Yet the British Navy has been unable to challenge control of this great stretch of seashore. The British offensive against this area, including the attack on so-called invasion ports and U-boat bases, is being made exclusively by the Royal Air Force. Similarly, the Nazi attacks on England's harbors and coastal fortifications are being made exclusively by the *Luftwaffe.*

The days when battle fleets steamed boldly within striking distance of enemy shores and proceeded to pound them into submission are now relegated to history. Today these fleets can approach only under the shield of a powerful umbrella of land-based air power and can remain only if that umbrella is strong enough to resist the enemy's aviation.

True, there have been isolated exploits of sea power in the old style, such as the naval bombardments in the Straits of Otranto, and of Genoa in the Mediterranean, or the bombardment of Brest. Those exploits, however, merely emphasized the truth of the new situation. In every case they were surprise attacks, made on a hit-and-run basis. They occurred at points where the defensive aviation was either unprepared or nonexistent, and the naval attacks beat hasty retreats before the adversary's aircraft could be mobilized.

In short, the struggle for possession of the coastlines, the initial offensive action, is by this time a function of aviation, not of navies.

3. *The blockade of an enemy nation has become a function of air power.*

Britain has learned the hard way that blockade, heretofore pre-eminently the task of sea power, has been taken on in ever-larger measure by air power. Though practically without a fighting fleet, Germany has been able seriously to hamper the flow of supplies to England, intercepting British commerce and men-of-war many hundreds of miles to the west of Ireland. As Hitler's bombardment and fighter aircraft extend their range, this threat to British shipping will grow, unless it is canceled out by counteraviation.

Countries in any degree dependent on overseas commerce must recognize and act upon the fact that aerial blockade is not only possible but is destined to be the only effective type of blockade. Given enough properly armed airplanes of adequate range, an enemy's lines of supply can be wrecked. Even the operations of raiding submarines become secondary as against the destruction sowed by airplanes.

Blockading aerial armadas, as soon as the necessary range is built into them, can harass shipping at *both* ends of the sea routes—Liverpool or London at one terminal, Boston or New York at the other, for example—and on the whole dis-

SHIP-BORNE AIRCRAFT. Engineering ingenuity solves design problems involved in operating airplanes from ships, as in the folding wings shown here. Such solutions impose encumbrances which make ship-based planes inferior to similar land-based planes.

FLOATING AIRCRAFT BASE. The aircraft carrier U.S.S. *Ranger.* Safety of an aviation base lies in dispersement of its facilities and aircraft—but the carrier violates this principle. It represents a maximum concentration of equipment in a minimum space, thus providing an ideal target.

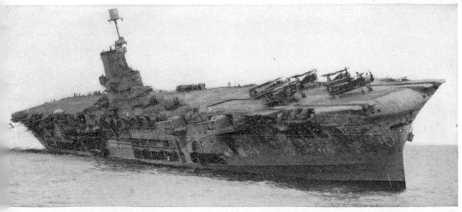

THE END OF THE *ARK ROYAL.* The British aircraft carrier going down after a torpedo attack, carrying its aircraft to the bottom of the sea. Aviation based on ships can be destroyed by surface forces through elimination of their floating bases.

Antiaircraft Battery

Listening Device of Warning System

Searchlights

Balloon Barrage

PASSIVE DEFENSE AGAINST AIR RAIDS. These offer additional haza for the attackers rather than a positive defense. In the final analysis, only power can fight air power.

tance between the terminals. What is more, their speed enables them to act as the directing and commanding component in co-operating with U-boats. Complete blockade by
air power has not yet been demonstrated, but enough of it
has been on view in this war to make this method the most
frightening of any held over an enemy's head. The countermeasure, of course, is air power fully capable of meeting and
defeating the blockading force in the skies.

According to official Nazi statistics, of the first 13,000,000
tons of British military and commercial vessels destroyed,
3,500,00 tons—about twenty-five per cent—were sunk from the
air. The German government is too concerned about maintaining the morale of its submarine command to deprive the
undersea arm of credit where credit is due; the percentage
assigned to aviation must therefore be accepted as true,
whatever we may think of the total figures. But it is an over-
all figure covering nearly two years of operations, during
which the share of the *Luftwaffe* in the blockade has continually expanded. There have been weeks in which the
*Luftwaffe* accounted for more than half the tonnage sent to
the bottom of the sea. A fair guess at this writing would thus
be that about a third of the destruction visited on British
tonnage to date should be chalked up to aviation.

The new principle was almost symbolically demonstrated
on September 11, 1941. It was the day on which President
Roosevelt made his famous broadcast announcing America's
intention to enforce the freedom of the seas. Even while he
spoke, the Germans were attacking a British convoy near
Iceland. According to official London figures, eight ships
were sunk—three of them by U-boats and five by airplanes.
More than sixty per cent of the losses in that instance were
thus attributable to the air weapon. It is still the custom of
old-line military men to talk of blockades and counterblock-

ades as naval strategies, but reality mocks their words.

Until aircraft able to strike at merchant vessels far out at sea is available, it is likely to concentrate on striking them in their ports of embarkation and destination, and on making the delivery and loading of goods as hazardous as possible. A total aerial blockade, effective at any spot in any ocean, as well as in the third dimension over the blockaded area itself, awaits only the inevitable extension of the striking range of air power.

Naval blockade had been able only to maintain an outside barrier, interrupting the external lines of communication. In addition, of course, they could carry armies across the water, land them under the shield of naval gunfire in the hope of severing internal lines of communication in a mile-to-mile conquest of territory. Aerial blockade is immeasurably more effective in that it effects both outside and interior breach of supply lines simultaneously. It is total and instantaneous blockade.

It must be remembered, of course, that just as the precondition for naval blockade was the elimination of the opposing navy, so the imposition of aerial blockade calls for the elimination of the opposing air power. Conquest of the skies, once again, is therefore the first objective.

### 4. *Only air power can defeat air power.*

Another vital principle which has been confirmed by the course of the war is that only air power can meet the menace of air power. The hope that antiaircraft artillery, balloon barrages, or other improvised terrestrial defenses on land or on ships could form a positive protection against attack from the air has by this time been largely abandoned. Such devices can confine the enemy to higher altitudes, thereby reducing the accuracy of his aim. It offers a supplementary hazard to the attacker, but is a palliative at best, not a cure. The actual elimination or even stalemating of an attacking air force can be achieved only by a superior air force.

The lesson that only air power can defeat air power is especially recommended to the attention of those who still like to fool themselves with theories of "defensive" equipment. The only defense against the menace from the skies is in the skies. Hostile aviation must also be destroyed at its source, in the enemy country, and that, too, is a task for air power.

The notion that ships can carry their own defenses against hostile aircraft, in the form of antiaircraft guns, balloon barrages, or even ship-based planes, is no longer seriously defended except by the stubborn or biased. Not all their antiaircraft defenses could save the British naval forces in the Battle of Crete from overhead punishment. Despite its first-class antiaircraft fire power, the *Illustrious* was damaged and put out of action by bombing planes. The German battleship *Bismarck* could not ward off aerial torpedo attacks. Nor could Britain's *Prince of Wales* and *Repulse* or Japan's *Haruna* drive off aerial destruction with their own antiaircraft fire.

Thus on the seas, as on land, the defense against aviation is equally good or better aviation.

5. *Land-based aviation is always superior to ship-borne aviation.*

Wherever in this war military aviation based on land has come into conflict with equivalent aircraft based on ships, the former quickly established its superiority. The reasons for this are purely of an engineering and aerodynamic nature. The airplane taking off from an aircraft carrier or other "floating base" is of necessity encumbered with special prerequisites which are built in at a heavy cost in performance.

Ship-based planes must be able to take off and land on limited deck space. They must be subject to retrieving by the carrier or warship whether they make forced landings at sea in the case of a landplane, or normal seaplane landings on water. In the latter case the aircraft must be seaworthy, hence heavier in construction. These and a host of other supplementary prerequisites call for supplementary mechanisms or design encumbrances, paid for in the quality of performance.

The limitation of landing speed, for instance, necessitated by the restricted landing area or rough sea, is achieved by reducing the "pay load" or striking power; or by increasing the wing areas, which normally means a larger plane. Since it must be accommodated to the elevator of the carrier ship, folding wings are called for. This in turn entails more mechanical gadgets, more weight, and still another loss in performance.

This vicious circle which condemns the ship-borne plane to relative inferiority is manifest in most other phases of design. Arresting gear for landing calls for additional strength in structure to take care of the sharp deceleration, and of the whipping force against the deck. All of these call for more rugged, hence heavier, structure, which cuts into quality factors for military purposes.

In relation to bombardment aviation, one does not need to be an aeronautical engineer to realize the inevitable superiority of land-based craft. An average ship-based dive-bomber or torpedo plane today carries a maximum of one 2000-pound bomb or one torpedo. Its land-based counterpart, the twin-engined bomber, carries two tons, or could be constructed to carry two torpedoes. The land-based flying fortress carries four tons of explosive over a range of 3000 miles. The British Stirling Bomber carries seven tons; our own B-19 and the Glenn Martin Flying Boat can deliver nearly twenty tons of explosive or twenty torpedoes. Unhampered in landing speed or size, these bombers must always exceed ship-based bombers in performance. Owing to the greater lifting capacity of a land-based plane, it can deliver torpedoes of vastly greater size and destructive power. Probably that explains why the *Bismarck,* attacked by torpedo planes from carriers, was only crippled, whereas the *Prince of Wales* and *Repulse,* attacked by shore-based torpedo planes, were swiftly sunk.

The carrier or floating airdrome provides, on the average, a landing space 100 feet by 750 feet. For contrast, the latest airdrome on *terra firma,* at Newfoundland, constructed especially to enable bombers to take off safely with heavy overloads, has a concrete runway 1200 feet wide and 10,000 feet long—approximately ten times the take-off area available to ship-borne bombers. The heavy bombing plane of the immediate future, patterned after the B-19 or the Martin Flying Boat, will have a span of 200 feet, or twice the beam of the average battleship or carrier; and bombers with a 300-foot spread have already been projected. Clearly, therefore, the striking power and other performance embodied in a land- or shore-based bomber cannot be incorporated in planes housed in or operated from any practical floating base.

The same conclusion is inescapable in regard to pursuit or fighter planes. The landing speed of ship-borne aviation is necessarily restricted, due to the small deck space and the need to hold deceleration within practical limits; in other words, mechanisms are essential to arrest the speed of the plane in landing within a short distance. Take a plane whose landing speed on board a ship is limited, let us say, to 80 miles an hour. If the same plane is permitted to land at 90 miles an hour, or ten miles faster, it can carry roughly ten pounds more for every square foot of wing area. The wing area of the average fighter being around 200 square feet, an additional 2000 pounds of useful load can thus be carried.

Part of these 2000 pounds can be put into heavier and more powerful engines to give greater speed and greater rate of climb. Another part can be invested in additional armament and armor. The rest can be put into additional fuel for range. Thus the carrier-based plane, if adapted to a land base, excels in speed, range, and fire power and defensive armor. This margin of advantage must hold good no matter how many improvements and refinements are developed in carrier planes—the same improvements in land-based craft will give higher performance. True, one naval air arm may be better than another—in this sense, for instance, America's naval air arm is peerless—but the very fact of attachment to a ship means that the aviation is inbred, restrained in a naval strait jacket, and hence inferior to land-based aviation.

Another important factor needs to be taken into account. The war has taught us that the safety of an aviation base lies in dispersement. The more widely the facilities and the airplanes are scattered, the less vulnerable they are to attack. Aircraft carriers obviously violate this principle of dispersement. They represent the maximum concentration of aircraft and base facilities in the minimum space, thus offering the most attractive and most vulnerable aviation target. A single well-placed bomb can bottle up an entire complement of airplanes, or prevent the whole complement from returning to base if they are in the air. Such was the case with the British carrier *Illustrious,* off the shores of Sicily. If the carrier is crippled and lists heavily, the aircraft are likewise doomed. For that reason, when the *Ark Royal* was struck by

a torpedo, off Gibraltar, it carried its aircraft to its watery
grave. There are, of course, an array of other considerations
which cut into the efficiency of ship-borne aviation. The carrier, for instance, is compelled to steer a direct course into
the wind to facilitate the take-off and landing of its planes.
This obviously simplifies the problem of accurate aiming by
aircraft attacking the carrier. Also, if the carrier is driven
from its position by the enemy, planes already launched
often find themselves unable to retrieve their base and are
lost.

Because the range of aviation is still limited, there are
ocean areas beyond the reach of land-based aviation. In these
areas naval aircraft have their logical sphere of operation—
as against the enemy's naval aircraft. Ultimately, when aviation bridges oceans those oceanic margins will be erased.
Floating bases will then be atrophied. The striking power of
ship-based aircraft will be insignificant against the support
offered by land-based aviation.

Navies of the world, of course, will always carry their
own auxiliary aircraft, even as they now carry guns and torpedoes. But this should not be confused with genuine land-
based air power. The argument is sometimes made that the
aircraft carrier is essential because it travels with the fleet,
whereas land-based aviation, powerful though it may be,
will not be on hand when needed. The argument is tenable
only in the in-between period before air power attains its full
range. When land-based aviation covers all waters directly
from primary bases, surface fleets will no longer dare to venture forth until mastery of the whole sky is assured, or without a powerful, land-based, long-range escort. The kind of
airplanes that travel with the fleet will simply be of no avail
against the enemy's attack from land.

Naval aviation is a temporary expedient, marking the transition of military aviation from its short-range infancy to its long-range maturity.

6. *The striking radius of air power must be equal to the maximum dimensions of the theater of operations.*

This concept has been substantiated, as it were, negatively: by the difficulties and failures which lack of the necessary range imposed on the Nazi *Luftwaffe.* Range deficiency has been the curse on Hitler's aviation. In the Norwegian campaign, for instance, the Germans could not stop the British from occupying a chain of coastal towns and were put to the necessity of expelling them after German aviation had been carried close enough to those towns. With adequate range Hitler could have taken control of all Norway from the outset. On the other hand, the British failure to hold Norwegian bridgeheads was due, in the first place, to the lack of range in their pursuits, without which control of the air cannot be kept.

The Low Countries, Belgium, and France were occupied to bring aviation within striking distance of the British Isles and their overseas life lines. In Hitler's relentless pursuit of British sea power, he had to move his air bases to the very rim of the continent. To approach the Mediterranean, Germany had to carry its *Luftwaffe* through Rumania and Bulgaria, step by step as it were, on the shoulders of its ground forces, until it reached Greece. Repeatedly Hitler was obliged to occupy one nation after another in order to bring his air force within striking distance of some main objective. With proper aviation range, occupation of some of those countries might have been unnecessary. In Russia, Hitler's handicap of short range in his *Luftwaffe* showed up even more sharply.

The basic advantage of air power in contending with moving objectives on the surface of the earth is speed and freedom of action. It is dynamic. But at the extreme limit of the operating radius, that dynamic quality tapers off and finally ceases. During the interval when new airdromes are being built, when new communication lines are being laid, when new supplies are being accumulated for the next take-off, the airplane in its action over land becomes static and hence as vulnerable as any other static target. In the final analysis, aviation cannot proceed beyond its intrinsic striking radius any faster than airdromes and ground organization can move.

The logic of this lesson is so startling that it paralyzes the imagination of people unprepared to accept the facts of air-power expansion to the ultimate circumglobular range. In the further development of military aeronautics it will be recognized that for maximum effectiveness air power must function directly, nonstop, from primary or home bases possessing strategic supplies. It must strike at the enemy in the air, on land or at sea, without way stations. These way stations or intermediary bases are at best a makeshift substitute for range, destined to be eliminated when that range is built into the airplane itself. In relation to the huge distances which will soon be compassed by aviation, it will make literally no difference whether a force takes off from the American mainland or from some island outpost a few hundred miles off the mainland. In point of fact the outpost, being dependent on outside communications for its fuel and other supplies, is less desirable as an operating point despite the fact that it is closer to the enemy target by a few hundred miles.

Floating airdromes, ship-borne aviation, are in a sense mobile intermediary stations. We have already noted that they are normally unable to survive when brought within the

radius of land-based aviation. The same thing is true of fixed
intermediary stations when they are within the radius of air
power operating from primary bases.

Since range and load-carrying capacity complement each
other, the striking force of aircraft is in inverse ratio to the
distance. Given two nations with approximately equal air-
power potentials, intermediary bases would fall almost automatically to the nation to which they are closest. The idea
that a European country could maintain bases in the West
Indies, let us say, against the United States is technically
fallacious. Because of the shorter distance, the American
striking force would be enormously greater. By the same
token, American maintenance of bases on islands close to
Europe against a European air-power nation is likewise ruled
out. (Only as long as the British Isles are unconquered, therefore, will it be possible or feasible for America to maintain
military way stations at places like Iceland and the Azores.)

"Steppingstones" for aviation, intermediary bases, are simply compensation for inadequate range. The task of holding
them, cut off as they are from the main sources of production and supply, would be too great to allow effective warmaking. The advantage would be too drastically on the side
of an adversary working directly from his home grounds.

Today the British Isles can be considered, in a sense, the
advanced base of the United Nations. But we know the difficulties of maintaining it, even with the help of the United
States, and despite the fact that the islands do possess immense local resources in manufacturing facilities and man
power. The British Isles, being seriously dependent on outside supplies, are definitely at a disadvantage against a self-
contained Continental power. (It is Germany's need to make
itself self-contained by acquiring ample sources of oil and
other essential materials which, more than any other factor,

explains its attempt to conquer Russia and the Near East.)

Advanced bases without the inherent advantages of the British Isles will be utterly impractical. True, the air potentials could be balanced if the entire supply, maintenance, and reinforcement of such bases were made by air transport, protected by a strong convoy air force; and if, in addition, enough aerial strength could be concentrated to maintain continuous and unquestioned local air mastery. The magnitude of the aerial-defense effort to shield a given point is not determined by the size of the point but the size of the opposing air force. Hence the defense of an advance base close to the enemy would call for an effort equivalent to the defeat of the entire enemy air strength. Under these circumstances it is sheer waste to maintain advance bases instead of hurling the full aerial potential directly against the adversary.

The entire logic of aerial warfare makes it certain that ultimately war in the skies will be conducted from the home grounds, with everything in between turned into a no-man's land. As soon as aviation exploits its full technical potentialities of fighting range, intermediary points will be abandoned, one after the other, like so many obsolete outer fortifications.

The military moral of these principles became increasingly clear as the war in the Pacific unfolded after December 7, 1941. In the Atlantic we had to occupy Greenland, then Iceland, in order to bring our air power to the scene of conflict and offset German aviation over that ocean. In relation to the Pacific, our aviation was even more backward. Our bombers, it is true, could fly to Hawaii, and thence to Wake, Guam, the Philippine Islands, but only one way, as a self-transport procedure, not as a two-way striking force. To dominate the water gaps between the islands of the southwestern Pacific from the air, our air force—bombers *and* pursuits—should have had a striking range equal to the largest water interval between any of the islands from Hawaii to Japan. It should, in other words, have had an operational radius equal to any theater of war from island to island. As long as we lack this minimal air force, we shall be gravely handicapped. Equipped with such a long-range air force, however, why attempt such a round-about strategy? Why expand the theater of operations to the entire Pacific, when air power of only slightly longer range could operate directly from Alaska and the Aleutian Islands? These, on the same continent with us, are in effect primary bases, permitting us to wage direct all-out air war against the Nipponese.

Summed up in a technical formula, all this means that a modern air force does not provide us with true air power until it has a striking radius equal to the maximum dimensions of the theater of operations.

**7.** *In aerial warfare the factor of quality is relatively more decisive than the factor of quantity.*

"Just planes" are not enough. Hitler and Göring counted confidently on overwhelming the RAF by sheer weight of their aviation equipment. We have seen how mistaken they were—how, in effect, a 25-mile edge in speed plus superior fire power decided the issue in the English skies in Britain's favor.

If you are faster than your adversary, you can engage him in combat at will—and can withdraw at will. The initiative is in your hands. You are able to start combat on your own terms and call it off at will. Next in importance to speed is fire power; once you have exploited the effect of a surprise attack or the advantage of relative position, whether you can continue to fight depends on whether you have superior fire power. In the absence of better speed and greater fire power, maneuverability and rate of climb become purely defensive factors.

In bombardment aviation, speed is secondary to load-carrying capacity and defensive combat fire power. The bombers which possess a greater bomb salvo, longer range, and a more powerful defensive armament can accomplish more destruction at a greater distance, brushing off the attacks of enemy pursuits. The fire power of bombardment aviation, of course, can be further enhanced by the fire power of convoying long-range pursuit planes. These vital military considerations were completely ignored by the German, French, and American military leaders. The demonstration was glaringly clear in the Battle of Britain, when Nazi bombers were shot down in droves. It was also demonstrated in the plight of our earlier Flying Fortresses, which, due to insufficient guns and their faulty disposition, proved extremely vulnerable.

Our aviation reverses in the Pacific were not, as popularly supposed, the result only of Japan's superiority in numbers. Press dispatches have described Japanese fighter planes powered with engines of 1675 horsepower, and carrying two 20-mm. cannons in addition to light machine guns. As against the American type apparently most extensively in use, the P-40, the enemy thus had an advantage of about 500 horsepower, which meant all-around better performance, besides the explosive action of 20-mm. cannon shells entirely lacking in the P-40. Had we possessed a quality coefficient sufficiently superior, we might have upset the Japanese air potential notwithstanding our quantitative handicap.

The efficiency of an air force is the product of quality and quantity. Not only specialists but the public at large must understand the elementary idea that the real measure of the

effective strength of aviation is obtained by multiplying the
number of planes by the coefficient of quality—not alone
the quality of equipment but the quality of men. If either
of the quality coefficients is zero, the effective strength remains zero even if a country has "clouds of planes."

The adding-machine conception of air power, which ex-
presses itself in undifferentiated statistics on the total number of planes planned or produced, rests on a delusion. Attention to this principle is of special value to Americans.
Because of our national talent for mass production and
standardization there is the danger that we may "freeze"
our aviation models too soon and too rigidly.

The rapid obsolescence in aviation, and the need to adjust
aircraft to special purposes or to overcome sudden innovations by the enemy, require a productive technique that is,
within reasonable bounds, flexible. Frequently the readiness
to produce better aviation, rather than the availability of an
inventory of actual aircraft, may become the crucial factor.
In one sense Britain benefited from its delay in building air
power. Having entered the production race late, it was able
to incorporate the results of later aerodynamical knowledge
into its pursuits, whereas Hitler's fighters had been "frozen"
for mass production years earlier. Like every other idea, this
can be carried to the absurd extreme of doing nothing. The
sensible compromise is to build as much as is necessary to
keep plant and personnel at a point where instantaneous expansion without confusion is possible, and to construct plant
facilities always with an eye to future developments.

Those who bet on quantity as the simplest and surest type
of superiority should not forget that a huge expansion of
numbers in weapons implies a proportionate investment of
American lives. Tactics and strategy based on qualitative
superiority will enable every American combatant to inflict

a larger total of destruction upon the enemy. It is important to note that every time we double quantity, we double the investment of American lives; but every time we double the efficiency of a weapon, we cut the investment of American lives in two.

The leverage of quality is something which we in America, in particular, should exploit to the limit. We have the engineering skills and inventive capacities to enable us to place reliance on superior performance—where it belongs— rather than to attempt to smother enemies by a mass investment of equipment and lives.

8. *Aircraft types must be specialized to fit not only the general strategy but the tactical problems of a specific campaign.*

The war to date has also brought into clear focus the principle of specialization as applied to air power. Naturally, there must be a well-balanced basic air force to cover all possible tactical contingencies with a minimum of types. But when a campaign is already defined, when the arena of action is known, narrower specialization of equipment must be considered.

It should be remembered that military aircraft are always a compromise among the primary factors of speed, range, altitude, and load-carrying capacity. An increase in any of these elements is unavoidably attained at a sacrifice in the other elements. Hence, to obtain maximum military efficiency in relation to a given target of vital importance, it may be expedient to design special equipment to answer the specific conditions defining such a target.

It may be that the standard range of the basic bombers is excessive for a certain target; in that case, the saving in fuel may be converted into larger explosive loads. More bombs cannot be put into planes not built for them, since that calls for additional space and mechanisms, necessitating much larger fuselages and consequently greater air drag; to design all basic bombers with such larger capacity would penalize them if they were called on to use their utmost range. The design of a plane must cut down on some performance elements in order to enhance others, assuring the best results for a particular task at a particular distance.

The German Heinkels and Dornier machines were used as all-purpose bombers; one day they struck at Dover, another at London, a third at the Shetland Islands. The destruction of the British capital was so vital to the Germans that they sacrificed 2300 aircraft in the futile attempt to achieve it. It would obviously have been more economical for the Germans to build a special fleet for this particular purpose. The same Heinkels and Dorniers, adapted to the special job, would have packed more than double the destructive wallop.

The principle of specialization underlines the importance of not merely outbuilding but *outthinking* all of our adversaries. More and more, we may be sure, aircraft will be planned for the accomplishment of definite purposes, even to the extent of taking a single objective, when its military significance warrants the investment. There will be not merely specific military characteristics for general strategic undertakings but extreme specialization of equipment for individual tactical purposes in specific theaters of operation. That is another reason why modern military leaders must have technological foresight as well as strategic and tactical foresight. They must be able to visualize not alone the tactical picture of the future operations but the specialized equipment demanded by that picture.

**9.** *Destruction of enemy morale from the air can be accomplished only by precision bombing.*

Another vital lesson, one that has taken even air specialists by surprise, relates to the behavior of civilian populations under air punishment. It had been generally assumed that aerial bombardment would quickly shatter popular morale, causing deep civilian reactions, possibly even nervous derangements on a disastrous scale. The progress of this war has tended to indicate that this expectation was unfounded.

On the contrary, it now seems clear that despite large casualties and impressive physical destruction, civilians can "take it." Provided they have the necessary patriotism and the will to fight, they can adjust themselves to the threats and the sacrifices much more readily than had been foreseen. On the whole, indeed, armed forces have been more quickly demoralized by air power than the unarmed city dwellers. (Of course, if populations are wiped out substantially or entirely, the game is up; we are dealing with large-scale destruction far short of such extremes.)

These facts are significant beyond their psychological interest. They mean that haphazard destruction of cities—sheer blows at morale—are costly and wasteful in relation to the tactical results obtained. Attacks will increasingly be concentrated on military rather than on random human targets. Unplanned vandalism from the air must give way, more and more, to planned, predetermined destruction. More than ever, the principal objectives will be critical aggregates of electric power, aviation industries, dock facilities, essential public utilities, and the like.

Unquestionably, the indiscriminate bombing of defenseless open cities will be used, but for tactical and not merely

morale reasons. For instance, the all-out aerial attack on
London was essentially provocative—aiming to draw the
whole British air force into combat with the intent of annihilating it. The Japanese bombardment of Manila had an even
clearer tactical purpose. General MacArthur's extremely limited aviation had already been divided into two sections to
support troops north and south of the capital. In order not
to overstrain this meager aerial strength, he wisely decided
to turn Manila into an open city. The Japanese, however,
attacked it all the same, hoping to goad the Americans into
splitting their aviation further by a last-minute defense of
the skies over Manila.

Should General MacArthur stay out of that trap, the Japanese no doubt calculated, Tokyo would at least gain a propaganda talking point—in claiming that the Americans were
not only ineffective but indifferent to the sufferings of the
Manila population. Incidentally, that is one more reason why
the general public should be taught to understand the principles of aerial warfare. They will then recognize that the
defense of one target or the failure to defend another may
have valid tactical cause. If America is attacked, our military leaders might at some juncture concentrate available
aviation to defend cities containing vital defense plants,
thus leaving other cities undefended. The inhabitants of the
slighted cities may feel outraged by such neglect, unless
they grasp the tactical importance of the operations and that
by absorbing destruction they are doing their patriotic duty.

In any case, the "panic" that was expected to spread
through a city or even a nation as bombs began to fall has
turned out to be a myth. Thinking on the subject of morale
therefore reverts to the basic idea that the will to resist can
be broken in a people only by destroying effectively the
essentials of their lives—the supply of food, shelter, light,

water, sanitation, and the rest. This clearly demands *pre-cision bombing* rather than random bombing. Bombardment from on high must fit strictly into the pattern of aerial block-ade, systematically wrecking the implements and channels of normal life until a complete breakdown of the will to fight and the ability to fight is accomplished.

A corollary of this lesson is that highly industrialized soci-eties are vastly more vulnerable to modern aerial warfare than more primitive societies. Urban populations dependent on public utilities, on great water reservoirs, on a constant flow of food and other essentials from outside their own communities, can obviously be more readily reduced to helplessness than populations accustomed to living on the soil. Industrialization provides perfect concentrated targets for enemy aviation.

It is well for Americans to realize that the United States presents the most vulnerable aerial target on the face of the earth. If only for that reason we have no alternative but to make ourselves the strongest and most effective air-power nation on the face of the earth.

10. *The principle of unity of command, long recognized on land and on sea, applies with no less force to the air.*

The air is not a part of the surface which it covers, but an element as distinct as land or sea. The notion that there is some mysterious distinction between air-over-land and air-over-ocean is a hangover from two-dimensional strategic thinking. Already that artificial differentiation, reflected in the United States and in some other countries in a corre-sponding artificial division of its air forces, has disappeared in the more advanced air-power countries. It is certain to disappear in the rest of the world, since it no longer corre-sponds to the facts of warfare.

The "air ocean" which envelops the entire globe is continuous and uninterrupted; it extends over prairies and mountains, rivers and oceans, deserts and icefields. Common sense and common tactical experience dictate unity of command. Military experts know that division of force spells disaster. To split an air command between other services, in arbitrary reference to the contours or character of the surface below the aerial theater of conflict, is like drawing a chalk line through the skies.

We have been sufficiently impressed, I trust, in all that we have considered with the axiom that conquest of the air is the *first condition* for operations below. It is a separate enterprise in a different sphere and must have a unified command. When air power fights an assisting action with ground forces it operates in specific localities. But when it is fighting for control of the air it operates simply in latitude and longitude, without reference to how wet or dry the terrain underneath may be.

There are three natural elements: land, sea, and air. Each of them must have an autonomous, independent organization in order that it may develop the last ounce of potentiality, the most appropriate equipment, and the best strategy without interference from either of the others. True co-ordination is possible only between autonomous but different members. Land, sea, and air services can be efficiently co-ordinated only when each is fully developed within its own sphere.

The absurdity of split command in the air was revealed for all but the blind to see in the first weeks of the war in the Pacific. The Japanese aerial offensive on Hawaii came as a single and continuous operation. It represented a single objective in the skies. Yet two different and almost unrelated air forces rose to meet the challenge: army aviation and naval aviation, each trained in a different military tradition, in different tactics, through different maneuvers. Even if one man were put in command of these duplicate units in the actual fighting, he would still deal with two forces having different military characteristics and personnel steeped in different military ideas.

Was the defense of the skies over Pearl Harbor to be regarded as merely a naval show, with the Army aviation grounded? Was the defense of the skies over the near-by Army base, Hickam Field, to be left to the Army aviation? Or were the two services expected to hold a conference to solve jurisdictional puzzles? If the New York area is hit from the skies, will the defense fall to the Navy's air arm at Floyd Bennett Field or to the Army's air arm at Mitchel Field?

What applies to the Hawaiian Islands or the New York area applies no less to the entire United States. The enemy in the air will represent a single objective, before it reaches our shores and after it is over our soil. There is no artificial line at which one aerial command bows out politely while the duplicate command takes over. We shall have two services milling in the same sphere, hunting the same quarry, but taking orders from two sources. Imagine the Battle of Britain under similar circumstances, with the Royal Air Force split into segments, one under the Admiralty and the other under the Army! That is precisely the situation which we face as long as we lack a homogeneous air force, under a single command; without these we cannot have air power, or assurance of victory.

11. *Air power must have its own transport.*

Aviation dependent on slow-moving surface communication lines for its supplies and replacements is an anomaly. It

is ludicrous to make an air force, moving at 300 or more miles
an hour, dependent on transport crawling along at ten or
fifteen knots. Furthermore, the main advantage of the aerial
weapon is that it ignores obstacles on the earth's surface. To
leave it in any way dependent on surface conditions for its
supplies and reinforcement is to impair its natural advantages. That is the case today in the Pacific, where our air
forces have been hamstrung because they have had to rely
on slow and uncertain sea communications.

Increasingly Germany has been using aerial transport for
aerial warfare. In Norway the initial troops, equipment, and
supplies were delivered by the *Luftwaffe*. In the Battle of
Crete the entire problem of transportation, including troop
movements, was solved by Hitler with airplanes. We also
know that Germany transported supplies, equipment, fuel,
and even light tanks through the skies to northern Africa.

It was lack of swift and sure transport which handicapped
the defense of the Hawaiian and Philippine Islands. Given
adequate air transport, including delivery of aircraft on their
own power, the Hawaiian defenders might have been reinforced in seven or eight hours.

The American aeronautical industry and individual designers and students of aviation for years pressed upon the
War Department plans for long-range cargo planes, long-
range pursuit and convoy fighters. They saw the coming need
for equipment that could reach all our outlying possessions
under its own power. These proposals were always arbitrarily dismissed as farfetched. Sometimes such ideas were
even resented as sacrilegious in that they cast doubt on the
ability of navies and armies to cope with transport problems.

Yet by this time it is obvious that air power must be fully
self-contained. It must rely on its own transport, being geared

to carry with it at all times reserve equipment, reserve supplies, and also, when necessary, troops through the air.

It will be possible for critics to take exception to one or another of these "lessons." In a good many events of the war the part played by aviation has been obscured by the absence of appropriate equipment; in others the official version of the event has been deeply colored, often unconsciously, by the mental slants of the old-style military men who did the reporting. Yet, after all discounts are made, the vitality of air power and its incursion upon textbook precepts and assumptions still remain. It is easy to dispute over this or that specific item in the account, but the total cannot be seriously challenged.

Reviewing our present aeronautical picture in the United States in the light of these lessons, we realize how far we have fallen short. We have no air power. We have only army and naval aviation developed and used primarily as auxiliary weapons for surface operations. Though navies can no longer approach hostile shores defended by genuine land-based air power, the fiction that our Navy is our primary striking force is still maintained. The neutralization of enemy air forces is now the precondition for attacking hostile areas, yet we have no long-range air power, and our available aviation is treated essentially as a defensive element. The range and striking power of our aviation have been artificially curtailed in order to avoid encroaching on the offensive functions of the Navy, which can no longer fulfill those functions. We are geared to mass production of fine airplanes but with tragically inadequate attention to their tactical suitability. While we are catching up with the enemy in many respects, planes on the production line today will unquestionably be obsolete by the time they are put into action.

Worst of all, our aviation equipment is built without specific relation to definite strategic and tactical problems facing us; it has not the range for independent action in the ever-widening theater of operations, being normally an appendage to slow-moving surface forces. We lack even a vestige of unity of command in the aerial sphere. As a matter of plain fact, we have neither air power nor airmen, but only flying soldiers and flying sailors who do not even speak the same military language.

# CHAPTER VII

# THE TWILIGHT OF SEA POWER

—— 1 ——

MEN RAISED in the rich naval traditions naturally have a deep emotional attachment to sea power. They resent doubts of its continuing and eternal ascendancy as they would a slur on their private characters. There is something of the old-school spirit and caste loyalty in their refusal—nay, their psychological inability—to admit any serious inroads on the navy's ancient domain by a new weapon. A doting parent is the last to recognize in his darling child shortcomings which are obvious to strangers—and navy enthusiasts are the last to acknowledge that aviation is displacing surface fleets in one after another important function of warfare.

A high-ranking Army Air Corps general, writing on the role of aviation, listed an array of glorious land and naval battles through the ages, from Marathon and Salamis to the Marne and Jutland. Then he added:

"It is but human that the older military services ... should regard the pretensions of air power with a measure of distrust, and should prefer that this new petitioner content himself with a subordinate status in a world at war."

There we have, in one amazing sentence, the strange attitude of certain groups in the older services. They treat a life-and-death problem of national security as though it were a question of dinner-table etiquette! How many more battleships will have to be sunk from on high before our naval diehards realize that inherited concepts of sea power must

be brought into alignment with the new conditions of the
air-power age? How long will it be before military bureau-
crats stop thinking of historical seniority and face immediate realities? The treatment of weapons and strategies in
terms of "new petitioners" and "subordinate status" would
be humorous if it were not loaded with menace to our national safety. Incredible though it may sound to the layman,
there are generals and admirals who in their zeal to uphold
the prestige of their particular service tend to forget the very
reason for the existence of that service. The fact that they
are well meaning and patriotic does not make their influence
any less harmful.

It is also human, I submit, for the "new petitioners," the
exponents of true air power, to regard the pretensions of
the senior services with a measure of alarmed impatience.
Precisely because we are on the firing lines of "a world at
war," questions of prestige and precedence must be cast
overboard. Neither Marathon nor the Marne can offer solid
and explicit guidance in a type of warfare that has come
into its own only in the past few years and is even now in
the early stages of its development.

We have looked at events since September, 1939, and
have seen how they shaped new principles of warfare, conditioned by the transfer of the conflict into the skies. Sea
power has been shorn of one duty after another. Fleets have
been stymied at points where previously they would have
dominated the situation. Nations strong in naval force have
been balked by a nation without any, and have turned over
to aircraft, of necessity, tasks which formerly only sea power
could undertake. Where a navy still operates essentially as
in the past, it is for one of two reasons:

   1. Because the action is in areas safely beyond the range
of land-based aviation, or

2. Because the enemy's aviation is inadequate, inferior, or nonexistent.

Under all other conditions, naval units either must withdraw to a safe distance or work under the shielding wings of friendly land-based air power. Battleships can venture into hostile waters which are protected by aircraft from primary bases only under an umbrella of air power equal to or superior to the total enemy aviation on such bases. To do anything less is to court destruction. But that sort of convoy is uneconomical and illogical. It is very much like conducting a machine gun to its task under an escort of Big Berthas. Once a country has air power enough to guard a battle fleet in enemy waters, why not unloose that air power directly at the heart of the enemy instead of wasting it to shield a less effective force?

Navies are no longer lords of the seas. Their authority is being rapidly restricted and in some respects wholly wiped out. Certain naval units may be salvaged for auxiliary jobs under the protection of air power. A portion may make itself felt against backward nations lacking effective aircraft. But the rest—especially the battleships—will be consigned to museums of outlived weapons along with the bow and arrow and the blunderbuss.

As a primary, self-sufficient branch of national defense, navies are already finished. References to naval might as our "outer defense" or "first line of defense" already bring curious echoes of a far-off past. The complacency with which we once relied on such slogans seems as tragic as reliance on the Maginot Line must now seem to Frenchmen. Those who have not caught up with the revolution in war science brought about by the advent of air power may dismiss as exaggeration talk of first-line warships destined for the scrapheap. Yet a consideration of the facts we have already touched on reveals that I am merely setting down the inescapable conclusion to be drawn from the experience of this war.

One of the air-power lessons summed up in the preceding pages is that navies have already lost their function of strategic offensive. Even their defensive usefulness, being limited to regions beyond the striking radius of aviation, must shrink as the reach of air power is enlarged. It is quite possible, therefore, to foresee the vanishing point: as soon as air power can strike directly across oceans, navies will be finally eliminated as a primary factor in warfare. At that point sea power will become a subsidiary function of air power. Navies, of course, will remain thereafter as an accessory service. As long as we have sea commerce, we shall have some sort of surface policing. But in the final analysis the safety of the commerce and the survival of those policing units will be guaranteed by the control of the skies above.

While the whole world looks on, the Atlantic and the Pacific are crumbling as barriers to aviation. In my own carefully considered view, the ultimate round-the-world range of 25,000 miles—enabling a nation to strike at any point on the face of the earth in any direction—is at most five years away. When that range is achieved, there will remain no major tactical task now entrusted to navies which will not be swallowed up by aviation. But as I have already indicated, in practice a 15,000-mile battleplane, having a striking radius of some 6000 miles, can give air power total dominance of the world, since such a radius covers all major nations with their capitals and strategic industrial centers.

—————————————— 2 ——————————————

THESE TRUTHS cannot be shouted down by rhetoric invoking the glories of naval history. It is a matter of sense, not of sentiment. The towering fact is that fleets no longer can approach hostile shores which are guarded by first-class aviation forces. For centuries one of the principal jobs of navies was to carry the conflict to the enemy: to attack the outer ramparts of a country, its coastlines and harbors and fortresses, whether as part of the strategy of eliminating the enemy's sea power or to establish bridgeheads for invasion. Now that job has been taken over by air power.

The British fleet has been unable to take offensive measures against any portion of the Nazi-held European continent. Except where the Royal Air Force is strong enough to control the air above, that fleet must remain at a safe distance—the distance being determined by the range of the enemy's aviation. The point of the story is that the picture would not be materially different if the British Navy were a dozen times bigger and stronger. As far as ability to assault shores defended by adequate aviation is concerned, the role of navies has not merely been diminished—it has ended.

The most impressive fact about the long Battle of Britain has been the virtual elimination of the armies and navies of both adversaries. In the all-air battle, the older services have remained impotent. Not all the strength and courage of the fleet could have saved the British Isles from aerial annihilation had the air forces been unequal to the task. The RAF fought the battle alone in the English skies and over enemy targets. Even the systematic bombardment of Hitler's so-called invasion ports and submarine bases near the coast—objectives within the easy reach of naval guns—has been carried out exclusively by British air power. It was neither the Army nor the Navy, but the Royal Air Force which has dammed the flood tide of millions of mechanized German troops across a narrow water barrier.

The grip of clichés on the mind of man is not easy to break. In England, as in our own country, the notion that "the country's chief defense is its navy" has acquired the force of a commandment handed down from Mt. Sinai. Doubtless it was being repeated through sheer habit in the British Isles even while air power was so clearly their main reliance. Yet we need only imagine the RAF out of commission—not a ship could then reach England, for all that the Admiralty could do. The approaches would be as Nazi-dominated from the air as the Skagerrak and Kattegat straits. Not a battleship could survive under the roof of enemy aviation long enough to interfere with German plans for invasion or for unhampered destruction from the skies without benefit of invasion.

British sea power was practically driven from the North Sea by Nazi aviation based in Norway. Whether Britannia's fleet can remain in the Mediterranean depends not at all on the size or skill of that fleet. It depends, in the final analysis, on whether British or Axis air power will obtain mastery of the Mediterranean skies. Assume that the last of Mussolini's fighting ships has been sent to the bottom of the Mediterranean by the British, but that Hitler's aviation has captured full dominion of the air overhead. That sea would then be utterly untenable for the "victorious" British Navy which would have to retreat from the aerial menace even as it did in the North Sea, or subject itself to a hopeless ordeal such as it faced at Crete.

In that epochal engagement at Crete the world witnessed a clear-cut confrontation of overwhelming sea power and overwhelming air power. Air power triumphed. That is the fundamental fact of the event, which no amount of fanciful "interpretation" can quite obscure. Its moral has been amply underscored by developments in the Pacific. The Japanese invasion of the Philippines was possible only because the defenders could not hold the skies. Had American naval units been massed at the scene they would merely have provided convenient targets for the enemy's air power.

Let us enlarge the focus of any of these pictures to the breadth of the Atlantic. The eastern portion, within bomb shot of German air power, has been made a no-man's land by long-range aircraft. Though Germany has as yet relatively few of its giant Focke-Wulf bombers in action in this theater of war, official sources in Washington by April, 1941, were crediting fifty per cent of the tonnage sent to the bottom of the Atlantic to air raiders. In the area under Nazi threat from the air, the RAF rather than surface convoys increasingly provides the only real protection to commerce.

Fully aware that the battle of the Atlantic is being gradually transferred to the air, the British, and later also the Americans, have sought to assure themselves of protection in the skies above the ocean. They began to install on merchantmen fighter aircraft, which are catapulted from the decks when enemy planes appear. Hurricane planes thus are often able to attack Hitler's four-motored Focke-Wulfe bombers, after which they alight at sea, forfeiting the plane, or make for the nearest shore if they have enough flying range left. As soon as the range of fighter aircraft is sufficiently extended, of course, such protection against enemy bombers at sea will be offered directly from land, rounding out air dominance in the battle of the Atlantic.

In a radio broadcast on May 6, 1941, Secretary of War Stimson drew a somber picture of England's plight at that time. The British Isles, he said at one point, "are threatened both by attacks from the air and blockade from the sea." He referred to the dire possibility that their government might "fall either from starvation or from attack." Then he added: "The life line of Great Britain is threatened. The high-water mark of the Nazi effort is at hand in the shape of an attack on the shipping which furnishes Britain with the means and the nourishment to maintain her battle."

That was a state of affairs unthinkable in the days of Mahan. A nation with an overwhelming preponderance of sea power was being slowly choked to death through employment of aviation by a country practically devoid of naval strength! The new relationship of weapons cannot easily be overlooked in that situation. The battleship faces an adversary who has lifted his striking force into a third dimension, into a medium which the surface vessel cannot penetrate. At best the striking power carried by the battleship loses all value at the shore line; whereas the same power conveyed through the air can be made effective beyond the shore line, over land, with the identical ease and identical results as over water.

Now imagine the operational radius of air power expanded three to five times—as it inevitably will be in the next few years. The Atlantic then becomes another Skagerrak, every bit as vulnerable as the North Sea. Unless our Navy is protected by superior land-based aviation, it must escape from the Atlantic—even if our enemy has no navy at all. America will then be in precisely the same strategic position as the British Isles today, with the Atlantic Ocean equivalent to the English Channel and its control, like control of the Channel today, depending on relative aviation strengths.

There will no longer be any warrant in common sense for

LARGEST AMERICAN BOMBER, DOUGLAS B-19, IN FLIGHT. The offensive initiative of battleships has been usurped by hard-hitting superbombers.

COVENTRY. The English city was wrecked by 500 Nazi bombers. The same number of bombers of the immediate future will be capable of demolishing 100 such cities at one blow.

BARRAGE BALLOONS OF THE FLEET. The advent of air powe
further encumbers the operations of naval forces.

carrying striking power slowly across the ocean by battle-ship when it can be carried faster, more cheaply, and more effectively by battleplane. In any case the battleship will be unable to perform this strategic errand unless and until air power clears the skies over the ocean of enemy planes and maintains a canopy of overhead protection over the entire span.

The 45,000-ton capital ship of the sort now being built by our Navy will cost approximately $100,000,000—a sum that could pay for the construction of 100 bombers capable of flying to a European target, dropping their explosive loads, and returning to America. Since each of these craft could carry about twenty tons of explosive—as much as forty German Stuka dive-bombers now deliver—their combined striking power would be equal to 4000 Stukas. Such, in simple arithmetic, is the economic equivalent in air power of a single capital ship only slightly larger than the *Repulse* or the *Prince of Wales,* sunk by Japanese airplanes in the Pacific.

The more closely we study those economic equivalents, the more impressive they become. A naval appropriation announced in September, 1941, totaling seven billion dollars, covered the construction among other things, of 17 battle-ships, 14 heavy cruisers, and 12 aircraft carriers. Estimating the cost of the batleships, cruisers, and aircraft carriers at an aggregate of some three billions, it means that for the same price we could build 1500 superbombers at two million dollars each—of a type having a 6000-mile effective radius (sufficient to reach any major capital in Europe or Asia), each carrying at least 50 tons of bombs.

Such an armada of aircraft would carry 75,000 tons of explosive. The magnitude of this force is suggested when we recall that the devastation of Coventry was accomplished with about 250 tons of explosive. Our theoretical armada could therefore achieve devastation 300 times greater, either concentrated on one point or distributed on 300 Coventries!

Now let us estimate the aircraft carrier as an economic investment. The average new modern carrier costs about $50,000,000, complete with all trimmings. It ordinarily carries approximately 75 dive-bombers or torpedo planes. Under operating conditions, about two thirds of the complement of aircraft is used in combat, leaving 25 planes in reserve—usually pursuits for the defense of the carrier. The striking force of 50 naval dive-bombers is expressed by 50 tons of high explosives or 50 torpedoes.

For $50,000,000 we could build at least 25 long-range torpedo bombing planes to provide aerial support to surface forces at any spot on the seven seas. Each of these planes would be capable of carrying 50 tons of explosive or 50 torpedoes, giving us a total striking force of 1250 tons or 1250 torpedoes—which is to say, 25 times as much as one carrier at the same cost. Since it takes approximately five torpedoes to dispose of a battleship, the potential destructive force of such a land-based squadron of huge bombers, purchasable at the price of a single aircraft carrier, would be strong enough to sink some 250 battleships. Under these conditions it becomes absurd to build aircraft range into "floating hangars" when it can be built into the aircraft themselves.

But that is not the whole story. Recent war experience has left no doubt that aircraft carriers are the most vulnerable part of the fleet. The whole carrier investment can be eliminated at one blow. A flight of 25 long-range torpedo bombers based on land may suffer casualties, but the great majority of them, if they possess adequate combat power, would live to repeat the attack again and again. In short, we could obtain about 25 times as much value, plus a vastly longer life span, for every dollar invested in carrier-based aviation if it were converted into long-range land-based planes. Besides, aviation brought to the scene of action on carriers can no longer venture into waters defended by powerful land-based aircraft, whereas the superbombers will be able to fight their way through to the target. The common sense of these facts is difficult to evade. Even if any of these specific figures should be challenged, the differential should still be sufficiently large to overcome the inertia of naval thinking in all but the hopeless cases.

Suppose, for the sake of argument, we consider types of planes already constructed instead of the two-million-dollar type which I took for granted above. The Douglas super-bomber and the Martin Flying Boat bomber carry almost twenty tons of explosive. In quantity production those planes could be built at about a million dollars each. For the price of the battleships, heavy cruisers, and aircraft carriers under the September, 1941, appropriations, therefore, we could have some 3000 of these planes, with an aggregate striking force of 60,000 tons of explosives. A single aircraft carrier translated into such airplanes would give us about 50 of the Douglas B-19's or the Martin Flying Boats, able to deliver 1000 tons of explosive projectiles.

No matter how the values are converted, the results are so staggering that it is really incredible how smugly we continue to hold on to outdated strategies and equipment, when the same tactical results can be achieved at immeasurably smaller cost, or with immeasurably greater effect.

It may be objected that aircraft carriers, with all their obvious faults, are at least always at hand when needed, since they travel with the surface fleet. The objection holds good in waters as yet immune to land-based aviation. For that reason such carriers should be an integral part of the fleet as long as they are needed at all. But once air power avails itself of the full present technical possibilities of aeronautics, there will be no such immune waters. Fleets will simply be unable to venture into the open seas until the air over the entire water expanse is in friendly hands. Besides, aircraft of the type we are discussing will be able to maintain constant vigilance over entire oceans, and will contact hostile fleets days before surface navies can possibly do so. Demolition of approaching naval forces will be undertaken, and normally completed, from the skies long before surface ships can come to the scene of action.

The idea that navies can carry war to hostile shores across the ocean under the protection of air power brought along on armadas of aircraft carriers and unleashed against the enemy is wholly unrealistic. We are already familiar with the shortcomings of ship-borne aviation and the vulnerability of its floating bases. But there are other considerations which make such an undertaking utopian and doom it to failure if directed against any nation with even a minimal amount of defensive aviation.

Ordinarily when the air power of a nation is hurled at an adversary, only the combat or fighter planes rise for defense. The bombardment aviation in such a conflict remains idle and subject to overhead destruction along with other static components of the defending air power. When the attacking air power is brought on board ships, the situation immediately changes to the great detriment of the attacker's position. The bombardment aviation in that case is no longer dormant and ineffectual. It becomes a significant defensive weapon by reason of its ability to eliminate the attacking aviation of all types—through the destruction of its floating bases.

Assuming that the carrier has brought one hundred planes,

an equal force is needed to dispose of them in the air. But one bombing plane, as we have already noted, can cancel out the entire force by crippling its "base," the carrier. In effect, therefore, a single bomber or torpedo plane can defeat a hundred ship-borne airplanes and may become a hundred times as effective as pursuit planes opposing the invaders in the sky.

More than that: normally, as the air lessons of this war have proved, only air power can defeat air power. But when that air power has been brought on ships, the situation changes. The entire naval surface and undersea forces of the menaced nation can actually grapple with the invading air power by attacking and destroying its floating bases. In short, when an attack is made by pure air power, only a fraction of its defensive strength—its pursuit aviation—is brought into play; but when that air force is brought by surface vessels, the whole defensive power—pursuits, bombers, battleships, submarines, torpedo boats—can be utilized to meet the onslaught. Besides, the strength of such an invading air force, if accompanied by a naval fleet, must be divided between attack on the enemy and protection of its floating bases, thereby reducing the potential that can be hurled at the enemy.

Invasion under the shield of ship-borne air power, it is obvious, is costly, cumbersome, and futile. Regardless of the distances, direct aerial attack from primary bases is the only means by which an offensive can be launched with hope of success today. Under no conceivable circumstances can navies any longer figure in a strategic offensive against enemy shores unless they are protected by shore-based aviation at least equal to the enemy's. In that case, however, the naval function can be only secondary if it can make a contribution at all. Air power strong enough to shield naval force can deal with the enemy more expeditiously itself.

I am not, let it be understood, advocating the abolition of the navy. It is obvious that at present, and until the time when true air power is available, navies will continue to play an important and indispensable part. At this juncture, for instance, the British and American navies still have a vital role in keeping Britain alive by holding open the supply lines to the British Isles. But it must be realized that the navy functions fully and freely, whether in blockading the enemy or defending its own merchantmen, only beyond the reach of aviation. It is able to make its present contribution only by reason of the insufficiency of that reach, and is consequently being more and more restricted as the range potential of aircraft is exploited more fully.

It should be pointed out that the vital, if passive, defensive task of keeping shipping lanes to the British Isles open has been imposed upon our navies by the special and peculiar situation of the battle area. As a comparatively small island, lacking essential natural resources and foodstuffs, England must rely on its foreign transport. If the British Isles were self-sustaining—in the measure, let us say, that the United States is self-sustaining—the British Navy would lose also this vital present-day and clearly temporary function. The statement is often made that though navies may have become partly obsolete for the British Isles, they are paramount for America on account of our geographical location. Exactly the reverse happens to be the case. Think of the British Islands expanded to the size of the United States and economically self-sustained, no longer in life-and-death dependence on overseas supplies. With the passive job of protecting ocean commerce reduced to the vanishing point, our Navy, no matter how colossal in size, would then remain unemployed while mastery of the air—the Battle of the U.S.A., parallel to the Battle of Britain—was being decided.

One of our military commentators, in a magazine article defending traditional naval ideas, pointed out that "today an insular power like Britain, close to a hostile or potentially hostile continent, cannot provide that secure base which is the one indispensable requirement of sea power." He credits the change to "a world made narrow by the plane." From this he argues that the United States, surrounded by oceans, "can and does provide such a base," and that therefore "our future greatness lies upon the great waters."

The flaw in this typically naval-minded reasoning is that it assumes aviation will remain frozen at roughly its present stage. It does not recognize that the world is being further "narrowed by the plane" every day, so that American insularity is as doomed as Britain's insularity. In three years, if not sooner, that doom will be a fact on our Atlantic shore and within five years on the Pacific shore as well; just about the time, that is, when our new two-ocean navy on which such military experts pin their faith will have been completed. It is the inadequate range of air power which still makes America "that secure base which is the one indispensable requirement of sea power," and this minimal condition for the very existence of sea power is obviously fading out.

Perhaps you have seen a lake being drained, crowding the fish into its contracting center where fishermen can scoop them up without effort. Even thus the progress of air power is "draining" water areas from the periphery inward, driving navies to the ever more shrunken center, seeking desperately to evade the tightening ring of doom. Soon it will be all "dry," with no margin of escape from air power. Today we are witnessing the twilight of sea power. Tomorrow the

whole epoch of modern history conditioned by that weapon
will be ended.

--------------------------------- 3 ---------------------------------

THE STALE argument of battleship versus airplane has always
seemed beside the point. Whether battleships are sunk outright or put out of action for six-month periods every half
year appeared to possess largely academic difference. Since
the beginning of the war, British and American shipyards
have been jammed with warships disabled by aerial bombing. With battleships like the *Prince of Wales*, the *Repulse*,
the *Haruna*, and the *Arizona* on the floor of the Pacific, that
old argument is ended once and for all. There is no room
left for wishful thinking or farfetched explanations. The
*Prince of Wales* was of the most modern type—the type
which our experts assured us was "unsinkable." Nevertheless,
it is worth looking at a few episodes and technical facts relat-
ing to the old controversy.

Fully two decades ago I had the privilege of serving as
technical consultant to General Mitchell when he demonstrated that a battleship could be sunk from the air by actually sinking one off Newport News. His experiment was
light-mindedly dismissed in the highest military quarters on
the ground that the ship was old and derelict. These quarters would not listen to our warning that while battleships
would be better armed and armored in the future, the striking power and performance of aircraft too would be raised
—and in the nature of the case at a much faster rate. The
result was that General Mitchell's idea of preparing heavy
long-range bombardment aviation against our potential enemies—an idea now universally recognized—was shelved for
nearly twenty years.

From that day to this, old-line military spokesmen have always found an alibi to match every new proof of the vulnerability of surface forces to overhead assault, and every new demonstration that the familiar functions of sea power have been curtailed or wiped out altogether by the advent of air power. Outwardly it has looked as if in their anxiety to preserve textbook military notions they deliberately refused to benefit from experience. But the explanation is not so simple. Such men, more likely, are honestly unable to digest the new experience. Minds thoroughly trained and set in a certain direction automatically reject facts that do not fit into their accustomed mental patterns. There was no rational explanation, from the point of view of an airman familiar with the facts of aviation life, for the passionate insistence that battleships were invulnerable to airplane attacks.

General Mitchell had to dispose of his battleship with a 2000-pound bomb dropped from a very low altitude, first because planes were unable to gain altitude with what was a tremendous load for that day; and second, because his sighting devices were too primitive for high altitude use. But long before the present war started both those factors ceased to operate.

The accuracy of bomb sights has been raised to a remarkable degree and is being constantly refined. Theoretically any sight works with a precision of ten minutes of arc, which is one sixth of a degree, giving a lineal error on the ground of approximately 100 feet from 30,000 feet. Under combat conditions, allowing for human error, accuracy in bombing at that height—which is comfortably above the ceiling of antiaircraft artillery—should be within half a degree, or roughly within a circle 600 feet in diameter on the target. From 20,000 feet the bomb should fall within a circle only 200 feet in diameter. That is about twice the beam width of a battleship or aircraft carrier. Hence a formation of three bombers, dropping their projectiles in a salvo with proper timing, can hardly fail to produce a pattern that must find its mark on the target.

Another fact should be noted, since it increases the vulnerability of surface targets at sea to air assault. As the size of the bombing plane grows, the pattern of bomb releases can be produced not only in the direction of the flight, but also in width. Take, for example, the B-19 superbomber. It has a wingspread of 200 feet, which is twice the width of the beam of a modern battleship or carrier. By locating the bombs in the wings, the breadth of the salvo pattern can be extended to 100 feet. Lengthwise, the pattern can be stretched to any desirable dimension by the timing of bomb releases in flight. Thus what previously could be accomplished only by a formation of bombers can now be managed by a single airplane. It can obtain a pattern of bombing hits 100 feet wide and, let us say, 600 feet long—which would completely cover a modern battleship.

No less impressive advances have been made since Billy Mitchell's days in the weight and effectiveness of the projectile. Our Flying Fortresses can carry 8000 pounds of explosive, in one or many missiles. Dropped from a high altitude, a four-ton projectile would strike a battleship at 1100 feet per second, producing a terrific impact. The B-19 could drop roughly 20 tons, which is to say a projectile of 40,000 pounds! And some of the planes now being projected will ultimately carry loads of 50 tons, so that theoretically they could deliver a projectile of 100,000 pounds. Such a mass hitting a battleship at more than 1000 feet per second velocity would jar all the mechanisms of the ship from their moorings and disable it completely even if the actual projectile did not contain explosive but bricks in a streamlined container.

As to methods of bombing battleships and other floating targets, the horizontal and the dive-bomber procedure each has advantages and drawbacks, and must be suited to the special tactical conditions. Dive-bombers are generally more valuable against smaller, faster-moving vessels. Though the present bomb load is very limited, there is no reason why it should not be increased. A direct hit on any ship except a modern battleship or cruiser is fatal, as this war amply proved. Battleships can be crippled beyond use by a direct hit or two, not only because of actual damage but because of the dislodgment of delicate apparatus essential for the functioning of the ship. Dive-bombers can also exploit the element of surprise. By releasing bombs at low altitudes they leave little if any time for the vessel to dodge the projectile. On the other hand, they are naturally more vulnerable to antiaircraft defenses, the vulnerability being in inverse ratio to the altitudes from which the bomb is released.

There is also the torpedo-carrying plane. Due to the fact that horizontal bombers have not been equipped with sufficiently effective projectiles, as could readily have been done, the aerial torpedo has shown up as the deadliest weapon against battleships. The planes fly low over the water and drop the regular naval torpedoes which, upon striking the water, proceed toward the target under their own power. To enhance the element of surprise, curtains of smoke are laid alongside the battleship. The crews manning the battleship guns cannot anticipate the exact spot from which the torpedo plane will dart to fire a torpedo and disappear again in the smokescreen.

Thus far in America torpedo planes have been employed almost exclusively by the Navy's air arm, which is another illustration of the jurisdictional red tape in which our aviation is entangled. Navies have no more natural monopoly on torpedoes than armies have on guns. True air power is able to attack targets on land or sea alike with any and all weapons and should not be artificially restrained. In his 1941 report to the President, Secretary of War Stimson described our Army Air Forces as a long-range striking force against hostile navies seeking to approach our territory. Yet those Army Air Forces are almost entirely limited to bombs, ignoring the deadly torpedo weapon. The nonsensical overlapping, contradictions, and bureaucratic handicaps of soldier-aviation and sailor-aviation operating in the self-same tactical medium becomes curiouser and curiouser, as Alice in Wonderland put it, as ranges are extended.

The rock-bottom fact is that there is no practical structure afloat, nor can any be produced with real tactical value, which could withstand the blows that modern aviation can hail upon it. The attack for maximum effect is tridimensional, employing all three methods: horizontal altitude bombing, dive-bombing, and torpedo assault.

When General Mitchell was making his fight for true American air power, naval diehards offered jocularly to remain on board any battleship he proposed to bomb from the air. In the perspective of time the offer sounds like one of those horse-and-buggy jibes at the newfangled horseless wagons in the early years of the automobile. But we do not have to go back that far for samples of deep skepticism about military aviation in high places, coupled with an abiding faith in the eternal validity of sea power.

When British, American, and Japanese battleships were already at the bottom of the Pacific, an article by the current Secretary of the Navy, Colonel Frank Knox, was still on the newsstands ridiculing those who suggest that "the battleship had been 'outmoded' by the airplane." Civilian officials, of course, cannot be held personally accountable for their technical military opinions. They merely give voice, loyally, to the views held by their top-shelf experts. And on that level the subordinate role of aviation is an article of faith, with little enough tolerance for heretics.

Admiral William V. Pratt was speaking for all the orthodox experts when he explained, on a radio program on June 11, 1940, why airplanes could never sink battleships: "A battleship is so heavily armored that when a bomb strikes it, the force of the explosion goes upward, into the air, and very little damage is done." Admiral Clark H. Woodward told a sad and simple truth about the upper naval leadership when he declared in a newspaper piece on October 10, 1940, that "the Navy is unanimous in its belief that the battleship is still supreme at sea." He warned that "exaggerated statements as to the effect of bombing planes upon battleships should be heavily discounted." The citations could be extended for pages. They amount to an eagerness to "save face" for the Navy, by blurring the lessons of experience.

It is not at all certain that even the tragic lessons of the initial months in the Pacific Ocean war will finally end the illusions of naval diehards. Their distrust and resentment of the new weapon are outside the field of reasoned conviction. The naval losses in the Pacific, however, have driven home the basic tactical fact that no battleship can any longer go about its business until the skies overhead have been cleared of enemy aviation. But once the skies above any arena of combat are in our hands, of what earthly use are the battleships? What, specifically, can they do that the victorious aviation cannot do more expeditiously? Whether the objective is an enemy vessel, a hostile shore, a coastal fortification, air power can attack it more quickly and more economically than any warship. Not only can it strike at surface objectives on the seas, as the battleship does, it can also strike at hostile aviation in the skies and at inland objectives, which no battleship can do.

The essence of the matter is that control of the skies—of the "air ocean" which envelops land and sea alike—will determine the final outcome of the present struggle. The nation or combination of nations which dominates the air over our planet will be able to rule the world, even as in the past the nations controlling the seas ruled the world. No victory on the surface of the ocean is permanent unless it is guaranteed by air power.

─────────────────── 4 ───────────────────

POLITICALLY, the British Navy still holds the upper hand in "jurisdictional" matters as against the air forces. This was evident in the attack on the Italian Navy in Taranto, and even more so in the disposition of the German battleship *Bismarck*. After Hitler's dreadnaught had been torpedoed and slowed down, it might have been left to the RAF for final disposition. Indeed, it offered a rare opportunity to test air-bombardment strength on the most modern naval target. Had the test been made, the British might not have risked the *Prince of Wales* and the *Repulse* in the Pacific. But it was a "naval show" and the honor of the final "kill" was left to cruisers firing torpedoes at close range.

At the Axis end of the struggle, it is quite conceivable that the Germans, having few battleships of their own and being fully conscious that enemy battleships no longer constitute an offensive threat against German-held areas, were not especially eager to sink them from the air. Why convince the Allies of the fallacy of their psychological dependence on sea power? On the contrary, the more that Britain and America could be led to rely on battleships, the better from Hitler's viewpoint. The Germans are so lacking in naval strength that, in relation to the Anglo-American bloc, their sea power is zero. Further increase of Allied naval forces could not make the ratio any smaller than zero.

Increase of British aerial strength, on the contrary, with its ultimate threat of mastery of the skies, is something that the Germans had reason to dread. It was surely not to their interest to divert Anglo-American energies and economic investment from naval to aerial construction. Germany had everything to lose and nothing to gain from disabusing our naval diehards of their error. Every Anglo-American argument for bigger and still-bigger sea power, every diversion of attention from the air to the surface, was a strategic victory for the nation which aims to attain world dominion on the basis of its air dominance. Our obsession with naval strategy gives the right of way to the Axis plan of universal control through air power, and it may be surmised that Hitler had no wish to disturb that obsession.

My suspicions in this regard were first aroused by photographs of bombings of British battleships in the Mediterranean. They showed from ten to eighteen bombs dropped on the target. So many bombs carried by one airplane cannot be of large caliber. The bombings, I became convinced, were deliberately intended to cripple rather than to sink capital ships. The illusion of battleship invincibility created by this process may have been a species of subtle Nazi propaganda to support naval as against aerial strategy in America and in Britain. Only the entry of Japan spoiled that propaganda. Possessing a real navy itself, Japan momentarily had too much to gain through weakening our naval forces and hence proceeded to dispose of enemy capital ships in a business-like manner.

Since our enemies, apart from Japan, have virtually no battleships, it is something of a strain on credulity that we should deplete our national resources for weapons to overcome nonexistent targets. The change that has come to warfare at sea may be surmised from the fact that the Japanese, in their conquest of the Pacific archipelago down to the brim of Australia, made little if any use of battleships; except for the *Haruna* episode, Japanese battleships were conspicuous by their absence. The idea is repeatedly advanced that if Hitler is victorious in Europe, including the British Isles, he will immediately proceed to build a supercolossal navy against the United States. Civilian statesmen, echoing the unthinking formulas of military men still living mentally in the era of 1914, are fond of evoking the picture of Germany utilizing the combined shipbuilding facilities of Europe and England for this purpose. The answer to this chimera, as Secretary of the Navy Knox has stated repeatedly, in line with the views of his admirals, is to build a supersupercolossal American Navy.

All this sounds plausible enough, but let us look at it a little more closely. If, as the argument assumes, Hitler should conquer the British Isles, it will obviously be by reason of his superior aviation, since he has no sea power worth considering. It will mean that he has taken those islands despite the fact that the defenders have practically a monopoly of sea power. It will be a demonstration, in effect, of the bankruptcy of sea power when confronted by superior air power. Having made that crucial demonstration, why in common sense should Hitler suddenly revert to the vanquished and obsolete weapon of naval power? Merely to justify the billions of dollars invested in American naval construction, or to avoid embarrassing our champions of sea power as the eternal and unalterable guarantee of national security?

Quite the contrary: it is only natural that a victorious Hitler would have even more faith in his *Luftwaffe* and more contempt for navies. He could be expected to devote himself more single-mindedly than ever to the construction of great air power of the kind which could ignore navies.

The same sort of traditional thinking, equally untenable in our day and age, is evident in nearly every public statement from naval sources. Recently the Secretary of the Navy, speaking at Indianapolis, warned Americans against purely defensive thinking, which he described rightly as the "Maginot Line complex." Yet in the same speech he exemplified the effects of that complex by asserting that "eventually we shall lock Nazi Germany up in an iron ring, and within that ring of sea power she shall perish." These, alas, are approximately the same words with which the French General Staff complacently referred to their frontier fortifications.

In both instances, they ignored the fact that rings of concrete or of steel, be they ever so thick and tall, cannot keep out the threat from the sky. The French hoped to surround themselves with a fixed wall; some of us hope to surround the Germans with a mobile wall of battleships—but the strategic principle is identical and equally fallacious. The French poured billions of francs into the concrete of the Maginot Line, their superfortress. We are pouring billions of dollars into the ring of steel, our supernavy. The only difference is in the substance: the French favored concrete, we favor metal. The ideas and the psychology behind both are the same, and unless we come to our senses in time, the same results may follow.

---------------------------------- 5 ----------------------------------

AN EVER-LARGER portion of sea commerce is likely in the near
future to be carried by airplanes, not by vessels. In intrinsic
value, if not in weight, transoceanic air commerce is destined in the nature of the case to surpass surface commerce.
Even now most American bombers are delivered across the
ocean on their own power, and pursuits could easily have
been built to do likewise, if those in charge of national-
defense programs had not let their prejudices blind them to
the opportunity. Such equipment had been proposed to
them, but rejected and ridiculed.

The war, however, has left no margin for doubt on the
matter. The mere thought of what long-range self-delivered
pursuits would have been able to accomplish in helping the
Hawaiian Islands and in relieving the Philippines is enough
to make one shudder at the blindness of officials who at this
writing were still at the helm, hoping to muddle through. In
the near future, it is certain, not only military aircraft will
have to proceed anywhere under their own power; military
supplies and man power for land, sea, or air services will
likewise proceed increasingly through the air lanes. One of
our foremost aviation engineers, Grover Loening, in an article in *National Aeronautics,* analyzed in detail the economic as well as military advantages of large-scale air transport across oceans. "In the immediately 'predictable future,'"
he wrote, "transportation of most armament materials, of all
troops and personnel, and practically all light or heavy loads
of destructive munitions, will have to be transported by air
and deposited by air in order to win a war across the Atlantic."

It has been estimated that the British Isles need some
25,000 tons of imported foodstuffs daily. Five hundred planes

of the Douglas B-19 size, carrying fifty tons each, could
keep the islands supplied more expeditiously than any
ships; food could if necessary be cooked in America in the
morning and delivered steaming hot in Europe in the eve-
ning. If transported in dehydrated form (especially such
items as vegetables, fruits, milk, eggs, dried meats), the
foodstuffs would have only from one fifth to one seventh of
their original weight. Through dehydration processes, only
5000 tons daily might keep England nourished, and only
100 planes a day could accomplish this miracle.

The fact that aviation transport of this sort is not available
is certainly no fault of aeronautics, which is technically fit
for the job. It can again be traced in the first instance to in-
grained reactionary attitudes on the subject, and also to the
fear of trespassing on the naval domain by raising doubts of
the ability of sea transport to cope with the problems.

But even transport by slow surface ships can be protected
against enemy attack far more efficiently from the air than
by surface convoys or patrols. Once the water highways are
policed by friendly air power, commerce will be able to
move under those canopies of aviation. The offhand assumption that ships must be protected by ships, trains by other
trains, and so on is at bottom absurd. There is no better form
of defense for traffic on any surface, land or sea, than a
strong roof of aerial might overhead, as already evidenced
by the installation of fighter aircraft on British ships.

The type of strategic thinking which continues, through
inertia, to rest on the old assumptions of sea power constitutes a brake on the full growth of the new "first line of defense." Minds that have not caught up with this reality are
incapable of grappling with the problems of national defense in the real modern world. Modern military aviation,
having shorn sea power of its offensive functions, leaves it

strategically crippled. This represents a fateful milestone
in the history of warmaking and therefore a turning point in
the power relations of the major nations. The implications
of the event add up to a fundamental change in the history of the immediate future.

Heretofore, sprawling world empires rested in the first
place upon superior naval might. Neither the governments
nor the admirals of the world have as yet conceded openly
that there has been a revolution in this respect. Nevertheless, that revolution is in full tide. Already neither the home
grounds nor far-off colonies can be considered impregnable,
or even defensible, merely because a nation possesses a magnificent navy. If those areas are within aerial striking distance of the enemy, they are vulnerable, regardless of how
large a fleet theoretically guards them.

Only air power capable of meeting the potential assail-
ant's aviation can guarantee safety. That means, in effect,
that every outpost of empire, if it is to survive, must be given
the protection of aviation that can be reinforced instantaneously to make it a match for the air power of the nearest
enemy. And what is true today will be a hundredfold more
important tomorrow, when the reach of the air weapon will
be enlarged to cover territories now comparatively immune.
By the unequivocal logic of this new situation, the empires
of the near future will rest not on sea power, as heretofore,
but on air power. By the same token, existing empires, including that of the United States, will no longer be able to
rest back on blind faith in adequate navies.

These empires are like great edifices, outwardly strong
and impressive. Those familiar with their interior structures,
however, know that they are built with wooden beams
which in time have become dry-rotted and termite-eaten. If
we want to save the structures, we have no alternative but

to replace the old-fashioned and outlived wooden beams
with powerful steel supports. The wooden beams—which is
to say naval strength—are unequal to the new tensions put
upon them, and the steel supports of air power must be
substituted.

The work of replacement goes forward inexorably under
pressure of the war. In America, the urgency of the problem is not yet so apparent to military leaders wearing
the blinders of traditional strategic ideas and still lulled
into a false sense of safety by broad oceans. But we, too,
must speed up the work of replacement. We must relinquish
the illusion of safety and accept the reality of the changed
conditions. And the time to start is *now*. The major European nations have been too preoccupied with immediate
short-range needs to devote themselves to the long-range air
power of especial significance in relation to America. As far
as that type of equipment is concerned, therefore, we would
be starting on equal terms with those nations if we start now
in the race for air-power supremacy.

For the moment, it is true, military aviation has made the
United States defensively stronger, since it has made us less
accessible to the navies of other nations. We all wish it could
be true forever. But we dare not shut our eyes to the fact
that this is a highly temporary advantage—we are passing
through a transition stage. Our temporary immunity is crumbling. The threat of enemy air power acting as a long-
distance offensive weapon, holding the menace of total destruction for its targets, is emerging. Only our own air power
—strong, truly unified, built in conformity with the new
strategic realities—can offer us adequate protection.

In the transition stage, while we are transferring from one
weapon to another, there is an overlapping of weapons that
is not only natural but necessary. Our nation is rich enough

to make the investment, to leave no margin of our national
security uncovered. But those who realize the immediate
potentialities of air power must inveigh against the obsession
of naval dependence to the detriment of an invincible air
power. Our basic national policy still rests on naval power
as our outer defense and on air power as a continental defense. The time has come to revise this policy completely.

Even if we follow the precepts of Captain Mahan in relation to sea power, we must note that he differentiates between the "fortress fleet" designed for defense and the "fleet
in being," ready to go anywhere for offensive tasks—which
is the only true defense. He explains that success will go to
the side which drives the adversary into a defensive position. To keep an enemy in a defensive position means to
take the offensive; but we know that navies have already
lost their offensive function. They are at best a "fortress
fleet" and what used to be a "fleet in being" has been absorbed by the striking air forces. Only air power can now
go beyond the defensive limits, into the skies of the enemy,
armed with far greater striking force than Mahan could
have dreamed—a striking power which does not stop at the
shore line but goes beyond, to attack the heart and vitals of
the enemy land.

Navies can still fight other navies. Within the framework
of their restricted functions, these navies must be equipped
with their own naval aircraft, the indispensable modern auxiliary. That, however, must not be mistaken as a substitute
for real air power. Clearly the time is approaching when
even the phrase "sea power" will lose all real meaning. All
military issues will be settled by relative strength in the
skies. Whoever has preponderant air power will automatically hold mastery of the seas, so that the concept of air
power will, by definition, include sea power and land power.

At that time, I dare to foresee, by the inexorable logic of military progress, the Navy as a separate entity will cease to be. The weapon it represents will have atrophied to the point where it is, at best, a minor auxiliary of air power.

The need, in short, is for a broader, more modern approach to the whole problem of America's national security; one that recognizes the changes in the science of warmaking enforced by the growth of military aviation. With the deepening twilight of sea power now unavoidably evident, it seems suicidal to make navies and an outmoded naval strategy the foundation of American national strategy. Those who insist on leading America in that direction are heading us for military disaster. They assume a fearsome responsibility before the judgment of history.

# CHAPTER VIII

# EUROPE'S AVIATION MISTAKES
# —AND OURS

## 1

IN FRANCE, during the critical months before the present war started, I frequently discussed defense problems with leading citizens of that country. I attempted to demonstrate the absurdity of the Maginot Line strategy and the dangers of unthinking reliance on the patterns of warfare established in 1918. Terrestrial obstacles, I argued, would be of no avail against onslaught from the air, directed against vital points far behind the fighting lines. Nothing short of first-rate air power, capable of striking at German life and industry, I tried to explain, could meet the impending danger.

Usually the French leaders were impressed; sometimes they were convinced. But in the end they would fall back on blind faith in the ineffable wisdom of their betters.

"What you say sounds logical enough," they would say in effect, "but surely the brilliant men on our General Staff must know what they are doing. They're the greatest military staff in the world. They must know why they are spending billions of francs on fortifications and why they stake everything on defensive strategy."

By this time we know too well how the brilliant French military brains, having been long confined in an antiquated strategic mold, could not rid themselves of disastrously outdated ideas. We mortals have a childlike faith in the ineffable wisdom of officials and notarized experts. That same pathetic confidence in titles and gold braid appeared when one sought to trace for laymen the picture of backwardness and arrested thinking presented by American military aviation. Among us, too, intelligent civilians and some credulous military men discount their own logical processes, deferring lazily to the officially anointed. "After all, they wouldn't be where they are if they didn't know what they're doing!"

Millions of Europeans have been shocked into awareness of the stupidity of their own brass hats by the tragic course of events. They are no longer reluctant to believe that their officials were ignorant of the facts of aviation life, often inept and sometimes corrupt to boot. Must we Americans, too, wait like hypnotized rabbits for the rattlesnakes of our cumulative errors to strike us? Must we wait for disaster to show up our mistaken ideas and false calculations?

American aviation has been repeating many of the major mistakes made by the nations of Europe, while imitating few of their virtues. Our military aeronautical situation as we entered the war was almost an epitome of Europe, especially western Europe, on the eve of the Second World War. Precisely as the course of the war across the ocean disclosed significant strategic lessons, so it exposed fundamental political and industrial mistakes. The experience of the Old World lies spread before the eyes of the New World, as precise as a chart, if only we cared to read and understand it.

In rehearsing my personal observations and experiences in the aviation world of Europe in the first half of 1939, my purpose is to underscore those features which, it seems to me, hold specific lessons for Americans. I spent the seven months before the outbreak of the war in aviation circles of France, Germany, England, Italy, and other countries. I was not merely studying the situation in the abstract but trying to sell American planes to Europe. Consequently I was brought into unusually intimate contact with aeronautical officialdom, from ministers down; with aviation manufacturers, designers, and rank-and-file pilots. I think I acquired not only a measure of understanding of their aerial equipment but some insight into the mental equipment and the social pressures behind the façade.

At that time, it should be recalled, air power had already scored some dramatic victories—without firing a single shot. The mere threat of unleashing this new weapon had sufficed to impose capitulation on the western democracies. Italy had won its first round with the proud British Empire in 1935. The British concentrated a mighty fleet in the Mediterranean in the hope of heading off Mussolini's Abyssinian adventure. But Il Duce announced his intention of blasting the fleet with his air arm, and Britain, after some panicky hesitation, cleared the sea lanes to the Fascist legions. Soon thereafter Adolf Hitler, again by merely flexing his aviation muscles, defeated France and Great Britain in a series of unfought engagements climaxed by the inglorious surrender at Munich. The nations with the most powerful army and navy respectively had thus been vanquished by the leading air-power nation!

It was against this background of aerial ascendancy in Europe that I saw the aeronautical picture on the Continent and on the British Isles. The automatic reliance on older weapons, the prevalence of "business as usual" and "politics as usual" in England and France, are the more astonishing when considered in relation to the blackmail exacted by the Axis on threat of using its fighting aviation.

France was living in a fool's paradise of false safety behind its "impregnable" fortifications. It was a paradise in which nearly everybody made fat commissions and complicated "deals," flaunting the kind of patriotism that paid dividends. Munich had awakened a section of the government and the public to the need for defensive steps, but most of the actual preparedness consisted of glittering verbal generalities.

Military aviation was organized as a separate ministry. But merely *formal* independence does not suffice. An air force that is a self-sufficient service in name has no value unless it is self-reliant in spirit and psychology—unless the nation which it is expected to serve regards air power without skepticism as a full-fledged partner, on a par with the traditional services. I found that French aviation, unfortunately, existed meekly, almost by sufferance, in the shadow of the French Army, whose prestige was not merely dominant but overwhelming. Aviation was just about tolerated and no more; in many respects it seemed more a political racket than a branch of the national defense. It had neither efficiency nor discipline. Worst of all, it had no clear overall aerial strategy. Airplanes were built or bought, accepted or rejected, without reference to a precise plan for holding the skies of France and conquering the skies of potential enemies.

Much has been revealed to the world about French aeronautical incompetence and venality since the debacle. But the fault went much deeper; it arose from the failure of the whole French people to recognize air power as its first line of defense. Aviation was run on frivolous and sometimes corrupt lines—primarily because aviation did not seem especially vital. A nation in the modern world which does not *feel* the advent of the new weapon in every fiber of its being is as helpless as the nation which, in another century, failed to sense the significance of gunpowder.

Inspecting French aviation factories, I was shocked by the pervasive dirt and lack of modern facilities, the cramped plants, the inadequate lighting and ventilation. Again and again I saw workmen arguing with foremen over blueprints, criticizing the designs; not infrequently mechanics indulged their artistic temperament by "improving" their work, instead of faithfully following the drawings. When the lunch whistle blew, I saw workers drop their tools in the middle of delicate operations, leaving engines suspended at precarious angles.

On the level of governmental authority, people were selected because of political drag rather than ability. At every turn one ran up against stone walls of political skulduggery: preferential treatment of certain companies at home and abroad, and a fantastic prejudice against foreign aviation, partly motivated by considerations of domestic business and partly by a childish patriotism. In general French aviation people were antagonistic to foreign planes not because these were worse than the home product, but precisely because they were indubitably better and thereby exposed the shortcomings of domestic types and the failures of officialdom.

It took me weeks and months to clear American planes—the kind of planes which might have saved the life of France!—through the multiple barriers of red tape and deliberate obstruction. There was an eagerness to "pick" on minor details and there was a shameless falsification of performance tests in the effort to "protect" French aeronautics against foreign competition or to make good on "deals" with favored foreign manufacturers.

Thus a Seversky pursuit which could easily go up 30,000 feet was reported by a French test pilot as unable to top 20,000 feet. Without even checking speed, an arbitrary figure was reported to the higher-ups; by planned coincidence it happened to be just below the record for French pursuits. The same sort of prevarication held true for armament, stability, and other essentials. For instance, a famous young French pilot, testing the plane in flight for the Air Ministry, made an obviously flawless landing. He approached me, with a sad mien, and exclaimed, "But your plane is dangerously unstable—and impossible to land!" Everyone present knew it was a diplomatic lie, uttered to protect his own previous selection of a comparatively inferior model. Some present were quite aware that eighty-five of these planes had been successfully flown by American Army pilots in all sorts of weather, landing on all sorts of terrain.

The ministry accepted the ludicrous reports uncritically in a bureaucratic spirit. Only after I forced the issue to the attention of members of the Chamber of Deputies and the Senate was I permitted to repeat the tests myself, with sealed instruments, showing up the extraordinary fraud. It was, at bottom, a fraud perpetrated by officialdom, not so much against an American manufacturer as against the national security of its own country and people.

That, however, did not break through the pyramided corruptions. It brought me only the satisfaction of a gallant apology by the Minister of Aviation. He begged us not to take the lying as a private affront, since it was the expression of a generic hostility to foreign airplanes. When I pointed out that certain American planes, irrefutably inferior to the one I had demonstrated, were being acquired in considerable numbers despite this antiforeign bias, his excellency shrugged his shoulders. The threads of the busy spinners of profitable cobwebs to snare their own country reached even across the ocean. . . .

The Minister also offered me the most curious and disheartening justification of the widespread lying that I have ever heard. True, he said, these pilots and officials falsified reports and perjured themselves. But they did so out of

"loyalty" to the French aviation industry! They were denying their country the planes that might save it from disaster,
and loading it with backward or obsolete models, but they
did so, thank God, for neatly "patriotic" reasons! How could
he punish people even willing to perjure themselves for such
high ideals?

Though it was common knowledge that the British Spitfires had a speed of over 360 miles an hour, that the Messerschmitt had a speed close to 350 miles, the French continued to fuss patriotically with their own Morane pursuit, even
enlarging their production of the model, with a top speed
of barely 280 miles. They slurred over the clear proofs of
obsolescence as complacently, as high-mindedly, as American officials were to slur over the backwardness of American
types in the following years.

Thus, episode after episode brought home to me the hopelessness of French aviation. The country was obviously taking a frivolous attitude toward the one weapon which, more
than any other, was destined to determine its future. Before
abandoning the fight, I called on the chief of the French Air
Force, General Vuillemin. Although I had requested only a
few minutes of his time, we remained closeted for hours. A
charming individual, he was as innocent of the potentialities
of the air-power age as a tenderfoot Boy Scout. For example,
when I talked about long-range fighters, General Vuillemin
was exceedingly vague about their possible use. Whereupon
I pictured likely operations in French Tunisia and Syria,
indicating how pursuits with a reach of several thousand
miles would become invaluable. The General finally warmed
to the idea. Then his face fell.

"But where could we possibly lay hands on such planes?"
he sighed.

"Why, just such a fighter is now in your hangar at Villa-coublay," I told him. "Surely your subordinates must have informed you about my pursuit."

"But that's impossible," the General assured me. "Here are the reports on your machine . . . below French standards in every respect."

And he drew from his desk another of those "patriotically" falsified reports. The plane's comfortable 3000-mile range had been trimmed down to 900 kilometers, or about 600 miles; its five machine guns had gone into the official record as only three machine guns; its speed—ahead of any other American or French model at that time—was set down as lower than a French Morane fighter's. For a while the General listened in embarrassment as I took this report apart. Then he said in a low, sad voice:

"I believe you. But I can do nothing about it. I cannot go against the whole Air Ministry. You are going to England. When you obtain the results of the British tests substantiating your claims, come back and we may be able to force the issue through the Chamber of Deputies."

But he did not sound very hopeful. No doubt he had vainly tried again and again to hew a path through the jungle of lies and self-deceptions. In any case, the picture of the head of the whole Air Force being fed with falsified figures and prevented from acquiring the best available equipment remained deeply etched on my memory. Though all its own planes were notoriously below British standards and even below the most popular American types in everything but armament, considerations of national pride and national profits prevented France from buying outside aircraft or undertaking the manufacture of foreign designs. The French possessed the semblance of a separate Air Force, as a conces-

sion to modernity, but their hearts were not in it. When the
country finally awoke to its aviation needs, it was much too
late.

Meanwhile French politicians and publicists deceived the
nation and each other by sneering at Germany's vaunted
aviation. I heard solemn recitals of the supposed weaknesses
of the Nazi aircraft from people whose business it was to
know better. Hitler's planes, I was informed confidentially
by French "experts," would bog down in sustained action;
their engines would explode; only one in a hundred had flying instruments; the Nazi substitute materials doomed them
to failure; and so on. There was little use in telling these
experts that I had inspected Hitler's military aviation and
had found none of these alleged defects. In the final analysis,
France credited any fairy tale that enabled it to malinger a
little while longer in blissful ignorance in that fool's paradise
behind the Maginot walls.

-------------------------- 2 --------------------------

THE BRITISH, I found, were far more realistic about the German threat. Munich, and especially the Nazi betrayal of the
undertakings made at Munich, had struck home and struck
deeply. Among British military and aviation men I found a
greater consciousness of the destined role of air power than
in any country outside Germany. But this consciousness was
in large measure vitiated by two sets of restraining forces.

The first and perhaps most influential of these was the
stubborn and routine faith of all Englishmen, high or low,
in their glorious Navy. To express serious doubt of the Navy's
capacity to protect the Isles and the Empire was a good way
of losing friends and influencing people to avoid you. However poetically touching this faith might be in the abstract,

in practice it served as a brake on the growth and the proper equipment of both the Army and the Air Force. Every intensification of war fears meant larger expenditures for the Navy, but only grudging appropriations for the other services.

British airplanes seemed to me the world's best as far as performance and military characteristics were concerned. They were often inefficiently designed, in that they were costly and difficult to build. Their workmanship was usually below the German or American levels, though easily better than that of France. But in point of speed, armament, armor, personnel training, and morale, the Royal Air Force held the lead. What it lacked, of course, was numbers. The separate Air Force was being kept on short rations, financially speaking.

Going through British factories, the co-operative spirit of British labor offered a pleasant contrast to the lackadaisical attitude of French labor. These British workers seemed eager to learn and truly interested in stepping up production. There were evidences in all aviation plants of excessive personnel—obviously an attempt to make up with sheer labor power for lack of experience in mass output and inadequate advance planning and tooling. But the picture as a whole was hopeful: there were all the earmarks of future orderly production.

Unhampered by other services in its internal development, the British Air Force, more than any other in the world, showed an understanding of air power as an independent military force. That understanding, as Hitler was destined to learn to his regret, stood the British Isles in good stead in their hour of supreme danger. But because the British people as a matter of course relied for their security in the first place and almost exclusively on sea power, their country was short on nearly everything pertaining to other military spheres. They were essentially naval-minded, generous in building up their sea power, but annoyed by the need to invest in ground and air equipment. In the main, moreover, military thought outside the RAF had not yet caught up with the concept of pure air warfare—the kind of warfare, that is to say, which they would face so soon in the Battle of Britain. Not until forced by harsh reality would vested military interests relinquish their assumption that aviation, for all its marvels, was somehow secondary and not the first line of defense. Their retarded thinking kept aviation numerically restricted.

The second of the sets of influences holding down British military aviation was entrenched in the business world of England: among the manufacturers of aircraft and their financial and political backers. Admitting that domestic production facilities were inadequate to meet the fast increasing aviation needs, these groups were nevertheless weighed down by fear of outside competition and of unduly expanded domestic plants *after the coming war*. They were less afraid of buying from America than of stimulating local aircraft industries in Canada or Australia or New Zealand—American competition could in due time be excluded, but Dominion competition would be a permanent drag.

Arriving in England with my pursuit models, I found complete co-operation on the part of the authorities. Air officials showed a sensible eagerness to acquire the best available machines, whatever their national origin. Unlike the Frenchmen, they were genuinely keen to learn from foreign achievements; the novel notion of a long-range fighter took their imagination instantly, since they could visualize its usefulness in the wide spaces of their Empire.

I spent a month at the British flight test station, during which time my American planes were put through their paces. The station, again unlike its French counterpart, was run with notable efficiency. Its crews showed a sportsman-like readiness to put in extra hours and undertake extra hard-ships. They took quite cheerfully the frequent practice air-raid alarms—a type of preparation that was not apparent in France. All the tests were made with absolute fidelity to truth, and without the slightest inclination to discredit for-eign models. The figures established by United States tests were confirmed and in several instances the American claims were even exceeded in the British reports.

Having encountered a little trouble in their Spitfire with respect to the ailerons, they seemed especially pleased to study the ability of the Seversky pursuit to maintain con-stant stick loads regardless of the velocity in dives. The Air Ministry cut through red tape quickly to permit me to fly the Spitfire in order that I might suggest solutions to specific problems. Up in the air in the British pursuit, checking its speed at critical altitudes, I was more convinced than ever that the Germans, for all their mass of equipment, would have a hard nut to crack when they ran up against the Spit-fires.

But military enthusiasm was repeatedly extinguished by the cautious calculations of some dominant aircraft industry leaders and financiers, reflected in the attitudes of their po-litical henchmen. These were willing, when pressed on the matter, to let their government purchase abroad training planes and even secondary fighting craft like those for coastal patrol. But the basic fighting aircraft, they felt, must be built at home. The technical alibi was that overseas delivery of for-eign planes was not dependable. Under the alibi was the reality of "business as usual."

In England, I stressed especially the advantages of the long range in my single and two-seater pursuits. In a memo-randum addressed to the Air Ministry, I wrote on April 8,

1939: "This feature, we feel, has a tremendous value for the colonial protection of the British Empire. Due to the scarcity of aerodromes and the great distances between them, it is imperative that the colonial air force, including fighters, possess a long range of action. Bases such as Iraq, Calcutta, and Singapore, will particularly benefit through such equipment. Long-range fighters will be especially effective in convoying bombers in their operations against hostile navies."

Recent developments in the Far East, of course, have fully justified my contentions. Furthermore, important as the quantity of aircraft available at the start of the war might be, I pointed out that the decisive fact would be the ability to produce planes faster than the adversary after war started. Hence I suggested the advisability of developing sources of supply throughout the British Empire, beyond the range of hostile air forces. Such planes, I said, if built in Canada for example, could be flown to the British Isles with full military load, ready for immediate combat. In the same letter to the Air Ministry, I also said that during the war the delivery of aircraft to the colonies should be made by air under their own power; and that the Air Force could not rely on transportation by sea, which during the next war would be extremely hazardous if not impossible.

The idea of building long-ranged planes outside the British Isles was warmly received by the Air Ministry. It was picked up by the newspapers and evoked considerable discussion. In business circles, however, the reaction was the opposite of enthusiastic. Indeed, soon thereafter a prominent British airplane manufacturer buttonholed me in a hotel lobby.

"It's a grand idea you have," he said, "of delivering planes by air from our Dominions and colonies. But it will never do. If you want to do business with our country, you'd better forget such ideas. Haven't you stopped to think what we're going to do with our own tremendously expanded aviation industry *after the war?* We must preserve our markets, you know."

In the dark days of national danger which were soon upon the British Isles, I often wondered whether that manufacturer and his friends realized their error. Had plants for long-ranged, self-delivered aviation been started in Canada at that time, a steady and perhaps decisive stream of fighters, as well as bombers, would have been flowing across the North Atlantic to the mother country just when they were most needed. Had it initiated a domestic aviation program at that time, Australia by this time would have been able to smother the Japanese in the Pacific; instead today the Allies must rely on reinforcements across thousands of miles of highly vulnerable communication routes. But the profit psychology had prevailed. The instinct to keep the outlying portions of the Empire economically dependent on the British Isles had triumphed. And this is only one example, from one foreigner's personal experience, of a mood which acted as a damper on unlimited aerial expansion.

---

3

---

IN GERMANY I saw the world's greatest facilities for the production of aircraft, and an independent Air Force not merely on a basis of equality with the other services but in some ways favored above them. Almost devoid of naval strength, long forbidden to train a large army, the country's creative energy and military thinking had been channeled into aviation long before the Nazis came to the top. By the beginning of 1939 Germany had clearly made up its mind that war was inevitable and was rushing preparations with characteristic thoroughness.

Aircraft plants were spacious and efficiently run, operations were disciplined, the specific designs were admirable from the standpoint of economical manufacture and effective maintenance. Workmanship was as good as in the United States. Although shortage of some materials existed, the substitutes in many instances proved even better than the original.

In point of military performance, I found the German planes distinctly inferior to those of Britain. The Germans had evidently decided to stake their fate on quantity rather than quality. Deliberately, quite aware that it would give their enemies a certain qualitative edge, they had "frozen" their designs early in the race, in the interests of mass production. They were counting on smothering the British, if necessary, by the sheer weight of their equipment. With enough planes on hand, they reasoned, they would be able to sacrifice equipment prodigally, giving up three or four for every one of the adversary's, and still emerge victorious.

The positive side of German aviation, its numerical strength and fine organization, had been readily seen and comprehended by foreign airmen investigating the subject. It was the side that was visible on the surface; Marshal Göring and his staff proudly displayed it to eminent American aeronautical personalities visiting Germany. The negative side, its qualitative deficiencies, could not be seen at a glance. It could not be grasped in the abstract but only in relation to the corresponding aircraft of other nations. Moreover, to recognize the shortcomings and visualize their likely consequences, the observer needed personal combat experience or at least a thorough grounding in the principles of aerial warfare.

Thus it happened that a number of American visitors, some of them high in aviation circles, were swept off their feet by the seeming grandeur of the *Luftwaffe*—swept off so completely that they either failed to see, or failed to evaluate properly, the importance of Britain's edge in quality.

I recall vividly a day when I was being shown through the magnificent Heinkel plant. Not only the scale but the luxury of the equipment, the buildings, the recreational facilities for workmen, were staggering. I had seen nothing like it anywhere in the world, not even excepting our best mass-production plants in America. Machinery and tooling were very like those used in the United States at that time. There were some interesting production wrinkles—automatic milling machines and explosive rivets, for instance—which have since then been adopted by the American aviation industry. All the buildings had underground floors, complete with bomb-proof shelters and air-tight sealing against gas attacks.

Outside the factory walls were the finished bombers, row upon row of slick, ominous-looking planes in battle paint, as if ready to roar into the sky at a signal. Honest pride, a bit smug too, was written all over the faces of the high officials who accompanied me. But I noted one curious fact in the course of the inspection—a fact the significance of which spoiled the impressive aviation scene for me from a purely military standpoint.

These bombers, while embodying the latest results of aeronautical engineering, were all seriously short on defensive armament (as I have already explained in discussing the Battle of Britain). Here, a quarter of a century after the start of World War I, in which we had already used twin machine guns to protect the rear of our planes, these Heinkels were virtually defenseless! As a combat pilot I was shocked by the inexplicable and inexcusable error—or worse, the German inability to foresee the tactical conditions under which bombers would have to operate. In particular I was horrified by this picture of tremendous industrial effort being canalized in the wrong direction. Having flown the Spitfire, it was quite clear to me that these Heinkels would fall easy prey to the British fighters. Nor was it merely professional horror: my mind naturally turned to American aircraft which, similarly, were beautifully designed but lacked the necessary combat power.

When I mentioned my reactions, my host smiled mysteriously.

During an inspection tour of the Leipzig factory which made Messerschmitts under license, I again saw amazingly fine plants, discipline, production. But again the margin of inferiority in fire power and speed were clearly discernible. The gasoline tank was poorly located: behind the pilot, exposing it to rear attack; also, while it was sealed against .30-caliber bullets, it was wide open to larger projectiles. There and then I was convinced that the Messerschmitts would be vanquished by the Spitfires. Without going into detail, I alluded to the 25-mile-an-hour edge in speed and the larger fire power enjoyed by British pursuits. Once more my host smiled mysteriously.

I thought that the official smiles covered some deep secret. Perhaps they possessed pursuits which they were not permitting me to see; perhaps they had a substitute for the conventional machine-gun armament; perhaps they had some more effective fire power hidden within their bombers, possibly in some kind of retractable turrets. In the first year of this war, however, it became clear enough that the smiles merely covered a superior—but in this case wholly mistaken —confidence in the advantages of their large quantitative margin.

The Germans, on the whole, discounted their French neighbors as opponents but looked with misgivings toward the possibility of a test of strength with Great Britain. I saw little if any enthusiasm for the coming war—only a resigned, fatalistic acceptance of the inevitable. Everyone I talked to expected a "tough" war at terrible cost in life and resources for all concerned. I learned that they were already planning long-ranged, four-motored bombers to intercept British shipping in the Atlantic hundreds of miles beyond the European shores. In this they were acknowledging the transfer of vital naval functions to air power—an acknowledgment which other countries failed, and in some instances still fail, to make. I was deeply impressed by the casualness with which Nazi aviation leaders discussed transoceanic ranges—"commercial," of course—with ultimate expansion to round-the-world ranges. It was not difficult to discern in such talk their mental picture of the whole planet dominated through air control.

To a larger extent than in France, the Germans had come to regard aviation as a self-sufficient service, equipped to cope with strategic problems on its own, without the aid of the Army or the Navy. The German *Luftwaffe* was geared along three distinct lines: for co-operation with the ground troops and tanks, for joint action with the German Navy, and for quite independent tactical actions. It was because of this recognition of the independent existence of the air arm—not merely administratively or formally—but in the deeper sense of a truly self-sustaining service—relying on its own air-borne supply and troop transports—that Germany had the upper hand over the rest of the world.

But this scheme contained flaws. There was a bias in the pattern and it was an army bias. Germany has been as army-minded as Britain has been navy-minded. The inevitable

consequence was a certain overemphasis on types of planes
best suited for co-ordination with the land forces. We have
already noted that this failure to carry the logic of air power
to its natural extreme stymied the Nazi aviation machine in
its greatest test: the effort to conquer the skies over the British Isles. It lacked the range, the striking power, the defensive armament, and the proper tactics for such missions—and
its masters seemed blissfully ignorant of these lacks.

We must recall, of course, that Nazi strategic plans had
been conceived years earlier, on the basis of relatively meager operational data. China, Ethiopia, and especially Spain
had served as proving grounds in which many tactical problems were indicated and a few solved. Yet the fighting in
those countries had not developed decisive aerial actions to
convince the less daring and less imaginative aviation experts. Possibly even men like Göring and Milch feared to
shoulder the responsibility of all-out audacity in their aerial
thinking. In any event, their planning went far enough to
give their country magnificent aviation for enhancing the
old strategy of mile-by-mile occupation of enemy territory;
it fell short of providing an air fleet capable of commanding
the "air ocean" at long range in defiance of enemy aviation.

Italian aviation, like the surface of nearly everything in
Italy, was misleading. Casual inspection, I must admit, in-
clined me to form a far better opinion of Mussolini's air arm
than it deserved. There seemed a promise of mass production; plants were well laid out, well maintained, with labor
disciplined and apparently efficient. But to this day, it remains a promise: Italian aviation has not asserted itself in
large force at any stage of the conflict. The Italian airplane
designs were fairly good, but the construction was chiefly of
wood and therefore earmarked as easy prey to the fire power

of metal adversaries. Clearly inferior to German, British, or American aircraft, the Italian planes were yet superior to the French in performance. And it was primarily for use against France that Mussolini was building his air equipment.

In one respect the Italians imitated their French neighbors, and that was in their puerile envy of any foreign craft superior to their own. It was no easy task to make a Fascist aviation official admit that something produced outside Italy was better than its Italian counterpart. They insisted, illogically, that their planes and engines were better than any in the world. Their reluctance to buy foreign airplanes—the one thing that might have saved them from a series of humiliating disasters—extended even to the aircraft of their ally, Germany. In the end they compromised on blind patriotism sufficiently to invite me to build Seversky pursuits in Italy, but refused to purchase American-made craft.

Italian bombers were apparently able to carry large explosive loads but were poorly armed. In general, it was clear that Fascist planes would fall easy prey to British or American fighters.

----------- 4 -----------

FOR THOSE more or less familiar with the equivalent phases of American aviation, the preceding pages must have made the deadly parallel with the worst elements in the prewar European picture unpleasantly obvious.

In the United States, as in France, there is scarcely a suspicion of anything resembling an over-all aviation strategy. Our Navy, being more dynamic in its thinking than our Army, has plans and principles for the employment of aircraft as a subsidiary of its larger undertakings—as an "extension" of old-fashioned sea power. The Army has not even

that much, but treats aviation essentially as "flying artillery"
or "more effective reconnaissance," as an improvement of
familiar textbook military precepts. Neither service has understood that the textbook precepts have been outlived. France
lacked an aviation strategy despite its separate Air Force.
We in America (at this writing) do not even possess any
agency with the responsibility or the authority to develop
such a strategy. No matter how brilliant the minds in the
Navy and the Army, they can give us only brilliant plans
for employment of aviation as adjuncts and auxiliaries.

Here, as in Britain, it is well-nigh blasphemous to question the traditional role of the Navy as our "outer defense."
Britain and France had prepared for a repetition of the
previous war. French military prowess would hold off Germany while British naval might strangled it by blockade.
American strategy, as reflected in current equipment, also
seems to assume a repetition of the last war, with modern
variations. We still concentrate on the idea of expeditionary
forces—bigger and better than in the past, with a lot of new
gadgets in imitation of Hitler's "surprises," but curiously
contemptuous of the strategic "short cuts" made possible by
air power. In absolute terms our aviation is longer ranged,
but in relation to our geographic position it remains tragically short-ranged. And of course it remains chained to ground
services, not even seriously considered for use "on its own"
in a sphere inaccessible to either of the older services.

We seem to be preparing against a phantom navy, on the
theory that nations which are doing extremely well without
naval power will reject their own experience and revert to
reliance on surface fleets. It has not quite dawned on our
military leadership that long-range aviation provides a "short
cut"—that battleships, the naval equivalent of the Maginot
Line, can also be ignored by air power.

In Germany to some extent and in France to the full extent, air power was handicapped by dominance of army mentality. In Britain it was handicapped by dominance of navy mentality. In America we combine the worst features of both: we split our air strength in two, subordinate one portion to the Army, the other to the Navy, and set them to competing with one another for the largest chunks of control in an element that is foreign to them both.

Germany's prime mistake—one that it is presumably correcting at breakneck speed—was in "freezing" types in the interests of mass output. We in America are even more prone to make the same mistake. Freezing of models for mass production is almost automatic in our country. The average American still thinks of airplanes—just airplanes—and is impressed with mere numbers, when he should ask at every point: What kind of planes? How well suited to the tactical purpose? How far beyond these planes has our research gone? What margins of plant facility are being prepared for the aviation of tomorrow?

Unfortunately we are more impressed with bulk statistics than with quality indicators. The news that we have transferred so many planes to England somehow has registered better than the additional news that the aircraft transferred is in many instances obsolete before delivery. Somehow the public has not yet been shocked into realizing the absurdity of the mass output under way, at this writing, of types of planes that have outlived their usefulness.

The fact that the outstanding figures in our defense plans have usually been production men rather than creative strategists offers almost symbolic proof of where we fail. This is no criticism of any individuals, but a commentary on the national attitude. These men may be productive geniuses. Their immense and well-deserved prestige unfortunately

means that their talents for greater output will condition the
program; they will overawe the tactical innovators and inventive geniuses whose ideas naturally tend to make current
output obsolete. In a sense it is as though the production
manager were put ahead of the chief engineer or designer
in a manufacturing plant. Plane types, of course, are selected
by military specialists, but the weight given to production,
especially at the expense of creative research and aerial strategy, deepens our dangerous national obsession with numbers.

In America, too, national defense is at many points hampered by fears and prejudices in relation to foreign models.
Knowing, as we do, that certain American aircraft types are
inferior to British planes in the same category, why do we
continue to build them in ever-greater quantities? After all,
with British drawings and tools available, it would take less
time to launch the manufacture of such established types
than to revamp and lift the face of existing types. At least
part of the answer is that some of the very officials responsible for the backward models are still in authority and find
it hard, psychologically, to make their own work obsolete.
They are humanly reluctant to admit mistakes and even
more reluctant to point up the admission by taking over
foreign designs.

Like the French, who persevered in accumulating obsolete Morane fighters, we have pet obsolete models which
we have been producing in vast quantities and defending in
perfumed publicity, though everyone knows they are tactically worthless. The Morane carried the name of a veteran
French pilot who was no more responsible for its misuse as
a tag on outmoded equipment than are the pioneers whose
proud names are attached to obsolete American models
kept mysteriously rolling from the production belts.

Our liquid-cooled engines, used in pursuits which are now

described as "the backbone" of American military aviation,
after five years of experimentation, develop only 1150 horsepower in production. Even at that level they are not yet entirely reliable. The situation was so appalling that national
pride gave way late in 1941 to the extent of putting into production imported Rolls Royce engines—but unfortunately of
a horsepower not exceeding our own. Yet for many months
we had available the British 2000-horsepower Napier Sabre
engine, a power plant of proved excellence. It had been
pushed around, postponed, hampered. Why? The only plausible explanation is the hesitancy to establish another and
perhaps better engine source competing with existing engine
plants *after the war crisis had passed*. As in Europe, there is
the continual fretting about the condition of business after
the war. Fearing the future, too many forget that, unless we
all buckle down to the main task, there may be no future
to worry about.

As in France, there is among us a tendency to exaggerate
the performance of our airplanes, attributing fantastic military characteristics to them, even converting deficiencies
into special virtues. For example, when the shortcomings in
fire power become too plain, in view of the appearance of
cannon on European planes, publicity beats engineering to
the punch and solves the problem easily by rechristening
certain machine guns "cannon."

And there is the same tendency to minimize the strength
of hostile nations. France kidded itself about the inefficiency
of German equipment, and we were led to believe that Japanese equipment is junky, that Japan would face aerial mas-
sacre if it tangled with us. Yet after a week of fighting in
the Philippines the American people were stunned by official acknowledgment that the enemy was in full control of
the air.

Our aviation industry as a whole is patriotic and high-minded and ready for sacrifice. It has aviation brains at its disposal equal or superior to any in Europe. It can produce· any kind of aircraft prescribed by our military leaders, with any type of equipment and any amount of armament demanded by our tacticians. Ultimately, therefore, the faults in our aviation picture must be traced to their source in the backward thinking of the topmost military officialdom. Not until there is American air power with a unified command, under farsighted officers with experience and knowledge, capable of planning true aerial strategies, can the American aviation industry have that official guidance so essential in a crisis.

Meanwhile, in many instances, the sort of "business as usual," which obsessed and helped finish off France and endangered England, remains a factor in America. The selfish and profit-minded elements (and every industry has them) are able to take advantage of the disjointed, amorphous state of our military aviation to foist on our poor, harassed military personnel equipment which, if woefully short on defensive values, is comfortably long on profit values. Through sheer inertia the business practices of peacetime have been carried over intact into the present period. But these competitive practices make no sense at a juncture when the industry's facilities are already overburdened and certain to remain overburdened for years to come.

Sooner or later the country will realize that many of the business talents which are admired in normal times have no place, and may even be harmful, in times of emergency. The reluctance to admit new companies or new units into a field of manufacture is understandable in a competitive world. It is inexcusable at a juncture when the best results and most rapid expansion must be obtained at any cost in the interests of national safety. The ability to chisel on costs and undersell the business opposition, even if it means a little skimping on quality, is normally regarded as a business asset. The shrewdness which helps to eliminate a weaker firm with a more attractive product brings bonuses to executives in peacetime. In an hour of national emergency, however, such business prowess is out of place. In the measure that it may deprive the nation of some needed instrument of defense, it is close to treason. Having seen what "business as usual" and "politics as usual" have done to France, we assuredly have no excuse for tolerating them here. Whatever the economic reasons that stopped us from developing Central and South America as sources of supply for strategic materials, it was a major blunder in the light of air power. The new weapon, as we have seen, makes it necessary to fight from primary—which is to say *self-contained*—bases. In leaving ourselves dependent on sources eight or ten thousand miles away for essential supplies, such as rubber and tin, we were clearly handicapping ourselves for modern war. It is our duty to develop all resources necessary for aviation in our own country, and by the same token to develop intensively all essential South American resources. Brazil, for instance, and its neighboring republics, with their immense potential stores of materials that make the hemisphere self-contained, should be integrated with our own industrial effort from the angle of air power. Britain failed to build up first-rate aviation industries in its Dominions and colonies, in part from fear of losing markets or creating postwar competition. Such dollar-and-cents considerations must not be permitted to detract from America's position as a primary air-power base.

Finally, even as in France, the officials in charge of procurement of defense materials have so many skeletons in their closets that they fear a far-reaching house-cleaning.

The backwardness of our aviation, as we shall see, was not due to lack of aeronautic brains or skills but to incompetence, shortsightedness, and conniving in high places. Many of the officials chiefly responsible are still in those places. The longer a house-cleaning is postponed, the longer those skeletons will remain unrevealed. In some instances, indeed, the adoption of new policies would so strikingly underline the stupidity of old policies that those who share the guilt naturally tend to keep things "as is." For them to do otherwise would be tantamount to committing political suicide. Military judgment is diluted by political expediency. The effort is in some cases permitted to go only so far and so fast, halting at the point where it threatens to expose past military errors or past commitments. Thus inertia and self-interest and honest ignorance have long combined to keep aviation in its comfortable old rut.

After the war began and the life-and-death seriousness of the situation was borne in upon them, the British made a wholesale cleansing of their procurement officialdom in the entire military establishment. They realized that, even if a few innocents were hurt in the process, they needed a new start and could not expect measures of improvement from the very people largely to blame for past mistakes. Those people had worked under normal conditions when old business and political attitudes prevailed, and inevitably carried these attitudes over into the war period. A no less drastic cleansing of our procurement divisions must be made in our country. All past commitments would thus be wiped out at one sweep, and the new chiefs could go forward to their urgent tasks without worrying whose toes or whose profits were stepped on in the process.

We Americans, in short, have little warrant for speaking too harshly of the shortsightedness and inertia of the French

or the Belgians, or for asking why England slept. The fact
is that even now, with the Second World War in its third
year and our country in it all the way, America has not fully
awakened to the new weapon and its implications for America's defense program. We build two-ocean navies in about
the same spirit that the French built their frontier fortifications, without reference to the new dimension of modern
warfare. Reluctantly, without conceding that a new military
age has dawned, we silence the annoying pleaders for real air
power by adding aviation as a kind of gadget to the elder
services; by establishing bogus "unified air commands" to
outflank critics; by making a great display of airplanes without admitting that airplanes do not necessarily add up to air
power. With us the champion of the new weapon, if he fails
to placate the self-esteem of admirals and generals, is regarded as a crackpot and treated almost as a disturber of
the peace.

The peak events of the war to date, as summarized sketchily
in earlier chapters, have not only been misunderstood but on
occasion have been deliberately distorted by interpreters to
"save face" for Army and Navy concepts. Our conventional
theorists have tried to measure three-dimensional events with
a yardstick suited only for two-dimensional surfaces. The
eagerness to "prove" that sea power is supreme and cannot
conceivably make way for air power, that ground troops are
destined forever to remain the decisive factor in war, has
been something to marvel over. Experts have fought to defend these inherited assumptions as though their private
honor were involved—as in a sense, psychologically, it was.

American military aviation, to put the matter bluntly, is
still in a primitive state—and this in the country where modern aviation was born and nurtured. This statement cannot
be refuted by statistics, since air power is not a matter of

numbers, but of proper strategy, tactics, psychological attitudes toward the new domain of conflict represented by the
air, proper military organization—all of it bodied forth in
the appropriate equipment. Those of us who have grasped
the meaning of genuine air power have a clear function to
perform. It is to hammer away, day and night, even at the
risk of making ourselves a nuisance, at the mind and con-
science of our country. We must awaken it somehow to the
realities of the new situation.

# CHAPTER IX

# THE ORDEAL OF AMERICAN AIR POWER

IN THE foregoing chapters we have traced the role of air power in the present global conflict and have noted the new relationships of weapons and the consequent revolutionary revision of traditional military ideas. We have witnessed the rapid decline of sea power and the panicky confusion of orthodox strategists under the new conditions. In these pages we have treated the tragic war events beyond our own shores cold-bloodedly, as though they were so much laboratory material for our guidance.

Now we must turn, with no less realism, to our own country and analyze the state of our military aeronautics before the outbreak of World War II and during the twenty-seven months of conflict before the United States became a full belligerent. It is a far from comforting picture. But for that very reason it must be faced unflinchingly. The sooner we reduce to concrete and unequivocal detail that vague feeling that we are an unconquerable nation, the healthier for our future. The time for bragging, and for dressing up faults to look like special virtues, is over. We must visualize the magnitude of the tasks ahead of us, estimate the technical and psychological obstacles on the path of victory, and proceed to overcome them. We must conquer ourselves to conquer the enemy.

There is no denying that there has been a tendency to slur over our aeronautical defects and "blow up" our accomplishments. The national genius for supersalesmanship played a sad trick on the American people, betraying them into complacency. For years they have been lulled into the belief that their military aviation was not only equal but superior to any in the world. In the light of what airmen knew then, and even laymen know now, about the backwardness of our military equipment for air combat, it is shocking to recall, for instance, that in the autumn of 1939 a national magazine boasted that "Our War Birds Are Best." Only our sedative adjectives, alas, were best.

The soporific process continued even after the European struggle had uncovered our shortcomings. Early in 1941, "sham battles" were reported from London in publicity stunts to save face for American airplanes. Unfortunately they were more sham than battles. With all due appreciation of British generosity in placating American feelings, only the verdict of real battles, in which machine guns rather than press agents do the talking, should be acknowledged. The achievements of American planes in action have been played up and the failures have been played down. On occasion palpable debits have been reported as though they were exceptional credits. Thus even the extreme altitudes at which our Flying Fortresses were obliged to fight—because of their serious deficiency in military characteristics for low-altitude operations —were presented to American newspaper readers as cause for special pride!

Such self-delusions are as dangerous as enemy attacks. Having entered a life-and-death struggle for survival, Americans must regard themselves as one great team. In the past we played under the rules of peacetime, in which business and profit were the guiding principles. Today we must play the game under the rules of war. Many procedures which may have been "good business" or "smart politics" before

Pearl Harbor have no place in the new conditions. Stupidity or indifference in matters affecting national defense is no longer an amiable fault but close to treason.

In presenting the bare facts without prettifying them, I am fully conscious of my responsibility. I recognize that the implications are serious. But I regard them as too vital for the safety of America to be passed over politely in silence or hypocritically in double-talk. It is not a question of blaming individuals or crying over muffed opportunities. It is a question of getting at the causes of past blunders and shortsightedness in order to remove them. The team must be reorganized in the light of past experience and new knowledge, so that the best abilities of all players may be properly used in a great pooling of our nation's human resources.

The widespread popular illusion persists that the world was caught unawares and startled out of its wits by the great size and terrific effectiveness of Nazi Germany's air forces. This provides a comforting alibi for the swift and humiliating defeats at Hitler's hands; it also furnishes a convenient excuse for American backwardness. But it happens to be largely untrue. The fact is that Germany did not throw into action a single aircraft type or unfold a single technique of aerial warfare which had not been thoroughly familiar to aeronautical experts long before the war started.

They had seen the Nazi aviation equipment in action in Spain, the proving ground for the aviation phase of World War II. They had seen it also at maneuvers and on display at aeronautical shows. They were familiar with it through German military and aviation journals. Every major government, including our own, was intimately informed on the development of the Nazi war machine.

The maneuvers which the Germans had carried out near

the French frontiers prior to the last crisis had been fully reported; I happen to know that the detailed reports in French translation were available to the General Staff of France. The Nazis on this occasion rehearsed their plan of action for surmounting the Maginot Line and their projected co-ordination of tank and dive-bomber operations. Subsequent war operations followed closely the patterns laid out for all to see in these maneuvers.

The Germans had made no secret of the uses to which they intended to put their new strength. The concepts of total war and *Blitzkrieg* were not "secret weapons" but techniques widely and openly discussed by the German military press and in a good many Nazi books and even over the air. Some perspicacious foreign military experts, indeed, had written extensively on the German strategic notions and weapons, especially on the Panzer divisions and Hitler's *Luftwaffe*.

Far from concealing his aerial might, Hitler was eager in the prewar years to impress the world with it. As a matter of policy, to overawe large and small nations, Germany showed off its aviation wonders for everyone to see, to marvel at, and to fear. American and other foreign fliers and designers of aircraft were given full opportunity to inspect the Nazi aviation setup, and every encouragement to report their observations to the outside world.

The responsible military authorities in Washington consequently were—or at least could have been—fully aware of the advances in fighting aircraft made in Germany, Britain, and elsewhere. They cannot plead ignorance. Moreover, our aeronautic industry and some farsighted military men made many recommendations for improving American aviation in precisely those fields where it fell conspicuously below European standards.

The current assumptions, deliberately encouraged by self-interested propaganda, are that it took the war to make us aware of our pathetic inadequacies in the air; that the mistakes of the military men in charge of aviation were invisible until a new war disclosed them; that their judgments had been competent for their time but unfortunately made obsolete by the war. All of which is nonsense. Some of the mistakes were so elementary that any novice in aviation could have exposed them if given half a chance. Others could not possibly have been made if those responsible had had a little knowledge of aerial warfare even as exhibited in the First World War.

Airplanes in later years were larger, faster, carried greater bomb loads, enjoyed broader range and larger striking power. Yet many of the tactical lessons still applicable were learned in 1914–18; certain principles of action were demonstrated which will remain axiomatic in air fighting. Yet American military aeronautical concepts, as bodied forth in the equipment that we possessed at the beginning of World War II, not only ignored but often defied these lessons of World War I.

The contrast between American and German or British military aircraft was in some instances so obvious that it must have required a special effort of the will to overlook them. Why then was the United States so dismally unprepared for the realities of the war? Why was our military aeronautical equipment inferior to that of the major belligerents?

Certainly it was not because we lacked aviation brains or suitable industrial skills. The impressive progress being registered at long last in some phases of our aerial defense program proves that there was no dearth of aviation talent. Moreover, the magnificent development of American commercial aviation stands as conclusive proof that it was not a paucity of creative or manufacturing genius which accounted for our lagging position. Whatever explanations may be offered, they cannot evade the simple fact that even by *imitating* German and British models, we might have reduced the differential between ourselves and Europe.

In the United States, lack of numerical strength can be reasonably and justifiably explained. Seeing no immediate prospect of war, placid in the knowledge that we harbor no aggressive ambitions or intentions against other countries, we did not regard a huge aviation inventory as necessary. But there can be no justifiable explanation for our lack of qualitative factors. There was no reason why we should have built deficient models and nurtured obsolete tactical principles of warfare.

Now and then there have been attempts to pass the buck to Congress, which failed to make adequate appropriations. While that may account for the small size of our air forces, it cannot account for the fact that our pursuit planes were ordered with two machine guns, when other nations were building them with eight machine guns. Where Europe had strong armor, we had none. When other countries were providing bulletproof and leakproof protection around their gasoline tanks, we did not. When Britain had powerful turrets in bombing planes, each carrying up to four machine guns, American bombers were either pathetically underarmed, or so ill-constructed that they could not use their full fire power. Skimpy appropriations cannot be blamed for such facts; it costs little more to build a good plane than a bad one; and no investment in original research and development was necessary, since even our popular aviation periodicals published full descriptions of the superior European models.

If we continued in stubborn blindness to keep our aviation unarmed, unarmored, and deprived of essential military characteristics, it is because we were afflicted by a species of psychological paralysis. The organizational setup and the psychological environment were unfavorable and sometimes hostile to aviation development. In England and Germany they had the good sense at an early stage in the game to take the development of air forces out of the hands of army and navy people. Men attuned to the rhythm and free-ranging nature of aviation were given the principal role in shaping air equipment and air defense. They could explore and develop the potentialities of their weapon in all directions without interference.

But in America military aviation was developed under unsympathetic control. It was tolerated, as a concession to modernity. The military leaders of our older services yielded to the spirit of the times and to popular pressure for air power as slowly as they could manage, and as if they were indulging an unpleasant fad. They allowed headstrong children to "play" with the new toy and occasionally gave lip service to the "future" of aviation. But always that future was conceived of as far off in the clouds of time.

Even today, in the face of repeated melodramatic proof of the dominance of aviation, the same old-fashioned strategists and commentators continue to write and speak of military aeronautics as only a branch of the existing services—just modern additions to surface forces. They seem psychologically incapable of recognizing aviation in its primary character as the new military force which, through domination of the skies, dominates the world.

It should be emphasized that this complacent underestimation of the aerial weapon does not extend to our military aviation personnel. In the main their very choice of profession usually meant that they had broken through the restraints of naval or infantry thinking. Aloft in their planes, they could not help becoming aware of the limitations imposed upon American air power by the arbitrary decisions of men raised in totally different traditions.

Unfortunately, the most emancipated minds, aeronautically speaking, could rarely reach the top rungs of the ladder of authority in a setup where aviation took orders from the older services. Under such conditions *political* gifts naturally were more useful than *aeronautical* gifts in reaching the highest level of command. What counted most was the ability to make adjustments between aviation facts and army or navy prejudices, between defense needs and the profit pressures of intermediaries with political leverage.

It is no accident, therefore, that complacent or shortsighted men, from the aviation viewpoint, tended to reach the top in the military bureaucracy. The setup makes it almost inevitable. An officer passionately convinced of the paramount destiny of air power, and openly defending that conviction, steps on tender political toes. On the other hand, the officer with a happy talent for handshaking and back-slapping normally rises to power. But that sort of politically minded personality rarely if ever goes with military or aviation genius. Nor is his job to be envied. He is caught between the realities of air power and the pressure of aviation personnel for better equipment on one side, and the orthodoxies of the older services on the other.

By and large the military aviation personnel, in both its land and naval segments, has chafed under the restraints on air power. No finer body of men has ever been assembled anywhere in the world. They are the men who have to fly and die in our aircraft, whether over land or over sea. Anything that limits the full growth of their aircraft and of air-power strategy is a direct blow at their morale and at our security.

The struggle of these aviation men against bureaucratic and narrow-minded military leadership provides a saga of heroism and heartbreak that has not yet been fully told. It is personified in the now familiar ordeal of General Mitchell. What the American public does not yet know is that General Mitchell's experience is only the most conspicuous item in a larger story. There are many other "Billy Mitchells" in our services—men who have fought against heavy odds for their conviction that our country can and should have air supremacy. Many of them spoke out. They brought down on their heads the lightning of disapproval from high places. They found themselves either in retirement or in "exile" on remote assignments.

The court-martial of General Mitchell was not soft-pedaled. On the contrary, it was staged and dramatized so that its moral would register with other "troublemakers" who might insist on talking aviation. And there is no denying that the intimidation has worked in many cases. It is that much more to the credit of the aviation personnel as a whole that it has not relented in its struggle to unchain American air power.

—————————— 2 ——————————

SUCH SPORADIC progress as has been made in aerial equipment may be attributed in no small degree to "fortunate disasters" which from time to time uncovered conditions which thereafter were remedied. Under the impact of some tragedy, aeronautical thinking would get a little more leeway. Then, as public excitement died down, the normal apathy in ruling military circles set in.

It was such a "fortunate accident" which exposed the woeful condition of radio and related instruments on airplanes. After General Mitchell's removal and the retirement of General Mason M. Patrick, our Air Corps began to deteriorate, sinking to an ever lower level of efficiency. Planes lacked the necessary modern equipment. Through the "housekeeping" agencies of the Army they were equipped with radio sets and other instruments unsuited for their tasks. Thus there was little opportunity for practical training in blind or instrument flying. Suddenly the Air Corps was jolted out of its somnolence by being called upon by the President to fly the mails, following the cancellation of airmail contracts by Postmaster General Farley.

Neither the President nor Mr. Farley nor the American people could possibly suspect that our air forces were dismally unprepared for the task. For years the War Department had considered radio beyond necessary equipment for communication with ground forces as a luxury. The instruments grudgingly given to them were normally selected by the Army Signal Corps. They were adaptations of the standardized types used on the ground—these procurement officers could not see why radio good enough for the trenches wasn't good enough for the air. To army minds the standardization of equipment in all branches seemed to be the paramount consideration.

Either through ignorance of the hazards involved, or in the frivolous hope that luck would save its men, the Army undertook the job. The result, of course, was that seven gallant Army pilots, good soldiers obeying orders, died as martyrs to bureaucracy and illogical procurement methods. From their graves these marytrs refute the claim—advanced not long ago by Secretary Stimson—that the War Department is divinely chosen to "keep house" for aviation.

As a consequence of the disastrous airmail episode, the Air Corps was given more elbow room in the matter of radio and other instruments. Today, if called upon to fly the mails,

our airmen could carry out the assignment without a hitch.
At the beginning of the present war, American airplanes, although deficient in so many other respects, were famous for
their superb blind-flying equipment and they have been able
to serve Great Britain in that sphere with admirable results.
I have not the slightest doubt that if airmen had been given
the same generous elbow room in relation to armor, armament, and other fighting prerequisites, we could have shown
equally satisfactory achievements in other fields.

But alas, armor and bombs and guns did not enter into
aerial delivery of mails, and the defects in those spheres remained concealed. There was no lucky accident to loosen
the grip of Army procurement. In fact, an Army ordnance
man displaced the air officer as head of the armament section
of the Materiel Division of the Air Corps. Purely ground
mentality continued to govern the military characteristics of
our fighting aircraft.

The appalling situation was perfectly well known to the
aeronautical industry and to the more farsighted Air Corps
leaders. But it required another "fortunate disaster"—the im-
measurable tragedy of another World War—to bring the facts
into the public light. The war startlingly disclosed that while
we possessed many airplanes with first-rate flying characteristics, we had practically no *military* airplanes in the real
sense of the word. It would be an insult to the dictionary to
designate as "military" craft so deficient in the basic qualities
necessary for combat.

The industry should not, in justice, be made to shoulder
responsibility for that. It had been besieging the War Department, year after year, with bold and practical military
ideas. Our engineers and designers and aviation salesmen
discovered soon enough that they only invited the displeas-
ure of the military higher-ups—even to the point of risking

the financial safety of their companies—with such ideas. They were in danger of being maligned by brass hats to their employers or associates as "nuisances" if not "crackpots." The more audacious and creative men were told in effect to "stick to their knitting"—which was to sell planes to the War Department and not to think of strategy and tactics. Is not the first law of salesmanship that the customer is always right?

Although dive-bombers were an American development, it took Hitler to show our Army how to use it. Since that bomber seemed "in competition" with antitank guns and other infantry equipment, it never became fashionable with the Army. But the observation airplanes, which seemed to the same experts merely an extension of "the eyes of the Army," found encouragement despite their obvious obsolescence under the highly dynamic conditions of the new warfare.

For nearly two years after the war started in Europe our Army Air Corps continued to build these observation planes. And few more damning indications of backward strategic thinking could be cited. Even by the end of the First World War it was clear that observation craft floating majestically over enemy territory, while chatting at leisure with artillery posts, were doomed. Only swift fighter planes, able to pound their way to the scene of observation and fight their way back, had any chance to do reconnaissance. Yet the obsolete gadget was being built and an Air Corps spokesman blandly informed the Senate Appropriations Committee, as late as May, 1940:

"We have 360 observation airplanes which are just as good which should not be taken out of the air anyhow, because they are just as good today as they ever were."

Not only were these relics of a primitive aerial day kept

FIGHTER INTO BOMBER. A Hurricane being loaded with bombs. Though even World War I showed this feature to be indispensable, specifications for American fighters just before World War II did not call for bomb racks.

EVERSKY P-35 MODIFIED FOR EXPORT. This plane carried two machine guns and 100 pounds of bombs over a range of 1000 miles. Modified for export under less exacting regulations, it carried four machine guns and 1300 pounds of bomb load over nearly 2000 miles.

Close-up of alternate installations of twelve .30-caliber machine gun
six in each wing.

Formation of these fighters.

Two of the four 20-mm. cannons installed in the wings.

SPITFIRE WITH CANNONS. Note the two 20-mm. cannons installed in the leading edge of the wings.

AMERICAN EAGLE SQUADRON. News picture published November 1941, showing a formation of American pilots somewhere in England– flying British Spitfires. Obviously they would have preferred American planes, but the quality handicap made that impracticable.

"in the air," but construction of the same kind of planes continued through sheer habit.

Infantry influence on the military factors in aviation often showed up in absurdities that outsiders will find incredible. For instance, European countries entered the war with planes that carried free-firing guns: as many as eight machine guns and cannon strung from one wing tip to the other. But American specifications, enforced on manufacturers by bureaucratic edict, placed the guns within fourteen inches from the eye of the pilot—ludicrously simulating the Army sharpshooter with a rifle on his shoulder.

On the basis of ample personal experience I can attest that the Army repeatedly refused permission to install machine guns in the wings, insisting that they must be in the fuselage, as close as possible to the pilot's eye.

Furthermore, we were limited strictly to two machine guns, both firing through the propeller, since that seemed right to an infantry mind. Under this technique the fire power of the machine guns is limited by the rotating propeller, thereby sacrificing a large part of the potential value of the armament. In addition, it is obvious that high explosive shells could not be used in this type of installation. But rules were rules, and what every airman recognized as fantastic nonsense remained "the customer's" unbending demand.

In the trenches, machine guns are "fed" only from one side. On aircraft this is unnecessary and impractical. But it required almost an Act of Congress to force Army Ordnance to permit machine guns on aviation to be fed from both sides. The poor American plane designers had to rack their brains and torture their plans out of shape to accommodate infantry types of ammunition boxes for one-side feeding.

By 1938, France and other foreign countries ordering American planes insisted that we install additional guns in the wings. But though these orders were carried out for other nations, the senseless taboos were not relaxed for our own air forces. As late as 1939, some pursuit airplanes were still ordered with only two synchronized machine guns. Moreover, for some inexplicable reason, light bomb racks, which had until then been standard equipment on pursuits, were removed.

Even in the last stages of World War I, we had learned in action that under certain conditions pursuits were the only planes that could carry out light bombing operations in daylight. Fighter planes had accordingly been equipped with bomb racks. World War II was to confirm that lesson, both the Germans and the British having found it necessary to convert pursuits into bombers for certain tactical purposes. In Libya, for example, Hurricanes fitted out with bomb racks played an important part in bombing mechanized ground forces. In "keeping house" for the air forces on the threshold of the war, our Army thus betrayed not merely lack of vision in this respect but a complete innocence of the history of aerial combat in the preceding war.

Our military aircraft have also been seriously handicapped by what we might call our "luxury complex." Because the naval and infantry people in control of air defense regarded it an indulgence rather than a critical necessity, we have built into our fighting planes many comforts and supersafety provisions at the expense of combat efficiency. For instance, after an unfortunate freak accident, which killed a pilot when his airplane turned over in landing, all our tactical airplanes were built with huge towers, like reinforced greenhouses, directly behind the pilot's head—at a cost of additional weight and reduction in speed. Our gallant military pilots, whose safety was directly concerned by this change, objected to these encumbrances. After all, under fighting conditions, the pilot's ultimate safety depends on the performance of his machine, rather than the luxury of its construction and excessive margins of safety. Their judgment has been completely vindicated by the fact that a mere twenty-five-mile speed edge of the British pursuits over the German Messerschmitts held off the numerical superiority of the Nazi air power.

It is a harsh thing to say and I say it with great reluctance, out of a sense of duty: much of our backwardness was so childish and unreasonable that it seemed deliberate. Those in charge ignored simple and generally accepted principles perfectly obvious to the whole world, as though willfully holding back our air strength. It required no profound grasp of the science of aeronautical combat to add guns, to protect gas tanks, and so on. I confess myself baffled by the whole strange business.

--- 3 ---

NOTWITHSTANDING rich potentialities in inventive skills, manufacturing leadership, and aviation personnel, we failed to attain aeronautical maturity because our military organization insisted on keeping the science of aeronautics in a strait jacket. I want to fix this fundamental fact in terms of concrete evidence. In order to avoid involving any other individual designer or manufacturer, I shall limit myself strictly to evidence drawn from my personal files. I do so, however, with the knowledge that my experience was not at all unique.

In fighting for certain improvements in the combat qualities of aerial equipment I was not acting on abstract "hunches,"

but drawing deliberately on my own combat experience as a
military pilot, merely translating the tactical experience of
an earlier day into larger technical terms made possible by
more recent aeronautic improvement.

Thus I always fought against the unreasonable and disastrous limitations put on the fire power of our aircraft. As
Commander of Pursuit Aviation in the Baltic Sea in World
War I, I had become convinced of the importance of armament. Our Nieuports and Spads had been equipped respectively with one and two Vickers machine guns. Find-
ing that this fire power was inadequate and that synchronized
guns were not always reliable anyway, I installed a third
free-firing Lewis machine gun on top of the wing, gaining
a distinct advantage over the Germans. The principle of
superior fire power remained indelibly in my memory. Years
later, when I had the opportunity to design and build a fighting plane for the first line of American national defense, I
was naturally eager to raise the armament factor.

I pleaded with the Army to let me mount more guns. To
placate the Army Ordnance man at the head of the armament branch of the Materiel Division, I even offered to install four machine guns in the fuselage, synchronized through
the propeller. I proposed in addition to build wing guns into
the Seversky P-35's already in service. The manufacturer undertook to double the fire power—and to double the flying
range as well, by providing additional gas capacity in the
outboard panels of the wings—for the negligible sum of
$1879 per machine in lots of twenty-one or $15,000 for one
experimental set. The War Department declined the proposal, asserting in an official letter that the price quoted exceeded the potential value of such modifications to the Air
Corps.

Next to an edge in fire power, I learned to value emergency range in pursuit airplanes. The extra reach offered a variety of advantages. It enabled pursuits to convoy and protect bombers in daylight expeditions. It allowed the exploitation of internal lines of communication to the fullest extent, for the easier concentration of the defensive force in the area under threat. Most important, it enabled this vital tactical equipment of the air force to reach any part of the theater of war under its own power. In all these respects the last years have confirmed overwhelmingly the deductions I had made from my personal experience in the earlier war.

In 1917, two of my fighter groups were stationed on the southern end of Oesel Island, one at the Tzerel Peninsula and the other at Arensburg. Our problem was to protect bombers in their expeditions against the coastal fortifications and German harbors along the Courland coast of the Baltic, on the south shore of the Gulf of Riga. The absurdity of our situation was that our pursuits were able to cover the bombers in friendly waters but, on account of insufficient range, had to abandon them over the enemy shores, where they needed us most—only to meet the remnants of the bombing force on their way back home. Right there and then I began to work on the problem of range extension for fighters, even including a scheme for refueling them in the air while in flight. Developments in the Japanese war on China and in the Spanish Civil War reinforced my point of view on this subject.

With all the earnestness of which I was capable I therefore urged the War Department to permit me to build additional gas capacity into our pursuits. On June 25, 1938, I wrote as follows:

"In connection with the value of additional gasoline tanks in the wings and the increased effective range, we are aware of the fact that there is a difference of opinion. However, the present employment of air power in Europe and the Orient has definitely shown the necessity for some sort of convoying protective force for bombardment aviation. Our proposal is made to enable the Air Corps immediately to begin to conduct tests of the combined operations of bombardment and pursuits to determine the type of mission where such combined operations, over long distances, is most advantageous. Whether such airplanes should be single-placed, two-placed, or multiplaced; whether they should be single- or multimotored; what their actual range should be can be determined only through actual tests."

Besides reducing such suggestions to writing, I expounded them personally in the office of the Chief of Air Corps. They were brushed aside and even ridiculed as visionary and as tactical heresy. I was told that the bombers would be built so fast that no pursuit would ever catch up with it, that even armament should be sacrificed for speed—and it *was* sacrificed to the point of making our airplanes virtually defenseless.

As to the utilization of interior lines for successful defense, I had always foreseen the day when the continental United States might be reduced by the advances of air power to an island surrounded by a hostile world, with attacks possible from any direction. I saw it as a larger-scale Oesel Island, needing constant defense of its entire periphery. Hence it was obvious to me that our interceptor fighters should possess the range equal to the maximum dimensions of the country. That would allow us to mobilize as much fighter aviation as necessary in any part of the country at any time.

Accordingly I wrote to the War Department in June, 1938, that the extra gasoline capacity which I was urging upon them "will provide a range to enable the concentration of pursuit aviation from coast to coast without stop. The necessity for the latter feature was demonstrated during the recent tactical maneuvers." My arguments fell on deaf ears.

Finally, I urged the importance of a range which would enable our pursuits to reach America's outlying possessions under their own power. Addressing the appropriate Army officials, I wrote:

"Another important aspect of such additional range is the problem of pursuit aviation in case of war. If our theories are correct and air power becomes supreme, we cannot depend upon naval protection for our warplanes being transported by boat. The Navy will not be able to afford the necessary protection for our transport. Therefore, thought must be given to transporting airplanes to the various possessions of the United States by air.

"To do that our airplanes must have an emergency range which would enable them, in time of war, to reach any possession of the United States under their own power. It appears that a certain small percentage of losses of aircraft, due to mechanical failure in movement under their own power, is less hazardous and provides more dependable transportation than moving the same equipment in bulk by transport. Therefore, the Air Corps must provide its own means of supply, free from dependence on surface vessels."

The Department thought so little of range that it would not risk the minor investment even on an experimental basis. My company made the investment itself in the hope of convincing officialdom. More than that, I decided to drive the facts home by actually flying my pursuit nonstop over long distances. It was specifically to demonstrate the feasibility of such range that I made long-distance hops and established new records between New York and Los Angeles, and between New York and Havana. Air Corps officials unfortunately preferred to dismiss as exhibitionist record-breaking

my carefully planned object lessons in modern tactical possibilities.

They were even willing to compliment me in order to discredit the idea. These flights proved nothing, they said, because "Seversky with his experience could fly a broomstick."
One of the highest officials also complained that it was "un-
dignified" for the president of an aviation company to pilot
planes and break records. To overcome all such absurd objections, I arranged to have the pursuit flown by a compara-
tive newcomer, Jacqueline Cochran, a young girl who was at
that time at the start of her brilliant career as a flier. After a
few trial hops, she picked up a fully loaded Seversky pursuit
and flew it nonstop from Los Angeles to Cleveland, a distance of 2000 miles, piloting by instruments most of the way.
She thereby won the coveted and hotly contested Bendix
race. But none of this could budge the Air Corps from its
curious prejudice against long range.

The more persistently I begged for the privilege of enlarging the reach of our military pursuits, the more unwel-
come I made myself at headquarters. A couple of years
later General Henry H. Arnold, in his book on air power, indicated that engineers were "frantically" at work on convoy
pursuits. The implication was that if we did not possess this
essential equipment it was through some act of God, rather
than through the blindness of officialdom. Had there been
more competence and less complacent indifference three
years earlier, there would be no need for "frantic" catching
up now.

Just to illustrate further the unimaginative conservatism
that prevailed in the Army Air Corps just before the war, let
us take, for example, the Army P-35 pursuit ship. That airplane carried two machine guns and 100 pounds of bombs
over a range of 1000 miles. This is a pitifully small utilization

of the plane's potentialities. Modified for export under less exacting regulations than our Army's, the same plane carried four machine guns and 1300 pounds of bomb load over nearly 2000 miles, with about the same speed. The increase in fighting capacity is evident. What applies to the P-35 in this case is applicable to practically every American fighting plane, built under those shortsighted specifications.

Both the Materiel Division of the Air Corps and the GHQ Air Corps officials were alert to new ideas, equipment, and tactics. But somehow all progressive innovations were stymied when they reached the office of the Chief of Air Corps —under the shadow of the General Staff and the Army. Had this uppermost bureau been less concerned with the crosscurrents of military politics and more keen to guarantee effective air power, American bombardment planes, convoyed by long-range pursuits, would have been winging across the Pacific immediately after the Japanese struck at Hawaii.

The refusal of the War Department to countenance additional range in fighter aviation, more than any other single circumstance, explains the American setbacks in the Pacific Ocean in the first months of our war with Japan. Pursuits had to be crated and shipped across an ocean infested with submarines and menaced by enemy air power, when they might have readily been flown to the scene of action—to Hawaii, Guam, Wake, Midway, the Philippines—under their own power. The public could not guess that this failure was the result of shortsightedness and not an aeronautical limitation.

Technically there was no reason why, years before the start of the Pacific war, we should not have possessed a canopy of air power—comprising pursuits as well as bombers —over the whole area. Our ships, and not the Japanese Navy, would then have been able to maintain a shuttle service of troop transports between the Philippine Islands and the primary base on continental United States.

The most alarming part of the story is that apparently the responsible authorities, even at this writing, are not yet awake to the importance and technical potentialities of range in pursuits. Clear proof of this pathetic blindness or amazing stubbornness was provided by testimony before the Senate Appropriations Committee in January, 1942. As reported in the press, Secretary Knox told of the difficulties of getting American fighter planes to the Pacific war areas. As he pointed out, this was not merely a tactical handicap in itself, but a great drain on our hard-pressed transport facilities.

The Secretary was referring not merely to existing pursuits but to the huge armada of projected pursuits for which he was seeking appropriations. His testimony revealed his honest delusion that the inability of fighters to fly to the scene of action was an act of God, an evil inherent in the science of aviation. He seemed to think that nothing could be done about it but to build more ships for transporting planes. Unwittingly Colonel Knox, at the behest of his aviation mentors, was therefore misinforming Congress! Had he been aware of the true facts he undoubtedly would have told the committee:

"At this moment, because of gross failures and ineptness in the past, we are stuck with fighters which must be taken apart, crated and shipped to the Pacific outposts. This mistake will now be remedied. The new pursuits will be capable of self-delivery!"

His failure to say this, his evident unawareness that long-range pursuits are feasible and possible, meant that the grip of the past was still strangling our air power in a time of supreme challenge and supreme danger.

——————————— 4 ———————————

ALL INSIDERS know that the inferiority of American pursuit
aviation at the time that hostilities opened abroad arose primarily from the Army's airplane-engine policy. It is to be
hoped that the whole curious and inexplicable business will
be thoroughly examined someday in the full glare of public
attention. Here I can no more than touch a few high lights
of the situation.

For many years the liquid-cooled plane engine had been
ignored. But suddenly Army policy in this respect swung to
the other extreme. For reasons that remain obscure even at
this late date, the Chief of Air Corps' office became obsessed
with the liquid-cooled engine, automatically and consistently
rejecting any others as far as fighters were concerned. Quite
aside from the merits of the engine, even a layman could see
that reliance on a single type and a single source of supply
was foolhardy. Even in the last stages of World War I, fighting airplanes had been adapted for powering with at least
two different kinds of engines, the installation being completely interchangeable.

With this experience in mind, and aware that America at
that time had only two major sources of supply—the Pratt &
Whitney plant in Hartford, Connecticut, and the Wright Aeronautical shops in Paterson, New Jersey—I felt that pursuit
craft should be built around an air-cooled engine, so designed
that either the Wright or the Pratt & Whitney installation
would be possible. Should one of these sources be demolished
by enemy attack or sabotage, the entire pursuit aviation would
not thereby be grounded. As early as 1936, when I brought my
first low-wing full cantilever all-metal pursuit plane for competition, I wrote to the government as follows:

"The detachable engine mount, together with the inter-

changeability of engines, is very important. It should be remembered that not only may a certain type of engine prove
faulty and unsuitable for use in actual combat work, but the
engine plant manufacturing that type of engine may be destroyed by the enemy. Under these conditions, the entire
pursuit force, depending upon these certain engines, would
be rendered useless. For that reason, it would be the height
of folly to allow the pursuit type of airplane to be designed
for one specific engine."

The office of the Chief of Air Corps failed to understand
this vital strategic consideration. In 1938 it not only rejected
the idea of interchangeable engines for all types of pursuits,
but went so far as to chain all pursuits to one type—and an
engine of highly problematical and experimental character at
that. It seemed to me incredible at the time that our national
defense should be subjected to such a reckless and headstrong gamble. This was the more strange when most aeronautical engineers agreed with me that both liquid-cooled
and air-cooled engines had their own merits and their special
drawbacks. Those in authority, however, were committed to
the single type, the Allison liquid-cooled, and it was impossible to break through their arbitrary ruling on the matter.

I made exhaustive studies of cowling and streamlining of
the air-cooled type, demonstrating that it could be quite as
effective as the liquid-cooled. Besides, it was a proved type
of engine and had nearly twice as much horsepower as the
proposed engine which had mysteriously become the court
favorite. In my letter of June 4, 1938, I proposed the construction of a plane equipped with an air-cooled Pratt &
Whitney engine, known as R-2800, of 2000 horsepower. Its
performance was 432 miles per hour at substratospheric altitudes, where I envisioned modern fighting as likely to take

place increasingly. My plan was to equip this craft with a turbo-supercharger placed in the rear portion of the fuselage. I could thus preserve the compactness and the tactically desirable location of the pilot in the Seversky P-35. These features the Air Corps personnel valued.

The Materiel Division was favorably impressed. But I was advised informally and in embarrassment that "Washington" would not even consider pursuits with air-cooled engines. I tried to argue the matter. On June 24, 1938, I wrote:

"While the liquid-cooled engine seems promising at the moment, we feel that in order to assure ourselves of a type proved and ready for immediate procurement in case of national emergency the development of experimental equipment, utilizing both types of engines of the highest horsepower available, is advisable. The function of a pursuit and interceptor fighter, in our scheme of national defense, is too important to rely on only one type of equipment, since, should it fail for any reason, the country would be completely deprived of this type of aerial defense. Therefore we feel that at this time it is highly desirable to conduct parallel experiments with a single-engined pursuit airplane built around an air-cooled engine, as well as a liquid-cooled engine of the maximum horsepower available."

Anticipating possible objections, I added:

"For the last year this company has been working continuously on the development of this design; the necessary wind-tunnel models have been constructed and investigated; mock-ups have been built and the company has to date spent approximately $50,000 on the research connected with this project. These experiments and preliminary work were done, not only to prove that a performance of the highest degree could be attained, but also to enable us to present to the gov-

ernment a design where there would be no question as to
practicability since all the aerodynamical, mechanical, and
structural problems have been satisfactorily solved."

The project also included comprehensive armor to protect
the engine and the propeller mechanism.

I went to Washington repeatedly to plead, in the name of
military common sense, that we develop at least one air-
cooled engine pursuit, in case something should go wrong
with the experimental liquid-cooled motor. I ran up against
a stone wall of bureaucratic stubbornness. As the whole
world now knows, the favored engine did not live up to the
extravagant expectations and the Army has been forced,
years too late, to take on also the air-cooled engine. The very
company which had been deprived of orders because it could
not accept the arbitrary decree in this matter, and had constructed such airplanes at its own expense, was swamped
with orders.

The same official who ruled that there must be no more
air-cooled engine pursuits years later boasted publicly about
the new Republic (formerly Seversky) P-47 pursuit built
around such an engine. In a recent speech, after mentioning
the Bell Airacobra and Lockheed P-38, he said that "eclipsing
both of these, however, is the new single-engine Republic
P-47B." The publicity implied that this was something new
in the way of pursuits, pulled at long last out of the official
magician's hat. The truth is that this plane was conceived in
1937, presented for consideration to the Air Corps in 1938,
only to be denied a hearing because it did not use the pet
engine. Its production was thus postponed until 1941. No
amount of self-congratulation by the very officials who prevented the construction of this plane until three years too
late can wipe out their responsibility for the delay. According
to the Truman Committee, the P-47 cannot be delivered in

appreciable quantities until the end of 1942, and production will not be in full swing until some time the following year. Yet this plane could have been in action on all fronts years earlier.

There, in essence, we have the ordeal of American air power, its development hindered by political or business considerations, and above all by strategic illiteracy in the new military sphere. The same resistance that retarded long range, greater fire power, and interchangeable engines also blocked suggestions for improving armor, for shielding the gasoline tanks, and so on. Top Army men, failing to grasp the tactical requirements, the hazards, and the countermeasures in weapons so far removed from their normal experience, paid little if any attention to their stepchild, the Air Corps. Though a scandal to intelligent airmen, the picture was kept out of the public view—until the "lucky disaster" of the new World War made concealment more difficult.

The war has jarred military aviation in the United States from its bureaucratic rut. The backwardness, for all that high-powered publicity could do, has been in large measure exposed. The facts placed before Congress by the Truman Committee in January, 1942, indicating that only 25 per cent of our aircraft could be considered equal to the best foreign models, represented a fair statement of reality. For all the crude buildup being given to inferior American types in the public prints, the American Eagle Squadron at this writing is still flying the British Hurricanes and Spitfires. Our boys, making their heroic contribution as Americans, would surely be willing to take additional risks to instill confidence in our equipment by using it themselves. But the tactical differential is too serious to permit them to do so.

The P-40's—called Tomahawks by the British—had been widely hailed as our first line of defense in the skies, and

cumulative evidence of their inferiority in action has been
openly resented on this side of the Atlantic. They consequently offer a fair test of American standards of realism
in relation to aircraft production. American newspapermen
confirmed what aviation men knew in advance: that the
P-40's were lamentably inferior to the British pursuits. Hundreds of these craft sent to England were not even uncrated
for months, despite that nation's life-and-death hunger for
fighter planes. They were adjudged obsolete and put "on
ice" for possible auxiliary uses. When some of them were
assembled in England as trainers with the Army co-operation
force, American publicity tried to convey that they were
being used with the regular Fighter Command over the British Isles!

For nearly a year the British did not know what to do with
these pursuits. Finally they sent them to Libya, where they
proved a match for the obsolete French and Italian airplanes.
In the British offensive in North Africa in the winter of
1941–42, the P-40's served well enough as a kind of cross
between pursuit and attack airplanes, flying at low altitudes
and dealing with Stuka dive-bombers and other inferior Axis
aircraft.

What had been advertised as the very backbone of our
pursuit forces thus turned out to be a mere accessory of the
land forces, useful within a most limited scope. It was a left-
handed compliment, indeed, which General George H. Brett
paid this plane when he declared, in a London interview,
that "the present operations in Libya at least ought to prove
the quality of our material for that theater of war." It was to
cover the faults with verbiage that the sham battles, alluded
to earlier, were staged. When the Messerschmitt, Hurricane,
and Spitfire installed cannon, thus further increasing their
fire power, the P-40 was brought into line most expeditiously

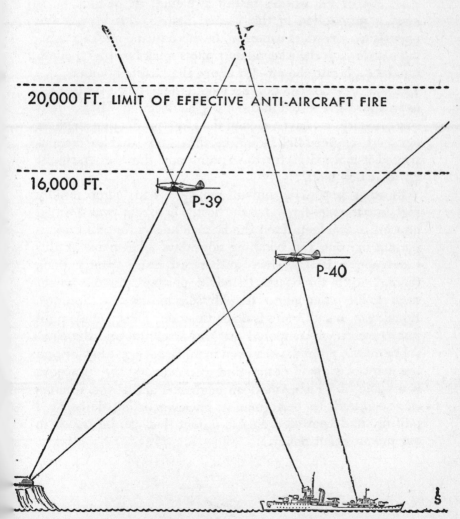

FLYING FORTRESS

MESSERSCHMITT

HURRICANE
SPITFIRE

30,000 FT.

20,000 FT. LIMIT OF EFFECTIVE ANTI-AIRCRAFT FIRE

16,000 FT.

P-39

P-40

RELATIVE EFFECTIVE FIGHTING ALTITUDES

and inexpensively by publicity men. They beat the engineers to the punch by simply rechristening the machine guns on the American plane "cannon." Unfortunately our enemies knew the difference.

On May 12, 1941, General Arnold grew quite impassioned in praise of an Army pursuit. "I can tell you," he exclaimed before the Women's National Democratic Club in Washington, "that one of the world's fastest airplanes, the Airacobra, is now in production in the United States. This remarkable plane is worthy of its name. . . . In this day and age our fighting planes with their keen, alert pilots must be able to climb rapidly high into the air—far above the hostile bombers. . . . That our Airacoba can do." Six months later, on November 29, in an address reported in the press, he declared: "In the pursuit category, we have reached the large production stage on our single-engined Bell P-39 Airacobra, a type that has demonstrated it is a match for the Spitfire and the Messerschmitt up to 16,000 feet."

In other words, the pursuit which was to "climb rapidly high into the air—far above the hostile bombers" was stymied beyond 16,000 feet. Even the layman knows that all the important fighting and bombing nowadays takes place at altitudes above 16,000, since antiaircraft fire is pretty thick there. Despite the boasts, therefore, our best pursuits would seem to be unequal to the Messerschmitts and Spitfires. Equality at low altitudes is no consolation. The general might just as well have compared the Messerschmitt and the Airacobra on the ground, with even more flattering results. From the point of view of design and workmanship the Airacobra is a plane of which American engineers and manufacturers can be proud. Its performance, however, is cut down by a pitifully underpowered engine—a fact that can be traced to our procurement policy.

LATEST ARMY PURSUIT P–47B. This plane, equipped with a 2000-horsepower air-cooled engine and supercharged to fight in the high altitudes, is today the white hope of our pursuit air force. Substantially the same airplane was offered to the Army in 1938 but was turned down because it was not equipped with the "pet" engine.

ARMY P–39 BELL AIRACOBRA. This fighter, with imposing fire power, is one of the finest in the world. It represents the most advanced tactical thought in engineering interpretation. It is seriously handicapped, however, by the performance of the engine with insufficient horsepower, which is the result of an erroneous and shortsighted engine-procurement policy.

VOUGHT SIKORSKY AIR-COOLED NAVY FIGHTER. At this writing, this American plane is the finest ship-borne fighter in the world.

AMERICAN ACHIEVEMENT IN BOMBERS. This Consolidated B–24, with added combat power and range, will be one of the world's most potent weapons of air power extant in the bombardment class.

CURTISS DIVE-BOMBER. This American dive-bomber of the Navy is the most powerful ship-borne weapon of its kind.

The engine situation could have been corrected, once the Allison engine had failed to serve as expected, by frankly adopting the best available foreign substitute. The British Napier Sabre, a 2000-horsepower engine eminently successful in the Spitfire and Hurricane, was at hand for immediate use. Unfortunately the Army steered around this and adopted instead the Rolls Royce Merlin, with horsepower similiar to the Allison's. Thus bad judgment in official policy in the past was perpetuated. If we had been able to deliver 2000-horsepower Napiers instead of Allisons and Merlins, such fighters could really have competed with the models of other nations. It is, after all, through the use of that superior engine that the British pursuits are now able to fight at high altitudes with speed in excess of 400 miles, carrying either four 20-mm. cannon or twelve machine guns.

What is gained by concealing mistakes and faults, in a historical period when facts not phrases will tell the final story? What is gained by cheerfully assuring the public that American pursuit aviation holds its own and is even better than any in the world? Enthusiastic publicity stories released by the manufacturer have boosted speeds of existing planes to over 500 miles an hour. Terrific diving speeds were palmed off as speeds on the level. Furthermore, these stories evoked visions of planes bristling with imaginary guns and cannon. The P-40-F was described as having 667 per cent superiority —a mighty impressive figure, until we learn that it is in comparison with the obsolete P-36. Had the comparison been made with the original Curtiss JN of 1914 vintage, the percentage would have been even more phenomenal. The P-47 is a promising plane that has no need of such fanciful promotion. Yet a columnist described it as possessing twelve machine guns and four .37-mm. cannon, synchronized to fire through the propeller. Which, of course, is sheer nonsense, there being no such armament.

But such fancies are soothing to ears aching for good news. However, they accomplish nothing except to fortify complacency through a false sense of achievement.

---

5

---

In the bombardment class, the picture was only a little better. In my opinion, the most promising type in production at this writing is the Consolidated B-24, although, like so much of our equipment, it lacks sufficient fire power. As a basic design, at any rate, it has strong tactical promise; fortunately the disposition of its structural and aerodynamic components permits improvement, so that it can be rearmed as an impressive bomber.

But the most publicized of our bombing airplanes was the Flying Fortress—a fine flying ship with a most misleading name. True, this craft has a long range, it carries an impressive bomb load, it is speedy, and it is justly considered a beautiful flying job. We have good cause to be proud of it. But precisely in the matter of impregnable defense, implied by the word "fortress," it did fall short. The defensive armament on this large airplane was less than that on the small single-seater Spitfire or Hurricane. Moreover, its guns were so disposed as to put the Flying Fortress at a serious tactical disadvantage. Only a small fraction of the total fire power could be used in any one direction. Until recently, in fact, it did not even have the rear turret that has long been standard equipment on all British bombers.

Responsibility for lack of combat power in the "fortress" cannot be laid at the door of its designers and manufacturers, who are not responsible for the purely military aspects of a plane. The shortage in armament can be traced directly to the notion that speed would serve as the best defense for bombers. This fallacy has been exploded by the war. Though the British Stirling bomber is somewhat slower than the Flying Fortress, it is definitely preferred in action because it carries a greater bomb load over a greater distance and has larger defensive fire.

American bombardment aviation would have advanced much further if the advice of able men like General Andrews had been heeded. In 1936 the GHQ Air Force under Andrews made its stand before the procurement board of the Air Corps for bombers of the four-engined type. General Andrews argued that they represented greater striking and combat power, and provided more defense value for every dollar spent, than a larger number of twin-engined bombers. The procurement board—headed by a nonflying Army man —turned down the proposal.

It was no secret among airmen that the Army was reluctant to undertake a program of long-ranged aircraft development, fearing that it might lead the Air Corps away from what the Army regarded as the paramount job of air power: direct support of ground troops. The delay in bomber development helps explain our margin of inferiority. It may be mere coincidence—but it happens that the officers who did not give up the fight, and submitted a minority report, were subsequently demoted. But those who sat on the fence, and did nothing to help the Air Corps procure these four-engine bombers, now actually receive credit for their ultimate development.

Publicity on the Flying Fortress, as on the P-40, has effectively protected the American public against the facts of life. Loose comment has emphasized the great altitudes at which the "fortress" attacks—as high as 35,000 feet. One report added that the resultant "invisibility" of the bomber

worked psychological havoc with the Germans. Why invisible
planes in the daytime are any more disturbing psychologically than at night, when they are all invisible to people at
the target, was not explained. The latest radio detector instruments locate planes at a distance of over 100 miles, according to the Roberts report on the Pearl Harbor Inquiry.
It therefore has no trouble spotting planes at 35,000 feet.
Every additional foot of height means a loss in the accuracy
of bombing. Besides, there are relatively few days when visibility permits bombing from that altitude, so that valuable
bombing equipment is left idle the greater part of the year.
The Flying Fortress was obliged to climb to superhigh altitudes because it was sadly deficient in armament and therefore sought to avoid encounter with pursuit fighters.

Publicity is no substitute for military characteristics. Thus
General Arnold had to admit, in an article in the *Military
Engineer* for December, 1941, that the Flying Fortress (B-17)
no longer can escape pursuits at any level. He wrote: "Recently on several missions the B-17 pilots flying at 32,000
feet and above have found Messerschmitts awaiting them on
their objectives and have received a warm reception, in some
cases much too warm." It took the British fighters to protect
the bomber at that height since our best American fighters,
as officially stated, were no match for the best Nazi planes at
altitudes above 16,000 feet.

Thus we went into the year 1942 producing fighting planes
with admittedly inferior military characteristics. Is it because a cessation of manufacture would be tantamount to
public confession of past blindness? It will be less embarrassing, of course, to keep things going without break until
the "catch-up" designs are produced. After that the outmoded models can be explained away as legitimate obsolescence.

It may be argued that we possessed nothing better at the time to substitute. In that case, why did we not stop making the obsolete planes and put the British Spitfire into production? It was then generally recognized as the best pursuit extant and after three years it still merits that distinction. In the foregoing chapters we have seen clearly what quality in aviation means—how it saved England in the Battle of Britain. The plight of the United Nations in the southwestern Pacific has been due largely to weakness in the air. That has been generally explained by Japanese numerical superiority. Had our qualitative potential been at the Spitfire instead of the P-40 level, the picture might readily have been vastly different. Little wonder that Major General Henry Gordon Bennett, commander of the Malayan forces in Australia, in a broadcast on March 8, 1942, demanded that the United Nations give Australia air support "better in quality."

The P-40 series is being built in increasing numbers. At the same time the road is being smoothed for a polite retreat from what was only yesterday touted as the backbone of our aerial defenses, with statements, to quote General Arnold, that "We no longer rate the P-40 better than a good pursuit trainer." The statement was made on November 28, 1941, yet nothing was done to eliminate that model from production. In point of fact, this plane has not even justified itself as a good trainer. It is known that the accident rate for the P-40 in routine training flights has been larger than for any other pursuit built for the Army. Where the casualties in the flying ranks are about as heavy in noncombatant flights as in combat, an airplane hardly qualifies as a first-rate trainer. The high cost per unit on this craft, moreover, makes it absurd to continue to produce it merely for trainer purposes.

The rock-bottom fact is that the same men responsible for the woeful backwardness of our military aviation are still in control. They would be more than human if they did not yield to the temptation to avoid candid admission of past errors. There are too many skeletons in the official closets: private arrangements, compromises to placate certain brass hats, blunders traceable to sheer apathy or honest ignorance. As long as the men and the system responsible for our weakness in the air remain, there can be little hope for world leadership in military aviation. In some instances those chiefly to blame for the backwardness have even been boosted to still higher peaks in our military hierarchy. No matter how earnest and able, new men who must work as their subordinates cannot achieve the clean, sharp break with past mistakes that is essential to real progress.

Obviously projects long pigeonholed and ignored are now being resurrected. That is part of the face-saving process, which will continue as long as men intimately identified with the whole history of failure and frustration in our military aviation remain in commanding positions. It is not altogether accidental, under these circumstances, that publicity to vindicate fallacious judgments has sometimes taken precedence over courageous action to undo the mischief.

There was no need, after the launching of our defense program, for high-powered salesmanship in behalf of aviation. Demand far exceeded supply. Yet the advertising and "public relations" campaigns went on without abatement. A magnificent job has been done to overcome nonexistent sales resistance by glorifying American models. Everyone was "sold"—the public, the editorial writers, the radio commentators—except, alas, Hitler and the Japanese, who knew the truth about American aviation only too well. The fantastic

performance credited to our aviation at home did not dis-
courage the Mikado from attacking us.

When the committee headed by Senator Truman disclosed
the qualitative lag of our planes, John Jouett, President of
the Aeronautical Chamber of Commerce, would have been
better advised to face the facts. Instead, he issued an am-
biguous statement of labored alibis. "The only yardstick by
which the merit of military aircraft can be judged," he declared, "is performance in actual combat. In every theater of
war to date, our American designed and built warplanes, including pursuits and bombers, have shown marked superiority on every occasion in combat with enemy planes."

At the time Mr. Jouett made this statement, the Allies
were inferior in the air on all fronts except the British Isles.
Presumably he was confusing the brilliance and valor of our
pilots—of which there can be no doubt—with the performance
of the planes. Besides, he told only half the story. The planes
which are, in fact, doing well in *secondary* roles are the very
ones which were regarded as the *primary* weapons of American aerial defense. It speaks well for British resourcefulness
that they have been able to fit our planes into various tactical
niches, thereby releasing their own superior planes for more
important jobs. If instead of planes we had sent wheelbarrows which proved useful in the Libyan campaign, it would
hardly justify us in praising the said wheelbarrows as first-
line aerial defense. The sad fact is that the pride and joy of
our aerial forces has found application in humiliatingly accessory roles. The sadder fact is that the moral of the story is being so patriotically evaded.

On March 12, 1942, a dispatch from Burma by foreign
correspondent Leland Stowe quoted an American pilot as
follows:

"Once we've got planes that are just as good in every way

as anything the Japs or Germans have, we'll really begin to
hand up some records. And once they give us planes that are
just a shade better than any Jap or Nazi fighter—well, brother,
I just want to be in on it when that time comes. It's going to
be a barrel of fun, I'm telling you. But it can't come too soon.
It's got to happen faster than anything ever happened in
America before. I hope to God the folks back home know
how much it will mean to us out here."

That is a more eloquent plea for quality in our aviation
than I can attempt—and a confirmation that we are woefully
behind in the qualitative factor. It does tear at one's heart to
realize that a spirit such as that pilot's, and precious American lives, are being endangered and wasted through inferior
aviation equipment.

It is about time we stopped bragging about our aeronautical superiority. If we continue to live in a fool's paradise of
self-congratulation and farfetched alibis, there is nothing
ahead of us but brutal disillusionment. The sooner we stop
patting ourselves on the back and clean our aviation house,
the closer we shall be to victory. In his talk to the Women's
Democratic Club in Washington in 1941, General Arnold
demanded a kind of moratorium on criticism of our aviation
setup, asserting: "I have no patience with the uninformed
and misguided croakers who look with thick-lensed glasses
for indications that the Air Corps is helpless; the Air Corps
is not properly trained and equipped; cannot be made ready
to fight; and is being furnished with planes inferior to those
of England and Germany." All he overlooked was that the
"croakers" were right.

Proof of this was not long in forthcoming, from the Pacific
theater of conflict. Here, for example, are a few revealing
sentences from an Associated Press dispatch out of Java,
dated March 7, 1942:

"Planes arrived, especially heavy United States bombers, which proved to be formidable weapons. Without sufficient fighter protection, however, and protection for the airfields, their value continually decreased. The fact that the fighters on hand were not of a quality sufficient to fight successfully against the excellent Japanese material made itself especially felt. Not only did their offensive power decrease, but the operations of the heavy bombers became riskier."

General Arnold concluded the speech, quoted on the last page, as follows: "Yes, we will have an air force in *time*. It is well on its way and will be *ready* when called upon." Inconsiderate enemies, unhappily, would not adhere to his optimistic schedule. They attacked *before* we were ready, and proved that our air force was *not* in time. The backwardness against which the "croakers" sought to warn had caught up with us.

Inexorable events are overtaking those who protect the moldy skeletons in official closets. Thus a report made in January, 1942, by a Congressional committee headed by Representative Harter of Ohio blurted out the whole sad truth about the ordeal of our air power. Ostensibly this report praised our aviation progress and the wishful-thinking press pounced on it as a consolation. Yet it included the direct charge that in the years before the start of World War II, the years when we should have been perfecting our aerial weapons, spokesmen for military aviation *had misinformed Congress as to our air strength!* The Harter report pointed out that in the middle of 1939 our aviation was exceedingly backward. We lacked fire power and other military essentials, the report attested, and ignored even purely American developments like dive-bombers and self-sealing gas tanks. Then it added:

*"All this despite the fact that Congressional committees*

*were frequently told our planes of that period were better than those of any other nation."*

As politely as possible, the report thus accused military aviation leaders of lying to Congress. Unfortunately it failed to follow up the accusation with a frank inquiry as to *why* this happened, whether it was still happening, and whether those responsible had been removed from spots where they might continue such mischief. The American people were jolted into awareness of the situation when it appeared recently that the Army and Navy Munitions Board twice refused Donald Nelson's request that the priority rating of aircraft be advanced. Not only was aviation listed below battleships and tanks, but even trucks! Aluminum for chairs on battleships was receiving higher priority ratings than aluminum for aircraft. Of course, public opinion supported him fully when Mr. Nelson overruled the Army and Navy view.

The clear need is to forestall events by seeking out the causes of our backwardness and eliminating them with relentless vigor. Human nature being what it is, certain officials resist a real housecleaning and renovation of our military aviation structure. It would expose too much, and would cut too cruelly into bureaucratic inertias and privileges. Our fighting men of the air services know that the very people who rammed inferior equipment down their throats are still in charge of the situation. That knowledge is scarcely calculated to raise morale. The most stimulating thing that the President could do to lift their morale would be to follow the example of England and clean house at the top—not in the tactical units, but among those who were directly responsible for procurement before the war emergency.

Senator Truman and his associates should be congratulated on the courage and candor of their report, insofar as it relates to the combat power of our aircraft. It proves once more that in a moment of crisis American leadership equal to the challenge is available. The American tradition of facing facts and correcting mistakes in advance, in the early stages of the war, will save us from weeping over them and seeking scapegoats afterwards as happened in France.

# CHAPTER X

# THE EMANCIPATION OF AIR POWER

1

THE CONTROVERSY over a separate and independent Air Force, organized as an equal partner in the great triumvirate of our land, sea, and air services, has been marked by an inordinate amount of bitterness and passion. This is not an accident; nor does it call for outcries of alarm. The intensity of the debate is really a measure of its importance. For laymen it should serve as a tip-off that this is no routine dispute over division of honors and authority. On the contrary, the problems involved go straight to the heart of war science, and on their solution depends nothing less than our victory and national survival.

To the average American the demand for an autonomous Air Department seems reasonable enough. His thinking is not complicated by military subtleties and political habits. He feels the common sense of the facts: a new weapon functioning in a different element calls for a specialized organization to meet its needs efficiently and expeditiously. Obviously air power has operated in several theaters of war without benefit of direct collaboration or support from either ground troops or naval forces, as in Britain and Crete. No less obviously, naval forces, including battleships, are committing suicide when they venture within bombing radius of hostile land-based aviation. The one nation whose aeronautic prowess has impressed him most, Germany, built it on the foundation of a separate *Luftwaffe*. Japan's successes in the first

254

rounds of the Pacific Ocean extension of the war—at Pearl Harbor, the Philippines, Sarawak, off Malaya (in the sinking of two British dreadnaughts)—were directly attributable to the air weapon.

But with the immemorial modesty of his breed, this average American doubts his own common sense in such matters. As one who has been exceedingly close to the whole problem for more than a quarter of a century, let me assure him that in this instance common sense happens to be a good guide. Precisely because they approach the subject with open minds and without deep-rooted prejudices, laymen are more likely to apprehend the basic facts than those raised in a military or naval tradition. They have nothing *to unlearn;* their emotions and loyalties do not get in the way of their thinking.

There is a kind of desperation in the illogic of some of the arguments against freeing air power from its present subordination to the older services. Even the coincidental fact that France, possessing an independent Air Force, was quickly defeated has been advanced by an Army spokesman to discredit air power. By the same logic, we should terminate the autonomy of the U. S. Army, since France fell despite its independent and much-touted army. The dismal showing of Italy, despite its independent aviation, is likewise cited. But it happens that Mussolini's land and sea forces have done no better. The simple truth is that a separate Air Force is not a wonder-working device to guarantee automatic military ascendancy, but merely the minimal precondition for successful modern warfare.

Another variety of farfetched objection voiced in high places may be described as "ideological." Unification of our aviation services under an independent setup, the story runs, implies a centralization of military authority suited to totali-

tarian regimes but at variance with the American spirit. Is
there in truth some mysterious quirk in the American system of democracy which makes it forever impossible for a
new weapon to attain a separate status? In that case, how
did the Navy evade permanent subjection to the Army?

Fortunately, the objection is wholly imaginary. The question of centralization is beside the point in this connection,
since it has quite as much pertinence for the Army or the
Navy as for an Air Department. A democratic system which
has survived two centralized independent services should
have no trouble surviving the establishment of a third.

This species of "ideological" argument really arises from
misunderstanding the problem of an over-all High Command. Germany had such a supreme military authority long
before airplanes existed; when aviation grew to maturity,
the *Luftwaffe* was added as a matter of course and became
a third independent element along with the Reich Army
and the Reich Navy. In the United States the co-ordination
has been much looser. It is formally maintained, however,
through an Army and Navy Board, which would automatically become an Army, Navy, and Air Board when aviation
is set up as a separate organization. There is no reason for
confusing this problem of centralized command with the
issue of air power.

Events, it is likely, will force upon the United States the
adoption of the over-all General Staff principle of conducting warfare. The emergence of air power must hasten the
process, since it undoubtedly "complicates" the problems of
co-ordination. Three major factors must now be brought into
perfect alignment in the interests of victory, whereas a generation ago there were only two. Life generally was simpler
and more easily co-ordinated before the advent of steam
power, telephones, and radio. War, too, has become increas-

ingly mechanized and intricate. But assuredly we do not remove the complications by pretending that the third factor of aviation does not exist. That would be like trying to restore transportation to its ancient simplicity by painting the locomotive to look like a horse. On the contrary, the splintering of our aviation, quite senselessly, into air force over-dry-surfaces and air force over-wet-surfaces makes the process a lot more complex.

Every confusion of the issue of a separate Air Force with the broader issue of unified command *for all the services* evades the facts. The creation, today, of a Supreme Staff on the European model would not alter the status of our air forces or solve the problem of unified command *in the air*. Moreover, such an over-all command of all our forces would be a futile anomaly unless the air weapon had at least equal representation and authority in its councils. There is not much sense in a High Command without a true and unified air force among the elements at its disposal. As far as the skies are concerned, it would be obliged to function as best it could with two distinct air services, each differently trained and in most cases with unlike equipment.

A High Command must select and combine the various military ingredients just as a painter combines colors to obtain the required shades. Every painter knows that he is hopelessly stymied unless he has *primary colors* for the mixing. He can never get the proper effects if some of his colors have already been organically combined beyond unscrambling. Even thus an over-all command would be stymied if it did not have primary military services at its disposal. Under present conditions, the air forces are organically combined with the other services beyond unscrambling.

Those who believe that we need such a command should realize that the immediate establishment of a separate Air

Department with the same standing as the War and Navy Departments is a necessary preliminary step. A High Command can be set up almost overnight when decided upon; it requires only the selection of the proper persons and their investment with the proper authority. But the full development of an organization to provide us with air power will take some time and should be started without delay.

Another set of objections rests on a misunderstanding of the scope of a separate Air Force. It assumes that the new Department would arbitrarily gather in and control anything that flies. Those who proceed from this false premise, those who advance such arguments, are like Don Quixotes fighting windmills. No matter how military aviation may be organized, neither the sea nor the land service can or should be stripped of airplanes logically and tactically a part of its operations. Just as the Navy has Marines and other adjuncts which, in a literal sense, are land troops—just as the Army has transport boats and other sea-going auxiliaries—so both the Army and the Navy would continue to possess airplanes for their own specific purposes.

The distinction that needs to be made is between *integration* and *co-ordination*. The U. S. Marines, for instance, are integrated with the Navy, whereas an Army division co-operating with fleet units in a tactical task is merely co-ordinated with the Navy, though it may be taking orders from an admiral. The Navy's own artillery, carried on its ships and planted on its naval stations, is integrated with that service; the Army coastal batteries, though intended to help the fleet in warding off assaults on our shores, are merely co-ordinated with the Navy.

In like manner, certain airplane auxiliaries should reasonably be integrated with the land and sea forces, as part and parcel of those military branches. That, however, does not affect the broader question of a self-sufficient Air Force, developed to conduct aerial war against enemy air power, and also capable of co-ordinated effort with the surface forces. Of course, differences of opinion will arise as to whether a particular aviation adjunct can be better developed as a component of the Army or the Navy, or as a part of the Air Force especially trained to act as a component when needed. Analogous problems have arisen in the relations between land and sea units, but no one insists, on that account, that development and administration of infantry should be made subordinate to the Navy, or vice versa.

Ship-borne aviation must be integrated with the Navy. Whether taking off from aircraft carriers or warships, it is intended primarily to operate in areas still beyond the reach of existing land-based aviation. It is physically as well as tactically joined to the fleet of which it is a part. It is as integral with the Navy as submarines or naval artillery or smoke-barrage apparatus.

But shore-based aviation (and this, of course, includes seaplanes and amphibian craft as well as land planes) logically belongs with the separate Air Force. Such aviation will include units especially developed and trained to bring maximum support to ships at sea—just as specially trained units of the German independent *Luftwaffe* have brought support to Nazi naval forces far at sea in the Battle of the Atlantic; just as Army coastal batteries co-operate in fleet tasks within the range of their guns across the waters.

The Army, too, may retain minor aviation adjuncts—certain aerial transport facilities and local reconnaissance auxiliaries, for instance. But in operations where Army and Air Force are components of a larger team, there is no more reason for the infantry to own and control the aviation than there is for aviation to own and control the infantry and tank divisions. Whether the Army or the Air Force will command a given operation will depend on the nature of the job to be done. The success of the operation will depend on how well each of these components has been developed in its own sphere, and how well they have been trained together. We can no more hope for maximum exploitation of aerial possibilities—in readiness for such operations—if development of the Air Force is subordinate to infantry minds than we could expect the best development of ground forces by subordinating them to naval minds.

There is an important distinction between naval aviation and Army co-operation units of air power:

Ship-borne aircraft are structurally unlike the standard planes. They not only operate with the Navy; they depend on it. They take off from ships and come home to roost on ships. They live with the Navy. But the types of aircraft likely to work with the Army in joint tasks operate from regular air-force airdromes; they are manned and maintained by the air-force personnel and supplied with fuel and ammunition through air-force channels. Structurally the planes themselves come within general air-force standards. Army co-operation aircraft works with the ground forces only at the moment of tactical operation—but it lives with the air force and administratively belongs with it.

The guiding mind of a High Command or Commander in Chief must be taken for granted at all times. That applies to the Army and Navy no less than to a separate Air Force. No military service in wartime acts on its own whims. Their co-ordination, however, does not require a merger of their internal organizations. Each derives its strength from its specialized personnel, its full sense of responsibility, its ability to extract the last ounce of effectiveness without interference from an alien mentality.

The task of the guiding intelligence is, in fact, enormously facilitated when it can deal with a self-sufficient air arm. There are then no leading strings held tight by the older services to hamper co-ordination. Air power would be available for use without bureaucratic impediments. The very principle of effective co-operation calls for true independence and equality on the part of the collaborating elements. There can be no co-ordination between a Navy and an Air Force subordinate to the Navy; in that case there can only be orders based on naval ideas and blind obedience by aviation.

———————————— 2 ————————————

In May, 1940, President Roosevelt, obviously speaking in accordance with the recommendations of his military advisers, made a statement in opposition to the emancipation of air power. It began with the assertion that "fighting efficiency depends on unity of control." This is a truism to which advocates of genuine air power not only subscribe but which they urge as a major reason for establishing a separate unified air force.

In the continental European *Blitzkriegs,* an army tactician could exercise command. The German Army in those operations used aircraft as overhead support for a ground campaign. But over England, with pure air warfare in progress, only a different species of tactical brain, adjusted to the special character of the air weapon, could direct the battle. That was why Hermann Göring, Hitler's aviation chief, took over at that point. But if Britain had not possessed an independent Air Command, who would have taken charge of the struggle? The Army, because the main target was on the ground, or the Navy, because the main barrier was a water

channel? Or would they have drawn lots to decide priority and jurisdiction?

Yet the United States, under analogous circumstances and
with the present form of organization, would face just that
ludicrous dilemma. Would Army aviation hand the ball—or
the bombs—to Navy aviation at the shore line and would
the Navy then carry the ball across the ocean, handing it
back to Army aviation to carry for a touchdown on targets
deep in the heart of enemy territory? Would a chalk line be
drawn through the skies and a "No Trespassing" sign put up
to keep out American aviators with the wrong kind of uni-
forms? In a continuous battle that raged across land and
across sea, in the unbroken "air ocean" that covers land and
sea alike, who would command, an infantry general or an
admiral?

When Japanese aviation attacked land and sea targets
simultaneously in the opening gambit of the Pacific war on
December 7, 1941, did they present us with an Army or a
Navy task in the skies? Though the attack constituted a single action, two sets of air forces rose to the skies—each under
different command, each with its own variety of training,
tactics, equipment, and psychology. In the following days
the public heard of Japanese ships attacked by American
"Army planes" and "Navy planes" and "Marine planes"—one
objective sought by three auxiliaries of two different services, in an element inaccessible to either of those services!
The same duplication, the same division of air strength, the
same confusion of authority exists throughout our national
aviation.

Incredible as it sounds, it is a fact that a few years ago
the Army and the Navy reached a gentlemen's agreement
under which Army aviation promised not to stray farther
than 300 miles offshore! Now that "Army planes" can cross

ocean distances, now that "Navy planes" take continents as well as oceans in their stride, the childish absurdity of the jurisdictional overlapping should be sufficiently clear.

The air, it cannot be too often repeated, is a separate element, distinct from land and sea—an element with its own space relations, its own laws and problems. It is a continuous and uninterrupted element enveloping the entire globe; strategically speaking every political division and every differentiation between air-over-land and air-over-water is artificial and meaningless.

The continuous and uninterrupted sphere of the air calls for a continuous and undivided *Air Command* and fully uniform air equipment, co-operating where necessary with the Army and the Navy, expecting their co-operation where needed. But each of those three commands should be organized and developed and administered as a powerful force thoroughly integrated and thoroughly free in its own element. Certainly the first condition for success in any campaign is unity of command. Unhappily we now possess only splintered aviation, none of it specifically geared for the primary task of taking and holding the skies for America.

This is the principle which President Roosevelt's statement overlooked. It went on:

"In sea operations the airplane is just as much an integral part of unity of operations as are the submarine, the destroyer, and the battleship, and in land warfare the airplane is just as much a part of military operations as are the tank corps, the engineers, the artillery, or the infantry itself. Therefore the air forces should be part of the Army and Navy."

On examination it becomes clear that the President voiced the official views of the existing military Departments. These military minds are confusing two categories of unity. No one denies that both the Army and the Navy need unity of command in their respective spheres. This includes authority over their various auxiliaries and authority over units of other services operating with them for specific tasks. If the sole function of aviation were to serve as the adjunct to the surface forces, the President's statement would be entirely correct. Actually it is true only as far as it goes—and unfortunately it leaves out of consideration entirely the most vital and decisive aviation which operates alone in its own element.

The President's Army and Navy advisers failed to explain —because they do not grasp this idea themselves—that coordinated action with other services is a *secondary function* of air power. The primary function of air power is to destroy the hostile air forces, to strike at the enemy directly across long distances—in brief, to take and hold the skies. That is as distinct an undertaking as the conquest and control of the seas by a navy used to be. The fact is that the tremendous expansion of the air weapon has opened a new world to conquest—the air—requiring strategy and tactics and equipment more complex and more specialized than any in the past. It has transferred the issue of victory or defeat to a distinctly new medium.

If aviation development followed the President's formula, the ground and sea forces would possess aerial adjuncts, but we should have no genuine air power at all. Among other things, the President's formula fails to differentiate between *tactical co-operation,* on the one hand, and *administrative and developmental integration,* on the other. Opponents of a separate Air Force can hardly mean that all services which work together tactically should be merged, since that would blot out the separate status of practically all existing military forces.

No one disputes the need for unity of control over any service in its own sphere—land, sea, or air—but that is altogether different from an artificial unity achieved by subordinating development and administration of the Army to the Navy; or of the Navy to the Army; or either of them to the Air Force—or the Air Force to both of them. If for some mysterious reason it is necessary to limit ourselves to two services, why discriminate against air power? The circumstance that it is the youngest is hardly a good reason; we are dealing with a realistic relation of forces and not a problem of respect for old age.

Air power today happens to be the only force that can frustrate enemy attack from the air, the only force that can reach the enemy beyond our shores, the only force whose support is indispensable to both the Army and Navy, but which is compelled to operate alone in its own sphere, where surface arms cannot penetrate. Why disrupt this paramount force? Why deprive it of the very unity of control everybody agrees is so essential to successful operations? Why distribute it for piecemeal development by other services?

It would be far more logical, in point of fact, to split the Navy. What Admiral Mahan called "the fleet in being"—the fleet that theoretically should go anywhere and do "the necessary" but today is unable to go into waters covered by land-based aviation—might be awarded to air power. Thus fast cruisers and submarines could be co-ordinated and directed from the air, as the *Luftwaffe* is already doing on the Atlantic. The rest of the naval forces, what Mahan designates as "the fortress fleet," could be assigned to the Army, under the aegis of the Coast Artillery. This would consist of the battleships which in their role of protecting the shores are, after all, merely coastal artillery of longer range.

I certainly do not recommend such a division of forces.

But I do submit, in all seriousness, that it would make more sense and would be less dangerous to the nation's security than the present splitting of our air forces, and the resultant absence of unity of command in the skies.

Taking cognizance of the growing common-sense public pressure for a separate Air Force, the War Department in the late spring of 1941 presented the country with a minor reform dressed up to look like a major reorganization. It announced the "unification of its air activities in a new unit to be known as The Army Air Forces." In informing Congress of the plan, the Secretary of War emphasized the "autonomy" of the new setup and its "unity of command."

This verbal garnishing was most unfortunate. Insofar as it created the illusion that the Army had made a "compromise" on the issue of self-administered air power, the public was being misled. Actually the reorganization merely revamped one of the Army's subordinate sections, while keeping it as subordinate as ever. The "unification" announced did not even touch the basic issues raised by advocates of an Air Department. No one can object to necessary internal reform of the Army's aeronautical structure. But there is every reason to object strenuously to an attempt to palm off a departmental reform, such as frequently occurs inside any service, as a substitute for a separate Air Force.

Under the reorganization, the Army continued to treat aviation as one more adjunct to its services. Ground generals remained the final arbiters of the fate of Army aviation, as in the past. The Army's record in the matter of aeronautical development scarcely encourages optimism, but even if it were to do a brilliant job, it would still be a job limited by the specific strategic concepts and the particular mentality of infantry generals. The reform was at best verbal—at worst it tended to mislead, mystify, and confuse the American people.

Similar confusion is exemplified by other Army acts that were in line with the new aviation age in form, but strategically backward in substance. I refer to the designation of able aviation officers to various theaters of operation. Such moves were announced with a great fanfare of publicity as "recognition" of aeronautics by our military leadership, and probably were intended as such. Strategically and tactically there is ample reason why the areas involved should be headed by airmen. They are regions representing natural arenas for the operation of modern air power, even with its present limited range.

The public assumed that these appointments made the strategy in the Caribbean, the Hawaiian Islands, etc., essentially an aerial strategy, as it should be. In a vague way the actions implied that air power had been given authority over the other forces. Nothing of the sort happened, of course. By reason of their appointment, the aviation officers were removed from the Army Air Forces and made generals of the line. Because of their knowledge and abilities, they could certainly make far better use of the available air equipment than nonflying generals of the line had been able to do. But they were responsible to the Army, and had to work within the framework of Army strategy and Army conceptions. They had no authority over the naval forces in their areas of command. Except for the fact that they knew more about aviation than other Army commanders, they had merely been taken out of the air and pinned to the ground, as it were.

To make the point clear, suppose the Philippines were under the jurisdiction of the Navy. Then suppose that defense of the islands developed into a predominantly land problem and therefore it was decided that ground strategy must prevail and that General MacArthur had accordingly been put in command. Now suppose, further, that the general is thereupon transferred to the Navy Department where he must take orders from admirals and is obliged to operate under naval strategic ideas! Could any arrangement be more muddled and unnatural? Would that constitute "recognition of land power" or only naval interference with land power? In assigning airmen to command, but removing them from the Air Forces and putting them back into the Army, where they take orders from generals, we have approximately that sort of unnatural situation.

As usual, in our process of compromise and "catching up," reorganization soon became unavoidable. Just as it took us about two years after the campaign in Poland to recognize dive-bombers, so it took us about three years to copy certain phases of the German war machine. But again the imitation was on a timid and limited compromise basis. The changes in Army structure made effective on March 9, 1942, were limited to and wholly within the old Army framework. Undoubtedly it meant another and significant step forward in the modernization and streamlining of ground operations. But as far as air power is concerned, the new changes were no more relevant than the preceding set.

True, our General Staff now provides equal representation for air officers; the fifty-fifty arrangement ought to result in better air-ground co-ordination. The air members, having had Army training, understand ground problems and can be most useful in formulating co-operative efforts. The ground members, however, having had no aviation training, can make no real contribution to purely air strategy. On the contrary, they will act as a brake on real aeronautical thinking and a constant source of interference. The air forces will be even more firmly tied into the ground strategy than before.

We are still left without genuine air power. As before, our strength is split into two sections, integrated with the older services, equipped with unlike aircraft, operating under a split command. The next Army reorganization and those to follow will be equally meaningless from the air-power standpoint, no matter how desirable they may prove in heightening the efficiency of the Army and the effectiveness of surface strategies, as long as they remain merely Army revisions.

At the Navy end of the picture, the same sort of illusion in regard to "recognition" of air power was created in the public mind by the appointment of Admiral King, who is rated as a naval aviator, as the Chief of all our naval forces. (Characteristically, the Navy outdid the Army in its adjustment to realities; in the March reorganization of the Army, the Chief of Staff in command of our entire land forces remained an infantry man without aviation background and training.)

The appointment of Admiral King guarantees that naval aviation *as an adjunct* will be more intelligently used. The effectiveness of the Navy under the able command of such a man will be raised, especially because he is an airman. But again this enhancement has nothing to do with true air power. Again, as in the Army, aviation will be even more definitely woven into the pattern of the surface service. Admiral King has been frank and emphatic in his refusal to recognize the independent strategic role of air power. He is a sailor to the core of his being, unwilling or unable to recognize that the air weapon is anything more than an implement and auxiliary of surface forces. His whole attitude on the subject of air power is implicit in a statement such as this:

"Air objectives are so nearly nonexistent that they are admitted to be remote of attaining even by the ultra-enthusiast

of air power. Since air power must rely on land [army] and
sea [navy] forces, it follows that the best use of air forces
is as components—and integral components—of the land and
sea forces. . . . The functions of naval aviation are derived
directly from the functions of the Navy. All the capabilities
and endeavors of naval aviation are directed towards the
promotion of naval efficiency and are designed to enable the
Navy better to perform its functions."

To anyone who has read this far in this book, the fallacies
packed into such a statement should be clear enough. As a
man passionately devoted to sea power, Admiral King fits
perfectly into the post assigned to him. He is a fine teammate in our top military command. But it leaves that top
command, as heretofore, without the third teammate: representation for a strategically separate air power—for the
obvious reason that we are still without such air power. The
designation of sailor-aviators to key posts in the naval forces,
like the designation of soldier-aviators to commanding jobs
in various arenas of conflict, slurs over the problem of a unified air force without solving it.

---

3

---

THE OFFICIAL propaganda here against emancipation of
American air power has thoroughly misrepresented aviation
facts in Europe. Whether the misrepresentation rests on sin-
cere ignorance or polemic enthusiasm, the effect in under-
mining American realism on modern warfare is the same.

Against my background of personal firsthand study of
German aviation, I feel justified, for instance, in asserting
that the American public has been given a peculiarly distorted account of Hitler's *Luftwaffe* organization. The Secretary of the Navy summed up the prejudices of his experts,

no doubt, when he wrote, in August, 1941, that "the *Luft-waffe* cannot be called a truly independent service, since all German forces—land, sea, and air—operate under a single High Command." The following month General Marshall made the same assertion in a speech. "The German air force," he said, "is not independent of the ground arms in the generally conceived sense." Others have offered the same stereotyped opinion.

What are the facts? If it is true that Germany does not have a separate air force, then it is equally true that it does not have a separate Army or Navy. If these critics seriously urge that we avoid the establishment of an Air Department on the basis of German experience, then they should logically urge the abolition of the War and Navy Departments as autonomous entities.

The elementary fact, I can attest from study on the spot, is that the *Luftwaffe* is wholly separate and autonomous. Its status is no different from that of the Navy or the Army in the Reich. The American public is being befogged through the juggling of words. The word "separate" is being confused with "independent." Also, "independent" in the sense of autonomous organization, administration, and development is being confounded with strategic and tactical independence.

The German Air Force is as distinct from the Army and Navy as those two services are from one another. But none of these services is independent of the High Command, any more than our Army or Navy is independent of our Commander in Chief and Congress. Every branch of the German military complex—land, sea, and air—has unlimited scope and authority for the independent development of its maximum efficiency, the best possible equipment, and the most appropriate strategy and tactics within its own element. At the same time, no effort is spared to achieve maximum co-ordination among any two or all three of the branches.

A naval attack on the separate Air Force idea declares: "In many respects the extent to which appropriate units of German aviation are integrated with and trained to co-operate with ground forces surpasses the integration and co-operation of air and ground troops in our own Army." Though intended to warn us against unified aviation, such a statement amounts to full corroboration of the claims of advocates of a separate Air Force. The fear that autonomous air power would be unable to co-ordinate effectively with our ground troops disappears in view of the German demonstration to the contrary.

There are occasions when the Army tells the German Air Force what its problems are and the Air Force provides the tools, personnel, and tactics to solve them. There are also operations in which the Air Force tells the Army what type of co-operation it requires on the ground—such as the acquisition of necessary advance bases—and the Army provides the men and the machines for achieving the assigned results.

It should be understood, moreover, that the German experience has by no means provided a rounded and definitive case study in three-dimensional warfare. In France, to be specific, there was no genuine confrontation of air forces in a struggle for the skies. The opposing aviation was so rudimentary that there was no fight of air power versus air power; in effect the air belonged to the invaders at the outset. The dive-bombers and other Army co-ordination aerial units therefore operated without opposition in the air.

But assume that the invading German forces had met opposing forces equally protected and supported from the air. We should then have witnessed an overhead struggle for air mastery along with the ground struggle. The action

of dive bombers and other co-ordinated aerial elements
would then have had a double relationship: to the ground
troops below and to the air power above. They would have
been sandwiched between two battles, called on to offer the
greatest possible help to the battle on the ground, while dependent for their own success and their own survival upon
co-operation from the aviation above them. Such double
synchronization would have been utterly impossible with an
air component divorced from the larger air-power organization. Critics of emancipated air power are therefore making
deductions from an exceptional and incomplete situation.
The fact alone that Germany, after its years of experience in
action, does not dream of turning over the development of
its Army co-ordination aerial units of the *Luftwaffe* to the
Army should set these gentlemen straight.

Propaganda capital has also been made here by opponents
of separate air power out of a series of circumstances in relation to the British Air Ministry.

As the first major nation with a separate Air Force, Britain
carried the absorption of existing air units too far. In their
pioneering fervor the British naturally made mistakes, including assignment of authority over purely naval aviation
to the RAF. In the not-distant future, when land-based aviation will cover all the seas, the aircraft carrier—today's "floating base"—will become atrophied. The British anticipated
this development by a good many years when they placed
their Navy's air arm under the RAF. By 1937 they realized
that there was no reason for the Air Force to control the
fleet's own aviation, and turned it back to the Royal Navy.

This reversion, in the view of American proponents of an
Air Department, was entirely justified. They point out that
Britain made this change in the peace years, and hence not
under the pressure of military events. But the change has

been vastly exploited here by Army and Navy spokesmen to make it look: (*a*) as though it were a confession that the separate RAF had failed, and (*b*) as though the change had been dictated by "blunders" in the current war.

Neither of these things is true. An organizational error by the RAF is no more a justification for the abolition of a separate Air Ministry than the many egregious mistakes made by the British Army—or by our own Army, for that matter—are sufficient reason for abolition of a separate Army. When Admiral Yarnell writes in a popular magazine that "The British have, after a tragic series of mishaps, moved to restore naval aviation to the navy," he is guilty of gross confusion. The "mishaps" which he alleges occurred since August, 1939, but the restoration occurred in 1937. The two sets of facts, even if they were as the admiral presents them, could have had no connection. Any "mishaps" of naval aviation in this war are clearly the responsibility of the Royal Navy, not the RAF. The juggling of the time element becomes exceedingly curious when we find many others doing it in almost the same phrases!

American official spokesmen, furthermore, point to the truly backward and inadequate equipment of the RAF for co-ordination with ground forces, and the general numerical weakness of the RAF.

No one admits this more readily than the Air Ministry itself. There is not the slightest warrant, however, for turning this admission into an argument against the idea of a separate Air Force. The insufficiency of aircraft certainly cannot be blamed on the Air Ministry, which naturally sought all the appropriations it could possibly obtain to enlarge its forces. It simply reflects the naval-mindedness of Britain, which kept both its Army and its Air Force on short rations until the realities of modern warfare became too overwhelmingly obvious to be ignored.

"We often hear that a unified air force would mean greater stimulus for military aviation and would insure better equipment," Admiral Yarnell wrote. "Yet certainly the condition of the RAF at the beginning of the war is weak testimony on both counts."

One can only marvel at the smugness with which old-line military men repeat such libels on the RAF. The quantitative lack, obviously, is no fault of the Air Ministry. And the most significant single fact about war equipment today has been the qualitative superiority of British aviation. RAF planes were, and at this writing still are, the best in the world. No greater praise of the system of separate aviation is possible.

If the condition of an air force at the outbreak of this war is taken as the test of the organization under which it developed, then the American system of aviation integrated with and owned outright by the Army certainly flunks out. Our military planes were not only small in number; they stood at the bottom of the list in point of speed, armor, fire power, and other military characteristics.

The RAF, too, lacked Army-supporting aircraft, thus again reflecting traditional British underestimation of the Army. Despite its separate Air Ministry, Britain had no satisfactory aviation to work with the Army for the simple reason that it had no real Army. The fact obtrudes that the only nation which did have proper Army aviation was Germany, and Germany developed aviation through its separate *Luftwaffe*. Speaking of the RAF, General Marshall stated, "More recently they have been improvising special groups to operate more closely with ground troops." He offered this as a count against a separate Air Force. All it means, however, is that the RAF, now that there are ground forces to work with, is developing Army co-ordination task units, precisely as the Germans had done and precisely as the separate American Air Force would do. The remarkable part of it is that General Marshall's army, with outright ownership of its air component, only recently began to develop dive-bombers for co-ordinated action on the *Luftwaffe* pattern; even later, that is to say, than the RAF.

Criticism can justly be directed also against the Coastal Command of the RAF. Such criticism was implied in Prime Minister Churchill's announcement at the end of 1940 that the Coastal Command aircraft would be substantially increased and that its operational policy would be under Admiralty command. But Mr. Churchill did not envision this as an argument against the idea of a separate Air Ministry— it remained for certain American military men to twist the event to their purposes. It has not occurred to the British to turn over the development of their Coastal Command to the Admiralty. It remains an RAF component co-ordinated in a naval enterprise, just as in other circumstances it might co-ordinate with Army operations or with operations of the RAF Bomber Command.

It is altogether right and necessary that pilots of the Coastal Command familiarize themselves in large measure with naval activities, and for naval officers to familiarize themselves in large measure with aviation matters. There is nothing new or remarkable in such duplication of knowledge, since all military services have areas of overlapping activities. Army coast-artillery men, since they are primarily designed to ward off hostile fleets, must know something of naval operations, and naval men must know something of the coastal fortifications which they must at times attack.

This, of course, can be carried to ludicrous extremes in any direction—and is, in fact, being carried to such extremes by certain opponents of air power. They demand that all pilots of aircraft flying over sea be naval men, in order that they may recognize different types and nationalities of ships below them. This is about as sensible as requiring all captains of ships to be airmen, in order that they may recognize the types and nationalities of airplanes overhead.

Again we have to draw the telltale line between special training for co-ordination with another service and organizational integration and merging with that service.

In the period immediately before our formal entry into the war, officially inspired American attacks on the RAF assumed the proportions of a major campaign. The purpose was patently to head off public pressure for a separate Air Force by discrediting Britain's separate Air Force. Only patriotic eagerness to save us from what seems to them a dangerous innovation could explain the extreme liberties the campaigners took with the facts of war events.

The British were in a most uncomfortable position, loath to quarrel with highly placed American personages, yet dismayed by "smearing" of the RAF on this side of the ocean. On November 10, 1941, they responded discreetly in a radio broadcast which singled out statements made by a retired admiral, Harry E. Yarnell, for refutation. Those statements, however, were largely a repetition of charges against the RAF made by Secretary Knox, General Marshall, Assistant Secretary of War Patterson, and others. Evidently London felt it politically more expedient to challenge an inactive admiral than active high officials in the United States.

One of the allegations running through the campaign was that the RAF refused or simply failed to respond to naval calls for bombers to attack enemy submarines or other naval

targets off the coast of England. Referring to Admiral Yarnell's reiteration of such charges, the London broadcast asserted: "This is completely untrue. Royal Air Force planes
have made more than 300 attacks on German U-boats."

There have been occasions when the RAF did not follow
up naval information that submarines or other targets at sea
had been sighted. The reason is that there have been more
targets and tasks than the RAF could handle at any one
time. Whether the bombardment of a submarine base on the
French coast, a concentration of aircraft for attack on England, an important industrial unit in the Ruhr is more important at a given moment than the bombing of a vessel
reported by the Admiralty is, after all, a matter of judgment
by the proper authorities. To present this as proof of the
inefficiency of the RAF is to stretch the facts.

Much of the campaign rested on the story that RAF failure to offer proper co-ordination to the Navy caused the
disastrous results at Crete. In this our critics ignored the specific assurances of Mr. Churchill that "co-operation and co-
ordination between services" in that area had been "carried
to a very high pitch." We have seen in a previous chapter
that the real difficulty at Crete had been caused by unwarranted reliance on sea power in the months of preparations.
There simply were not enough bases on the island to enable
the RAF to operate. The meager fighter force available lacked
sufficient range to co-operate in a theater of combat 300 or
more miles from its African bases.

Practically all the other accusations against the RAF are
equally ill-founded. If it has made mistakes, they certainly
do not derive from its organizational independence. Most of
them can be traced to the original neglect of aviation in respect to its numerical strength. Nor should it be overlooked
that the British, like ourselves, lack an overall High Com-

mand, and that most of the confusions blamed on the RAF
may be traced to that fact.

––––––––––––––––––––––––––– 4 –––––––––––––––––––––––––––

THE COMMON denominator of all the objections to an independent Air Force is that the United States has built air
forces of a sort under the aegis of the two other services and
can therefore improve them without limit under the same
monitorship. It would only complicate further an already
complex picture, the argument runs, to set up a "third" aviation when we already have Army and Navy aviation.

The answer is that *at present we have no air power at all.*
We have a miscellany of airplanes, good, bad, and indifferent, but no air power in the sense that we have defined the
idea in these pages. If the production program of 185,000
planes announced by the President in his great address of
January 6 is carried out in full, we shall be no nearer genuine air power—since those planes will not reflect a unified
aerial strategy to be used by a unified air command. They
will still be merely weapons of the Army and the Navy. Far
from being a "third" aviation service, a separate Air Force
would be the first and only agency to provide us with genuine air power. We now possess a variety of aircraft that comprise a first-rate naval arm, and an amorphous mass of Army
planes with great latent possibilities. But these accessories,
no matter how large they may become, would still remain
weapons of the two services, unfitted both physically and
psychologically for the tasks of pure aerial warfare.

The very fact that an air force is "naval aviation"—conceived and nurtured to suit the needs and the tactical principles of sea power—excludes it from the category of real air
power. The things which make aircraft "the best naval avia-

tion in the world" often destroy their value for pure aerial
warfare. We have already examined a few of the technical
limitations which always make airplanes based on ships inferior to equivalent designs for land or water take-off.

Over and above such technical handicaps, it should never
be forgotten that designing and broad-gauged conceptions
such as real air power calls for are overshadowed from the
start by naval preferences and naval tactical notions. In the
nature of the case, aviation tied to an older, slower service is
foredoomed to become inbred and freakish. It is as though
a high-powered gasoline engine or Diesel motor were installed in a horse-and-buggy. The addition might conceivably facilitate the horse's job. But it would remain a horse-
and-buggy, not an automobile. Its performance would never
go beyond the limitations of a horse.

Aviation of the fleet may be splendid naval aviation because it has been developed by the Navy. It would be splendid agricultural aviation if developed by the Department of
Agriculture for the purpose, let us suppose, of dusting the
fields against farm pests. When the airplane is used to spot
law violators and to act as a flying police car, it should be
assigned to the Police Department. Similarly, the aerial
equipment attached to the Army or to the Navy as adjuncts
belongs under the wings of the existing services.

None of this has any logical connection with the kind of
independent warmaking aviation under consideration. The
need is for air power that navigates in its own medium, ex-
pands freely in accordance with its own tactical laws, operating independently in some tasks and teaming up with the
other military services in other tasks. We have seen the
growing role of air power. We are conscious of the almost
limitless horizons of that enlargement. Shall we deliberately
endanger our chances of victory by failing to make room for

this growth, by holding on desperately to old prejudices and frozen organizational forms?

The mental timidity of orthodox military leadership—the time lag between weapons and tactics—was described decades earlier by Admiral Mahan:

"Changes of tactics have not only taken place *after* changes in weapons, which necessarily is the case, but that interval between such changes has been unduly long. This doubtless arises from the fact that an improvement of weapons is due to the energy of one or two men, while changes in tactics have to overcome the inertia of a conservative class; but it is a great evil.

"It can be remedied only by a candid recognition of each change, by careful study of the powers and limitations of the new ship or weapon, and by a consequent adaptation of the method of using it to the qualities it possesses, which will constitute its tactics. History shows that it is vain to hope that military men generally will be at the pains to do this, but that the one who does will go into battle with a great advantage."

It is that great advantage which is being denied to America by military men who have not taken the pains to revise their thinking. Mahan wrote in preaviation days in relation to sea power, but his logic is so clearly applicable to air power that were he alive today, I am convinced, he would be on the side of General Mitchell.

Practically every argument against unchaining and then unifying military aviation can be applied with as much, or as little, plausibility to the Navy. Take, for example, the oft-repeated contention that air power cannot "hold" a conquered area. To begin with, an enemy so thoroughly battered from above that it loses the strength to strike back does not necessarily have to be "held." It can be left to dig out of

its ruins—perhaps with the kind and profitable assistance
of the conqueror—since it has been neutralized for generations to come. Aside from that, does not the same contention
apply to the navy, which likewise cannot occupy a nation,
but must depend on the army to do that? The routine retort
that a navy can transport the needed army is no longer valid,
now that navies are barred from enemy shores by air power.
Besides, there is Crete as proof that aviation, too, can transport occupying forces. Because the final step is sometimes
taken by a foot soldier, does anyone insist on this basis that
the navy should be made subsidiary to the army?

No one does today. But the inquisitive might go back to
the debates on a separate and independent Navy Department in the last decade of the eighteenth century, before the
Navy was given an autonomous status in 1798. It is an en-
lightening experience. You will find that the War Department used substantially the same arguments for holding on
to the naval forces that are now being used against emancipation of air power; and you will find, too, that the spokesmen for genuine sea power used about the same reasoning
in support of their thesis that is being advanced today by
advocates of a separate Air Department.

Reading the *Congressional Record* of April 25, 1798, I
thought I was listening to typical current objections to the
freeing of air power. Congressman Livingston, for instance,
grew ironical about the silly business of a separate Navy.
"To carry this idea to its full extent," he explained, "it would
not only be necessary to have separate departments, but also
a great variety of subdivisions; they must have . . . commis-
sioners of gun barrels and of ramrods." How often have we
heard the same type of irony from naval men asking if we
also wanted a separate department for submarines or naval
artillery!

Congressman Macon pointed out that "he believed the building of the frigates had mostly been carried on under the direction of the captains who were to have the command of them." A century and a half later modern Macons are arguing that aviation is being developed by airmen who fly it, though there is no separate department for it. The current "ideological" arguments, implying that a separate Air Force is somehow against the grain of our Constitution, was voiced in 1798. The *Record* reports that Representative Williams was "alarmed" . . . "when he saw they were about to add a grand department to our government, not contemplated by the Constitution." Even the recent claim that the separate RAF has been at the bottom of Britain's trouble had its prototype in those far-off days. Representative Livingston exclaimed that this "practice of Europe had proved itself to be a bad one, as the navies of those countries had proved the ruin of them."

On the other side of the debate were men like Representative Otis who insisted that "the services of the War and Naval Departments were . . . perfectly distinct," adding: "As well might a Merchant be set to do the business of a Lawyer; a Lawyer that of a Physician; a Carpenter that of a Bricklayer; or a Bricklayer that of a Carpenter," as expect Army men to lead the Navy. And Representative Sewall declared that "It was well known that an officer might be well acquainted with the business of the army, without knowing anything about a navy." Navy men opposing separate air power might recall the fact that the bill authorizing the formation of a separate Navy passed the House by the narrow margin of 47 to 41.

The basic strategic plans of the United States at this time are predicated on the independent as well as the co-ordinated activities of the Army and the Navy. The air arm of each of these has a place in the pattern, just as other auxiliaries of the two services have. I venture to state that no matter how brilliant such plans may be, they are destined to failure when confronted with an enemy strategy based on all three services, each of which has had unlimited scope to create tactics and corresponding equipment. Until we have an Air Force, entrusted with the task and the authority to develop a specific strategy for taking and holding the skies, our plans must remain two-dimensional in conception and therefore, notwithstanding the physical participation of aircraft, seriously if not fatally handicapped in an epoch of three-dimensional warfare.

The technology of war advances with such rapid strides that it quickly outstrips the mental pace of humdrum old-style leaders. Today tactical vision must be coupled with engineering vision. Military leaders must be able to foresee both the new equipment and the tactical implications of that equipment. Only those with the creative imagination to keep them a few long steps ahead of the immediate technological-tactical picture can match the world we are living in. Even men trained in aviation have difficulty in visualizing the air power of tomorrow; how helpless, therefore, are those trained in totally different fields, who psychologically are incapable of considering the air as a separate tactical sphere! That is why a realistic program calls for an unequivocal separation of new weapons from old assumptions, especially in relation to air power, the newest, the fastest-growing, and most revolutionary military force.

A new military art, such as is inherent in aviation, must not be restrained by subservience to old military leadership, which is another way of saying old military conceptions. To do so is to lose the war by default. I am not reflecting on the intelligence or the patriotism or even the professional competence of the Army and Navy strategists. I am simply taking note of the natural and unavoidable fact that they think as infantry and naval leaders and can never fully release their minds for aerial warfare. Like the French General Staff which was preparing competently for a repetition of the war of 1914–18 with modern trimmings, our own leadership prepared for a somewhat more complex but essentially similar operation as in 1917–18. They accommodated aviation to their strategy, instead of accommodating their strategy to aviation. Only 100 per cent airmen can conceive and carry through a 100 per cent aerial strategy.

———————— 5 ————————

It is argued now—as it was in 1798—that the actual planning of aviation is entrusted to airmen, even if they work within the forms of the older services. No one doubts that talented aviation brains are at the disposal of the Army and the Navy. But those in any degree familiar with the operation of great disciplined military organizations know that the views, the prejudices, and the honest tactical fixations of the topmost leadership must always prevail.

Even if never expressed in words or orders, those preferences percolate down through the ranks. They make themselves effective in the subtle pressures of obedience to authority, loyalty to superiors, and honest hunger for promotion. To the extent that an aviation idea infringes on the traditional sphere of an older service, or throws doubt on the efficacy of that service in a given situation, it is slowed up and frequently doomed to premature death. The channels through which it must move are adjusted to the needs and the inertias of an older tradition. Military services, like everything else that is alive, are instinct with a will to survive which fights, consciously or unconsciously, against every reality that limits their functions.

The most talented air strategist or designer cannot contribute all that he has when he is condemned to work within the framework of limited and essentially false basic plans of strategy. It is not merely a matter of "guts" in speaking out. No one can deny the importance of discipline in the armed forces. Once he has made his recommendations to his superiors, an aviation officer feels it his soldierly duty to say no more—even if he is heartbroken by the manner in which his deeply felt views are filed and forgotten. On the whole, high-ranking military men in recent years have tended to be more outspoken than in the past. But the new candor has not affected the discussion on air power. That subject is ringed with a taboo.

The crucifixion of General Mitchell is still vivid in the minds of Air Corps officers. They know full well that the political forces responsible for it are still effective, despite the fact that the events of this war have fully vindicated General Mitchell's views. To put it bluntly—as airmen do among themselves—everyone in the Air Forces knows what is coming to him if he dares raise his voice against the outmoded ideas of the military hierarchy. The American public does not suspect that there are many lesser General Mitchells in our services who are paying a price for their advocacy of ideas beyond the grasp of generals and admirals now in command. The aviation industry, too, is effectively silenced. It does business with the same generals and admirals. Moreover, it is sworn to stringent secrecy in a manner that precludes practical criticism of aviation policy. With these things in mind we are better able to savor the unconscious irony of the words when a Navy memorandum states:

"No officer in the Army or Navy who is even slightly familiar with his profession fails to realize that aviation is a major and essential component of both services. Moreover, the airmen who are most vocal in urging the formation now of an additional independent air force are men who are not in the Army, not in the Navy, and are either unfamiliar with or not keenly interested in the broader aspects of national strategy, national defense, and the science of modern warfare."

It does not take a mathematical genius to figure out why the most vocal airmen are not in the Army and not in the Navy! The personal tragedies of those who dared to be vocal are only minor items in the larger tragedy of an American air force condemned to domination by the older services.

This is not rhetoric. It is the living reality which every creative aviation man confronts from day to day. Taken together, it adds up to a sinister reactionary force—almost a conspiracy of circumstances to clip the eagle wings of American air power. There is no cure for it except the emancipation of that service. There can be no makeshifts or compromises. The responsibilities and opportunities for putting our country in the first place among air-power nations must be transferred fully to men committed by their experience and their innermost convictions and enthusiasms to the air power of the immediate future.

As I have already indicated, there is no dearth of such men. We have, I would estimate, at least a thousand of them with roughly a quarter of a century of experience to their credit in every department of the science and the art of military aeronautics. We have an aviation industry capable of matching the challenge of such leadership in terms of designs and production. All that is lacking is the official setup properly to channel the industry's efforts. The morale of our fighting airmen can have its finest tempering only under conditions of an independent Air Force on a par with the Army and the Navy. Until then our aviation personnel, the world's finest, will feel the limitation of their status.

The importance of morale is so generally understood that I need not apologize for raising the question of the morale of airmen. I refer to their sense of identity, their awareness of a paramount role in the scheme of things. I refer to the profound inner warmth of "belonging" to a group which is fully recognized by the country. For airmen, staking their lives day after day, morale means a heightened consciousness of personal responsibility, pride of colors.

The present setup tends to blur the aviator's identity and make him feel an "also-ran." Under the backward system of divided air forces, airmen are necessarily overshadowed by the traditional prestige of the services to which they are artificially attached. The combat pilot, deeply conscious of the paramount role of air power, naturally resents the misleading implications when he reads that "the Army" has sunk so many Japanese naval transports off the Philippines, that "the Navy" has taken heavy toll of enemy ships in the Pacific. He knows that these achievements should have been credited, simply and plainly, to aviation.

Pick up any of the British war posters, official or civilian, and note how always and everywhere the airplane and its pilots are to the fore. In the United States, by contrast, soldier, sailor, and marine, even the coast guard, are to the fore —the aviator frequently forgotten or displayed in the auxiliary position which he, in fact, now occupies in the formal organizational sense.

I note such trivia not for their intrinsic importance but as symptomatic of a condition under which, I am able to attest from close-up personal knowledge, the average military airman now chafes. He is a sailor-pilot or a soldier-pilot, rather than a full-fledged member of his own military branch. From the angle of morale, the establishment of an independent Air Department would act as a wholesome and well-deserved stimulus.

In the abstract, the most diehard of admirals will usually concede that aviation has a limitless future. As a practical proposition of planning for that future, the imagination of such an admiral—or general—is certain to be paralyzed by the doubts and fears bred by his limited knowledge or his reluctance to offend superiors.

A convenient case in point is provided by General Henry H. Arnold, head of our Army aviation, in a recent book on air power. Admitting that the air forces of all countries will eventually be separated from land and sea forces, he writes that in America "This long step should be taken, if it is taken at all, only after careful planning and mature thought, and not with zest for radical reform. There should be a stage of gradual evolution as against another knife-cutting of binding ties." But almost in the same breath he contradicts himself by writing: "We shall be fortunate if our time for that reorganization of independent air force comes in the relative calm of peace or at worst in the preparatory and not in the fighting stage."

This sort of double talk, if it is not the product of honest confusion, may be a device for conveying the truth to those who understand, without offending the powers that be. The general surely knew when he wrote that we were close to the reality of war and that there was no time for the "gradual evolution" he proposed. He must be quite adequately aware that twenty years of delay—from the time when General Mitchell first demanded independence of aviation—have brought an evolution of approximately zero. Evolutionary processes, too, can be arrested by artificial restraints.

Apparently the general could not muster the boldness or the clarity of perception to demand action now, and contented himself with a verbal formula that leaves us exactly where we were. The same hopeless ambiguity pervades the public expressions of other airmen. They give enough lip service to the idea of an independent Air Force to create a popular, journalistic impression that they favor the idea (as undoubtedly they do in their hearts), but cautiously postpone its actualization to some vague future. The total effect, unhappily, is confusion worse confounded. If aviation men in the highest places cannot speak candidly because of political pressures, they might be better advised not to speak at all. When someone with the personal prestige of General Arnold is obliged to hem and haw on the issue, it is easy to understand how much more inhibited lesser officials must be.

At bottom the objections to true and independent air power derive from a flaw in vision. The critics are unable to see the potentialities of air power beyond the horizons of its present equipment and its present tactics. They do not take in the full majestic sweep of the inevitable progress of aircraft; they base their thinking on aviation as they know it today. It is, in many respects, the same sort of limitation of vision which cost the largest part of Europe, in the last three years, its national freedoms. Not only developments around the corner, but immediate possibilities which trained aviation minds know to be simple and sober realities, orthodox strategists dismiss as fantastic and farfetched.

Aviation is the firearms of the twentieth century. Imagine an island nation so small that it can be surrounded entirely by naval gunfire from all directions. You have then a strategic picture analogous to what confronts the largest of nations today under the weapons of superior Air Power, when it can be attacked as a totality. Under these circumstances it is a lunatic anachronism to divide our air forces and entrust the broken parts to other services. The eventual emancipation of air power from what an Air Corps general has called its "subordinate status" is inevitable. With that emancipation will come a blossoming of aviation talent, a heightened morale among the aviation personnel, a long-delayed chance for American air power to come into its own.

Meanwhile every week of delay is a costly and futile restraint on that unfoldment, and a postponement of victory.

# CHAPTER XI

# ORGANIZATION FOR AIR SUPREMACY

1

WITH SEA power declining and air power in the ascendant, the emphasis in our thinking and planning must be shifted from the obsolescing to the emerging weapons. The major portion of the resources and energies invested in war preparations must go toward the creation of a long-range air force to give us true air power. Clearly an agency especially dedicated and geared to this central task is indispensable.

It must have the requisite knowledge, experience, skills— and, above all, the *authority* corresponding to the importance of its purposes. Aerial warfare increasingly will affect not alone war strategy but the details of everyday life, from the character of our architecture to the clothes we wear and the food we eat. The job is so broad and so vital that it warrants the immediate establishment of an Air Department, with a Secretary of Air at its head.

This Department, in every respect on a basis of equality with the War and Navy Departments, will represent the first and biggest step toward world leadership in the air. There are, of course, no short cuts to national security. It cannot be enacted by Congress. Nations with separate air forces have been defeated notwithstanding, precisely as nations with separate armies and navies have been defeated. The proper organization is essential, but it will not automatically solve the problems of aerial defense. The need for intelligent planning, intensive research, superb personnel, streamlined organization of tactical forces will not be ended with the emancipation of American military aviation from its present subordination to outside services. *But the basic conditions will have been created, at long last, for meeting that need.*

The transition from the present divided and chaotic military aviation to a truly unified air power will require the complete and enthusiastic support of the President as Commander in Chief, as well as of an informed public opinion. The man selected as Secretary of Air will shoulder the most significant responsibility entrusted to one person in our generation. He must be equipped by experience and natural endowments for the vast and important undertaking.

But beyond that he should be someone with the personal prestige in the government and in the eyes of his fellow Americans to act with firm authority. It must be hoped that the other services, realizing their own dependence on impregnable aerial defenses, will co-operate in the effort. But human nature being what it is, they may be expected to fight for some of their traditional prerogatives. There will be inertias of the past whose pressures must be overcome. It will call for a personality of great strength, progressive military ideas, and robust practical imagination to meet the challenge.

The unnatural segmentation of our air forces is at present too often a source of misunderstanding and jurisdictional competition between the Army and the Navy. The elimination of this anachronistic issue should help to make these two services and the third independent service a team of three, with confidence in themselves and in one another. It should promote easier co-ordination. There will no longer be puerile questions as to how far beyond a coastline Army planes may fly without offending the self-esteem of naval aviation. There will be no more artificial problems about authority over long-range Army planes while spanning oceans en route to their land targets. Neither will there be any arguments as to whether a particular target constitutes a legitimate objective for Marine aviation, naval aviation, or Army aviation.

The present Army and Navy Board would, as a matter of course, be turned into an Army, Navy, and Air Board. It would constitute a supreme staff under the President as Commander in Chief. However, the President may reasonably decide to create his own staff or Board of Strategy, composed of leaders of the three military services, supplemented by representatives from such other branches of the government or from civilian ranks as he may deem necessary. However the problem of an over-all command is solved, it does not affect the issue of separate and unified air force, as we have seen in the preceding chapter. Here we are dealing with the organization of the Air Department and its air force, regardless of what form the topmost command of all our military forces may take.

The Air Secretary would be surrounded by a group of specialists, picked solely with reference to their abilities. Thus he would have an Undersecretary for Air Force, charged with the development of the fighting air forces, their personnel and supplies; an Undersecretary for Civil Air Defense, concerned with the total organization and preparation of the nation to resist and endure enemy aerial attacks; and undersecretaries for other subdivisions, possibly including one for Civil Aviation.

Whether civil aviation should be included within the authority of the Air Department, or whether it should be supervised by a board like the Maritime Commission, is an open question. There is no question, however, that the development of commercial aeronautics must be intimately aligned

with aerial defense. Civil aviation should not be hamstrung
by military domination. It must continue to enjoy the opportunities for expansion under commercial incentive which have
made it the greatest nonmilitary aviation in the world. At
the same time, thorough co-ordination of civil and military
aviation must be obtained in the interests of national safety.

Because of the difference in physical conditions, the alignment must be far closer than that between the Maritime
Commission and the Navy Department. Even in time of war,
the Navy seldom uses commercial facilities for its operations.
Air power, on the contrary, will of necessity use all the
commercial-aviation facilities available. Their development
must be scientifically meshed into the military-aeronautical
structure.

The air forces and civil aviation, for instance, should aim
at standardization of radio-navigation systems and equipment. Military pilots must feel themselves at home when
using commercial equipment for blind flying and blind landing. In like fashion, the commercial pilot who switches over
to military service in an emergency should be familiar with
military facilities. The regulations and instruments for the
control of airport traffic or landing procedures, the marking
of runways, beacons, and all other facilities should be carefully accommodated to the needs of aerial defense.

The popular notion that commercial airplanes can be built
with a view to transformation into warplanes ought to be
exploded once and for all, since it is a constant source of
confusion in the public mind. Let it be understood that it is
about as easy to convert a passenger plane into a bomber as
to convert an ocean liner into a battleship. Modern combat
equipment—armor, armament, bomb racks, and so on—are
structural parts of the basic design of the warplane; they

cannot be artificially added as an afterthought. Commercial and combat planes are different breeds of aerial animals and no magician can make them interchangeable.

But none of this applies to transport for war purposes. Passenger planes can be readily adapted for use in moving troops. Freight planes can similarly be adapted for the transport of military freight and supplies. There is no call for military control in the interests of such adaptation. Commercial planes will, in the nature of the case, be built for maximum efficiency at minimum cost, which will make them no less suitable from the military vantage point.

In general, I believe that while technological facilities for operations must be brought into line with military aviation, there need be no intrusion on the commercial and administrative side of civil aeronautics. Whatever the form of official supervision, co-ordination is inevitable in planning airplane types, personnel training, and ground arrangements with an eye to maximum value in military terms.

--------------------------------- 2 ---------------------------------

THE PROPOSED Bureau for Civil Air Defense would exercise functions not unlike those of the present Harbor and Rivers Control of the Army, although on a much more extended scale. Our national construction undertakings—housing, factories, bridges, tunnels—and our communications must hereafter be judged also in terms of resistance to aerial attack. This bureau would be called on to authorize and supervise all civilian building from this angle. It would also work out air-raid-precaution methods, organizing the entire country for maximum preparedness to meet attacks from overhead.

The air force proper would be commanded by a Chief Air Marshal, his rank and status being equivalent to those of the

Chief of the General Staff or the Chief of the Bureau of Operations. He would have his own Air Staff, headed by an Air Marshal. Additional air marshals would command various divisions of the air forces, such as a Striking Air Force, a Defense Air Force, Air Supplies and Ordnance, and other essential functions of the organization. The Chief Air Marshal and his marshals would constitute an Air Council. The titles are not important. I use them arbitrarily for the sake of convenience.

In order that air-force ranks may correspond more closely to the spirit and the tactical divisions of the aerial service, designations would necessarily differ from those of the Army or the Navy. Probably the present British system of ranking and titles could be adapted to suit American tastes: Marshal, Vice-Marshal, Air Commodore, Group Captain, Wing Commander, Squadron Leader, and so on. The arrangement could be modified in line with the experience of the RAF and the peculiarities of our own problems.

The Air Department would absorb the present Army Air Forces in their entirety. All shore establishments of the Navy —except those necessary for the maintenance and training of ship-borne naval aircraft—would also revert to the Air Department. The present Bureau of Aeronautics would remain a part of the Navy, its authority covering only the development, construction, and training of aircraft and personnel of the fleet air arm: ship-based and auxiliary planes. The rest would have to be transferred bodily, with all equipment and personnel, to the new department. It may be objected that long-range, shore-based patrol planes should remain with the Navy, since at this stage they seem to be a necessary naval adjunct. It must be borne in mind, however, that, like the extinct army observation planes, this long-range patrol aviation can operate because great expanses of ocean are still free of hostile aircraft. Once the air is infested with the enemy's fighting planes, observation will turn into aerial combat, which is the unequivocal function of air power.

Marine Corps Aviation might remain, as now, a part of the Navy, controlled by the Bureau of Aeronautics. But the Marines, too, will be equipped only with aircraft carried by ships. All Marine land-based stations, equipment, and personnel beyond the ship-borne adjuncts would be absorbed by the unified air forces. Coast Guard aviation, with all its equipment and personnel, would likewise be absorbed by the unified air force.

No modern air-power organization is worth its keep unless it provides the widest scope for research and experimentation, to the point of actual development and construction of experimental equipment, instruments, fuels, engines, airdromes, armament, building materials. The problem here is to organize the broadest facilities for governmental enterprise while encouraging private enterprise to the utmost. Neither political nor "ideological" barriers must be tolerated on the path to American aviation leadership. *Not for a moment must we forget that a great advance in the quality of equipment by any nation may alter the balance of forces in the air at a single blow, regardless of the numerical ratio.*

What if a new fuel, so light and compact that it solves the problem of range, were suddenly developed? What if stratosphere flying on the reactive-propulsion principle became a reality overnight? What if some new alloy, like beryllium or even lighter, were adapted for aviation use? What if the efficiency of engines were raised to cut down gas consumption to a fraction of the present consumption? It was not so long ago that I flew with engines consuming 0.7 pound of gasoline per hour per horsepower at cruising speeds. Recently, in long-range pursuit flights, my engine consumed only 0.35 pound—a decrease of 100 per cent—which means double the range, double the striking power, or a combination of both. Another such doubling of engine efficiency would, at one sweep, give the present Condor type of Nazi bomber, with a range of five to seven thousand miles, a range of ten to fourteen thousand miles—more than enough to lay the entire United States wide open to bombing, even with the existing Axis aviation equipment. The same kind of transformation would be achieved if the specific weight of fuels were cut in half.

Only recently, the world heard of Nazi bombers taking off by means of catapults on the rocket principle. The procedure should enable the planes to rise with enormous loads, implying greatly enlarged range, larger bomb loads, greater speed, or all these advantages. The rocket take-off should also enable heavy planes to operate from island outposts where big airfields are unavailable. Given the nature of the aerial weapon, progress may be expected to move not only by evolution from A to B, but by revolution from A to Z. Revolutionary changes in equipment can be made overnight—but the organization to exploit them requires time. In this respect, nations which have separate and autonomous air-power organization enjoy a terrific advantage over us. They are in a position to utilize instantaneously all new scientific possibilities.

It would probably be desirable to combine the National Advisory Committee on Aeronautics and its facilities with the Materiel Division at Wright Field into a single research and developmental section of the Air Department. This all-important effort should be headed by an aeronautical scientist of the highest type, a man of proved vision and creative ability in the domain of military aeronautics. He would of necessity become a member of the Air Staff, because equipment and strategy are indivisible. New types of planes or armament provide tactical possibilities, and new tactics call for revision of equipment. The work of the Air Staff and of the research organization must be closely integrated. Aeronautical-research facilities must be directly related to practical experimental planning. The compilation of purely theoretical data should be combined with the boldest kind of practical development.

Some aviation manufacturing companies already have experimental divisions segregated from their main production effort. The tendency merits public encouragement in the interests of national security. Each large company should have an experimental engineering division, if possible with its own plant and tools, where research is conducted not alone on new models but on new methods of production, new materials, new principles of flight. These semiautonomous developmental efforts would be in continuous touch with the research sector of the Air Department, for the purpose of maximum co-ordination and maximum official assistance.

The aviation industry has on many occasions been unjustly charged with making excessive profits by people who did not take into account the huge outlays in research and experiment that had to be absorbed. The separation of experimental units from the main production enterprise would make possible public subsidy without hampering the freedom of creative individual effort.

In addition to research undertakings by major companies, it may be found useful from time to time to finance independent experimental plants for designers or engineering units of proved ability. The products of such individual plants could then be made available for mass manufacture by the existing companies best fitted to undertake the particular jobs. Such experimental plants have brought immense aviation values to Germany. Both Heinkel and Messerschmitt made their most vital contributions through small companies engaged in developing and improving airplane types on the basis of small production orders, with large-scale manufacturing conducted by others.

At this stage in the history of air power, with all nations straining in the race for equipment for transoceanic, interhemispheral warfare, research and development are of the utmost importance. We must always maintain leadership in the efficiency of our weapons.

Scarcely one of the activities so sketchily indicated here is even thinkable until all military aviation is drawn together into a single agency, through an autonomous Air Department.

----------------------------- 3 -----------------------------

THE MECHANICS of the actual creation of the Air Department and its independent air force represent an operation of great magnitude. I have no wish to minimize it. At the same time there is no call for magnifying difficulties until they block our clear vision of what needs to be done and done quickly. Admittedly it would have been more reasonable and more comfortable to undertake the reorganization at an earlier stage, when our aviation was extremely limited and when no international emergency existed. The most propitious time was in the years when General Mitchell sacrificed his military career in his struggle for an independent air setup. But we must face conditions as they are, recognizing that further postponement will make the change more difficult, not less so.

As a practical means of minimizing confusion, waste motion, or costly errors, I recommend a scheme familiar to aeronautical manufacturers. Before actually building a new plane, we first construct what the industry knows as a "mock-up."

All the kinks and bugs are smoothed out in this elaborate "dummy" design before it is translated into reality. The idea can be adapted to the problem under discussion.

Specifically, the necessary legislation authorizing the formation of an independent Air Department would provide the requisite appropriation and authority for the immediate creation of a theoretical or organizational Air Department Council. It would be headed, logically, by the man selected as future Secretary of Aviation, who would surround himself with associates likely to assume portfolios as undersecretaries. The theoretical Chief Air Marshal and his staff would likewise be composed of the group told off for the real assignments.

The Council would proceed to work out in complete detail the entire organizational structure, with every man in place by actual name and actual rank; with every piece of equipment earmarked for its proper niche in the setup. We should thus have, in effect, a "dummy" Air Department which would begin to function in detail, to the extent of going through all the motions. Its Secretary would sit in with the President's Cabinet as an ex-officio member. The Air Marshal would be an ex-officio member of the Army-Navy Board. All the designated officials would take part in all meetings and activities pertaining to the war effort.

The "mock-up" Air Department would establish relations with the Army and Navy and make, in theory, all the necessary transfers of equipment and personnel and all the necessary adjustments of organization as defined by the action of Congress. Difficulties and contradictions would in that way be ironed out in all earnestness, but only on paper. Detailed decisions would be arrived at, but not put into operation until the whole plan, down to its last item, had been worked out and approved by the Commander in Chief.

There are those who fear that the creation of a new military department in the midst of a war may cause delays in the war effort. Their fears are unfounded. The new organization, being free from the routines, the tangle of red tape, and the strong inertias accumulated by the older departments in a century and a half of existence, will be modern, efficient, streamlined from the outset. Administered along lines of modern business practice, the new Air Department will be so much faster moving, so much more efficient, that it will quickly compensate for any minor delays or dislocations occasioned by the process of transferring and unifying our aviation.

Simultaneously with the development of a physical and personnel structure, the Air Department Council would set itself to plan a strategy of national defense with air power as the dominant element. Naturally, the aerial strategy proposed would be subject to consultation with the highest overall military authority, and co-ordinated with the general plans.

It is not within the province of this work to outline in detail any specific plan of war strategy. In time of war, indeed, that is outside the province of any published work. All that can or should be attempted is to indicate the general principles upon which, in the writer's view, a strategy for victory should be predicated. Those principles have already been emphasized in the preceding pages, but we may summarize in broad terms.

The strategy would arise from the fact that in terms of offensive initiative navies can no longer approach enemy shores, impose a blockade, or keep open their own lines of communication. Those functions must of necessity be guaranteed wholly or in the main by air power. For purposes of planning we must assume that the United States has been transformed into an island surrounded by a hostile world which, in turn, is ringed with strong air power. Under these circumstances our surface forces are immobilized and condemned to relative or total inaction until we can break through that ring by eliminating or at least neutralizing the enemy in the skies.

We must be fully prepared to defend ourselves against direct aerial attack on the nation as a totality from any or many directions. Physically and psychologically our air forces and our population alike must be attuned to resist attempts at destruction from the skies. And we must make ready for nothing less than all-out aerial war on the enemy directly from continental United States. Our attacking strategy should be devised to defeat and destroy all hostile air power, after which we can clamp a tridimensional blockade on the enemy —a blockade in which continuous blasting of his interior lines of communication and his economic mainstays is an integral part of the procedure.

Should occupation of the air-blockaded regions be considered desirable, air power must be amply equipped for the aerial transport of troops and materials and the maintenance of lines of supply and reinforcement. Mass invasion can follow by surface vessels, which could then move under the protection of our air mastery.

Even such a thumbnail sketch of a true air strategy makes it easier to visualize the organization and weapons that correspond with the new realities. The essence of the matter is preparedness to defend ourselves against assault from any direction of the compass—and likewise to strike in any direction at the heart of any adversary. With Japan across one ocean and Germany across the other, with our continent accessible to both enemies across the Arctic, the need for *circular* disposal of strength should be apparent. Our aerial preparations must be based on the concentric or peripheral principle. Every nation nowadays must regard itself, in relation to air power, as a fighter fully surrounded by enemies, ready to trade blows in any direction.

The traditional geographical patterns of military organization, fixed by the nature of surface combat, must be ruthlessly brushed aside in planning air-force organization. Since the entire nation becomes a single target, the old checkerboard types of regional-defense units familiar on the ground lose all meaning. Those in charge of our air defenses will have cut loose from older geographical concepts and will think, as already suggested, in latitude and longitude and altitudes, disregarding surface configurations down below. For the more complex space relations on the surface they will substitute the idea of the entire air space around the planet as a continuous ocean without real boundaries.

The concentric and radial organization best conforms to this idea. Air defense will be circular—and air offense will radiate in all directions. Naturally, we cannot avoid regional divisions for purely administrative purposes and for local operations. These we shall describe below, with special emphasis on the protection of specific strategic objectives. But tactically we must be geared for instant concentration of air power where it is most needed. An attacking force arriving from the east, having accomplished its mission, may then turn back and retrace its path; but it may also keep on going westward, or it may turn at right angles to retrieve safety across the Pole.

Our Air Command headquarters should therefore be located somewhere near the geographical center of the country, but naturally within the best possible area for effective communications. Wherever it is, this headquarters must be planned as an impregnable citadel—an underground world

where the mind and nerve centers of our aerial defenses will
be protected as they function along the lines so brilliantly
improvised in England. A bombproof sunken fortress, it will
be the skull enveloping the brain of air power. It will have
the plotting tables, signal services, information exchanges
that will provide the Air Command with an uninterrupted
and accurate picture of the entire air ocean.

The recent division of our Army Air Forces into four geographical segments, each having its own well-rounded complement of aircraft, was closer to modern realities than the
former haphazard regional divisions. Yet it no longer corresponded to pure aerial strategy. In a sense we were wrapping
our available air forces into four separate packages—like ice-
cream bricks containing an assortment of flavors. When the
call to combat comes, we shall not necessarily have to move
the entire assorted "brick," we may need only the chocolate
or vanilla ingredients. It will be impossible to extricate them
for use if they are permanently packaged with the other
flavors. It should be possible to throw the full weight of all
of any type of force in any direction that tactical problems
require.

---------------------------------- 4 ----------------------------------

Assuming an organizational framework corresponding to the
character of aerial warfare, we must now consider the actual
types of equipment needed for successful prosecution of the
war.

The chief value of unchained air power is that it will at
last permit the elaboration of an air strategy, over and above
the employment of aviation in joint tactical undertakings
with the surface services. It will be a strategy, as I have
indicated, of disarming the enemy from the air. Having

knocked the weapons out of his hands and reduced the enemy to impotence, we can starve and beat him into submission by air power or turn him over to navies and armies for handcuffing.

The detailed performance, characteristics, and designs of every type of aircraft are conditioned by the over-all strategy or by the specific campaign for which we arm ourselves. One of the lessons taught by the war, as we have seen, is that aircraft types must be specialized not alone for the general strategy but for the specific task in view. Today, because the whole world is at war and our aerial objective must therefore be dominance of that world, it is possible to outline specifications for equipment essential to compass this broadest purpose.

I do not propose to be too specific, however. We are at war, and no information beyond what is generally known in the aviation world should be made public. Where my proposed equipment and aeronautical innovations go beyond the present aeronautical scope, the reader will understand, I trust, that I am not indulging in dilettante flights of fancy. My every proposal is wholly practicable *now*. As I remarked in another connection, things that seem "fantastic" to the uninitiated are frequently quite normal and even commonplace to the specialist. Wherever, in what follows, I assume the solution of some aeronautical or armament problem it is because I have actually solved it through years of study and stand prepared to translate it into equipment. Although several of my suggestions are likely to be attacked as "visionary," they are in every case realities which I have worked out fully for practical application.

Theoretically, adequate air power must have a striking offensive reach clear around the world; and ultimately, without doubt, aviation will attain that circumglobular range.

For practical immediate purposes, a range of 15,000 miles should suffice. Forty per cent of the maximum range, or 6000 miles, would then be effective striking radius. Operating from the periphery of our country, that striking radius would include the vital centers of all major nations, giving us—in conformity with the axiom of effective air power—a striking range equal to the maximum dimensions of the theater of war.

What should be the range of defensive aviation? How far from our primary bases should defense aviation reach out to meet the foe? At the present stage of aeronautical science, a more or less definite answer can be worked out. Since aircraft is a compromise among such factors as speed, range, and military load, the striking power is of necessity in inverse proportion to the distance. Hence the logical limit of the striking radius for defensive aviation is half the distance to the enemy bases. From this halfway line inward the defensive strength of our aviation becomes more effective because of the contracted distance. The range of defensive aircraft, in other words, should be theoretically half of the offensive range.

It must be remembered, however, that such defensive advantage will gradually diminish as fuels become lighter or their use more economical, so that the fuel load shrinks in ratio to the total load. Assume, for example, that planes could fly without fuel: then there would be no difference between defensive and offensive aviation, and their relative strengths would depend exclusively on quality and quantity elements.

At this point it may be appropriate to comment on those who throw up the sponge, having understood that aviation over short distances is more effective than over long distances and noted that long ranges are necessary for American air power. They are as illogical as if, in the sea-power era, they had stopped naval building because the navies of potential

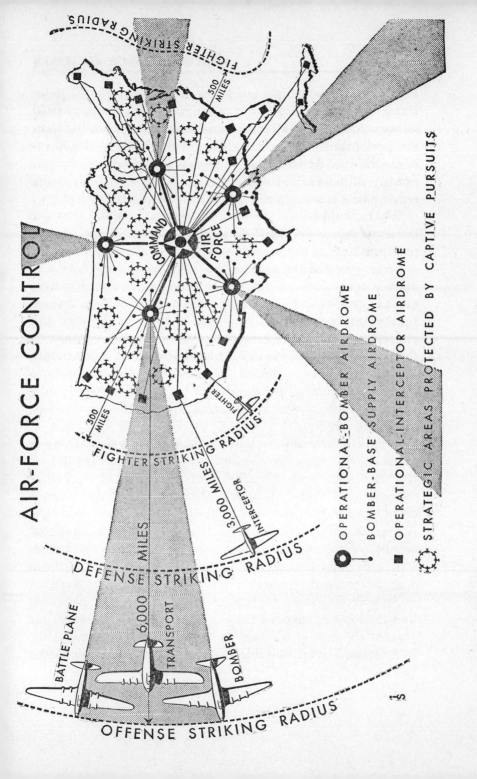

# AIR-FORCE CONTROL

FIGHTER STRIKING RADIUS

FIGHTER STRIKING RADIUS

500 MILES

COMMAND

AIR FORCE

300 MILES

FIGHTER

FIGHTER STRIKING RADIUS

3,000 MILES

INTERCEPTOR

DEFENSE STRIKING RADIUS

6,000 MILES

BATTLE PLANE

TRANSPORT

BOMBER

OFFENSE STRIKING RADIUS

- OPERATIONAL-BOMBER AIRDROME
- BOMBER-BASE SUPPLY AIRDROME
- OPERATIONAL-INTERCEPTOR AIRDROME
- STRATEGIC AREAS PROTECTED BY CAPTIVE PURSUITS

enemies were just as big and just as strong. For any weapon, it is a question of building more and better and faster than your enemy, thus making up for physical limitations by more audacious thinking, greater strategic ingenuity, and greater economic wealth. If the technological and intellectual components of two nations are identical, then the last resource is economic: sheer quantity. In our own case, our duty is to utilize fully all these elements to achieve unquestioned superiority. Air power, like older weapons, has to maintain its lead in the race for supremacy.

In analyzing equipment we must take for granted: (1) that our air power is geared for world operations and therefore must have a striking reach of at least 6000 miles, reckoning from the frontiers of continental United States; and (2) that we may expect attack from the enemy's primary bases as much as 6000 miles away. Under these conditions the air force proper will be divided into a *Striking Air Force* and a *Defense Air Force*. The Striking Air Force will be subdivided into a *Battle Force, Bombardment Aviation,* and *Transport Force*. The Defense Air Force will be subdivided into an *Interceptor Combat Command,* a *Fighter Command,* a *Captive Pursuit Command, Reconnaissance, Interior Transport,* and *Ground Defense*. In addition there will be the vital Co-operation Air Forces, to serve as an element in ground or naval task groupings.

Naturally, I do not insist on these particular subdivisions or labels. The Ground Defense probably could be combined with the Captive Pursuit Command into an Air-Raid Defense. There is no reason why the exterior and internal transport services should not be united. There are a good many other possible variants. I have set up the plan merely as a convenient device for indicating, in general terms, the military characteristics desirable in each category of equipment.

While planes must be planned for special purposes, it is also important to hold down the number of types of craft to a minimum. The actual diversity of models will represent a compromise between the two extremes of specialization and standardization. In what follows I must, of course, limit myself to basic types.

Cutting across the categories as listed above, there will also be a division in respect to altitude. The best mechanical performance can be extracted from a plane if it is designed for the air stratum in which it is expected to operate. Most equipment will consequently have to be divided into a *sea-level* force operating from the surface to an altitude of about 30,000 feet, and a *strato force* having its maximum performance potential from 20,000 feet upward into the stratosphere.

### Striking Air Force

This force will consist chiefly of two types: battleplanes and combat bombers. Together they will provide long-range bombardment aviation accompanied by suitable pursuit and convoy fighter craft. Its task in the first stage will be to destroy the opposing air force, both in the air and on the ground—that is to say, its facilities and sources of potential replacement.

An invading aerial battle force possessing only combat power, however great, can be ignored by the defenders, who may simply refuse to rise for the duel. Therefore the attacking armada must also possess bombing force, carrying the threat of serious damage to the enemy aviation's ground components. The opposing force will thereupon be obliged to rise and accept the challenge or be demolished. Contrary to the popular idea, the initial bombardment is not entirely or even primarily an end in itself but a device for coaxing enemy air power into action.

At this point I must take exception to the theory propounded years ago by the great Italian aerial strategist, General Douhet, which has been followed blindly by some American writers on the subject. Douhet's view has been summarized thus:

"While such a force can be composed of bombing planes and combat planes, both bombing and combat power can be integrated in one plane: the battleplane. This type is not a combat plane to which bombing power is added, but a bombing plane to which combat power is given. It offers the military and psychological advantage of functioning as an integrated unit capable of both bombing and combat, in place of a team unit composed of two types which may easily become separated and one of which can only combat while the other can only bomb."

If Douhet were alive today it is likely he would concede that the current war has disproved his concept. In theory it would be an ideal condition if the same plane could incorporate maximum bombing and combat qualities. In practice this cannot be achieved. Unless aeronautical science removes present engineering and aerodynamical limitations on aircraft, bombing capacity must be sacrificed for combat power or vice versa. Moreover, the present-day airplane because of its wings, control services, etc., cannot be designed to provide maximum fire power in every direction; underprotected "blind spots" will remain and will unavoidably be exploited by the enemy. In addition, the task of bombardment dictates a course of flight, maneuvers, and formations which may be quite unfavorable from the combat angle.

There is no real alternative today to separation of the bombing and combat functions, although this does not imply that the bomber must have no combat ability or the fighter no bombing equipment. The initial attack on an enemy nation must take the form of a combat action by a force possessing provocative bombing power. I submit therefore that the backbone of the air force, in direct contradiction to Douhet, should be *a combat plane to which bombing power is added*. This combat bomber should, besides, be fully protected by pure combat planes, so that it can proceed to its bombing targets unmolested.

The defensive job, being embodied in a separate unit, would shield the bombing force from any direction in accordance with the tactical needs, just as destroyers shield a battleship against torpedo attacks. The convoy fighter may be viewed as a "detached turret," hence capable not only of rotating in any direction but of being moved around the bomber in any position.

The combat bomber and its accompanying battleplanes are similar types of craft, the principal difference being that the battleplane, since it does not carry explosives, can carry maximum fire power. The bomber, on the other hand, sacrifices fire power to make room for bombs sufficient to warrant defensive action by the enemy. The fire power in these planes should be capable of maximum concentration in any given direction.

Once the opposing air force has been defeated or neutralized, heavy bombers can be brought into play. These should be designed for the greatest bomb loads, the combat task being entrusted to convoy battleplanes. The bomber, having carried the precious cargo of explosives across thousands of miles, must not be diverted from its mission. It must be thoroughly shielded while it goes about its main business, without wasting fuel or time in fighting off combat craft.

The combination of heavy bombers and battleplanes can

justly be described as *a blockade force,* because their job
amounts to systematic destruction of exterior and internal
lines of communication, annihilation of aviation and other
military industries, and crippling of facilities essential to the
existence of the enemy nation. As the aerial strength of the
adversary wanes, the intermediate bases which until then had
been untenable could be utilized as operational airdromes
for the shorter-range bombardment forces. That would make
it possible to bring to bear upon the enemy the maximum of
destruction in the minimum time with the necessary continuity of action.

No provision has been made in this outline for a strategic
reconnaissance force. As long as the hostile air power is in
existence, unmolested observation is out of the question. The
curious assumption that planes can still hover over hostile
territory is a hang-over from primitive aeronautical days. At
present observations can be made only by the speediest and
most powerful units, which must fight for the needed information. Hence battleplanes will also provide the equipment
for strategic reconnaissance.

These combat planes are as yet in the early stage of development. As a matter of fact, only one attempt has been
made thus far, in the form of the Bell YFM-1A or "Airacuda."
It can well serve as an example of American creative genius
at the industrial end—hampered and perplexed by confused
tactical thinking at the military end. The Airacuda has been
redesigned repeatedly and still has not assumed definitive
form. It is always referred to by officials as a long-range pursuit *or* escort or convoy fighter—although the military character of these categories is as different as day from night.
Since the fire power of the Airacuda is directed mainly forward, it can never be an efficient convoy fighter.

Combat planes can and should be designed for exceptional air-borne vitality, so that the destruction of portions of the wings or the control surfaces will not necessarily wipe out the buoyancy or stability of the craft. This can readily be accomplished, although little if any thought has as yet been given to the problem.

Conceivably, the present control of equilibrium through movable plane surfaces will be supplanted by dynamic controls enabling artificial redistribution and control of pressure as the balance is upset by damage to any portion of the plane.

Safety fuels will be developed to resist incendiary shells. Quite possibly engines of the fuel-injection type will be evolved, to operate both on high-octane fuels and crude oil. This will enable us to store high octane in armored parts of the plane for take-off and combat purposes while noninflammable heavy oils are used for approach and return.

Turrets housing the guns need not necessarily house the gunners. Firing can be remotely controlled, synchronized, and operated from a number of battle posts located for the best possible visibility. Thereby the deployment of armament can be made most advantageously, limiting the number of "blind spots," though the armament of course would still be accessible for servicing and repair in action.

The battleplane, requiring no space for bombs, may ultimately carry all its engines, as well as the crew, explosives, and high-octane fuels, in the fuselage—all enclosed in an armored nacelle.

Propellers may be driven by shafts or remotely controlled hydraulic transmissions. "Spare" propellers could be made available for clutching into operation should any of the active ones be destroyed. As a matter of fact, the propeller may be dispensed with altogether, as promising recent experiments suggest.

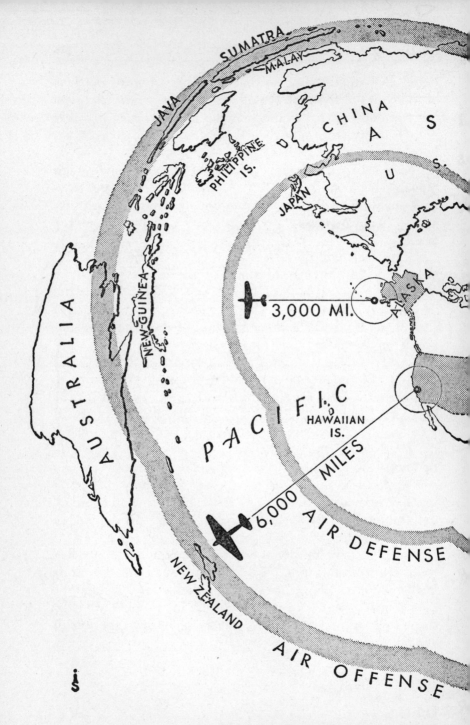

AIR CONTROL OF THE WORLD

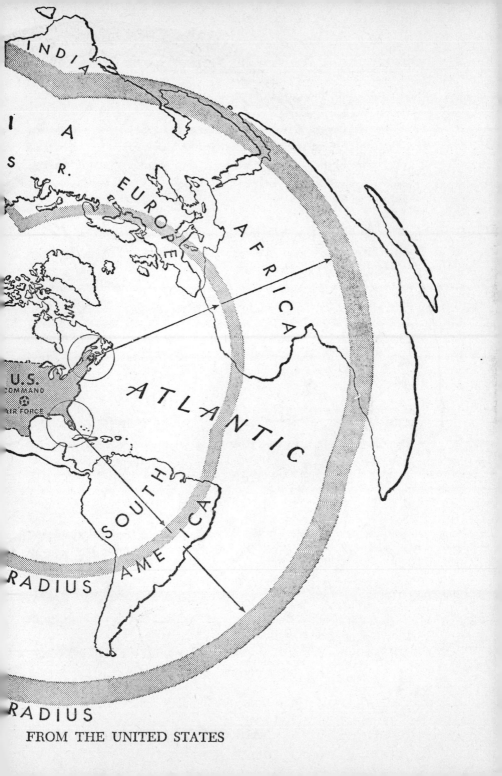

Strato-planes would of course have armored nacelles that are supercharged.

Future planes, I believe, will not have armor put on as an afterthought, as it were. The armor will constitute a structural part of the aircraft: it will not be an overcoat on the body of the plane, but the body itself, thus saving great weight.

Misgivings have been expressed about the ability of huge planes to survive against short-range defensive aviation. They are unjustified. In general, the bigger the plane, the thicker its armor, the greater the number and the larger the caliber of its guns; larger caliber, in turn, means longer range of effective fire. A large plane represents a more stable and more comfortable gun emplacement, as well as a platform for more elaborate and hence more accurate fire control as compared with the relatively ineffective sighting of the present pursuit. Usually, indeed, the pursuit will find it difficult to penetrate the long-range fire of the superplane close enough to use its own guns. After all, once aircraft are locked in combat, in an artillery duel, superior fire power decides the outcome. Thus one large plane, if properly designed and given suitable military characteristics, can account for a greater part of the opposing air power than several small planes.

This, of course, will lead inevitably to enlargement of defending aircraft commensurate with the growing size of the attacking aircraft. And there we have the elements of an arms race in the air like the one which the world saw in connection with sea power in the preceding military epoch. The nation with the greatest economic strength, industrial capacity, and engineering ingenuity will have the advantage in the race, as always through history.

Since the initiative of operation lies with the striking force, the bases where they are stored and maintained need not be operational bases. The force can always be transferred to operational bases for take-off on attack missions. Its actual location between missions would be governed by considerations of safety: facilities for camouflage, inaccessibility to enemy planes, superior administrative facilities, and so on.

Operational airdromes for the striking force will need no facilities except runways and fuel pipelines running to remote reservoirs. For all types of aviation, indeed, pipelines must be developed in order to minimize hazards of overhead attack. The attack forces, in particular, will require this sort of servicing because of the tremendous gasoline loads they must take on board for transoceanic assignments. When we visualize continuous long-range aerial operations involving the use of millions of gallons a day, it becomes obvious that direct and continuous flow of gasoline to airfields is necessary. Overland transportation and service would be utterly inadequate for the magnitude of the needs.

The Striking Force must be completely self-contained in the matter of transport of supplies and personnel. The air force also will provide transport for air-borne troops, equipment, and supplies.

### Defense Air Force

Our defensive organization, as already indicated, should be concentric in concept. The commander of each type of defensive force would therefore control a circle or ring, with subcommanders in charge of sectors of this ring.

The outermost ring would be the special responsibility of the Interceptor Combat Command. As its name implies, it will possess the necessary equipment for seeking out and vanquishing enemy aviation at a distance from our own territory. Since hostile aviation will attempt to reach us from varying altitudes, this force, like the striking aviation, must contain both sea-level and strato-planes. Obviously this force must consist almost entirely of combat types of aircraft, which should have a range of 7500 miles and a striking radius of 3000 miles.

The basic plane in this force will approximate the battle-plane, but it will be somewhat smaller and will have a different disposition of armament. Where the battleplane requires an even distribution of fire power, the interceptor has to concentrate its fire primarily on forward shooting, at some cost in rear fire power if necessary. It will be a fast and highly maneuverable craft that can take full advantage of the elements of surprise, initiative of attack, and selection of favorable distances and positions. It should be noted that, paradoxically, offensive aviation must have maximum defensive fire power, whereas defensive aviation must have maximum offensive fire power.

As an outer circle of defense, charged with continuous vigilance and distant interception, this Command will always have to be in "patrol" readiness. When the enemy's presence is discovered, attack must follow immediately to ascertain the strength and dispositions of the approaching air force. The combat readiness must be maintained, moreover, in the entire ring, because even if attack is expected only from one direction, the enemy's retreat may follow a totally different direction. A vigilant "alert" should be maintained around the entire country, not only in the segment supposedly under threat. The whole Interceptor Command must be flexible and under unbroken control from Air Headquarters. It should be pliably organized to permit concentration on one sector or many, as dictated by tactical exigencies.

Should enemy aviation penetrate within some 500 miles

from American frontiers, it will be met by the Fighter Command, comprising airplanes very much like our present pursuits. Whether single-seaters or two-seaters, single- or twin-engined, they must have consistently high performance. This second concentric ring—counting from outside inward—would comprise the area from our frontiers to about 500 miles out to sea. Its airdromes should be close to the shore lines, and control of this ring of air power, too, must be centered at Air Headquarters. Though the striking-combat radius is only 500 miles, an emergency range of 3000 miles is essential. This range would enable the fighters to reach any point in the United States without refueling, thus utilizing fully the advantage of interior lines for quick concentration of available Fighter Command strength where it is most needed almost instantaneously.

Finally we come to protector or home-defense aviation, which I have called the Captive Pursuit Command. The name derives from the fact that the planes will be of short range and permanently attached to specific localities or targets. As the enemy striking forces proceed over our soil to their objectives, the Captive Pursuit Command rises to attack the invaders as they pass overhead. Here necessarily the concentric principle can be disregarded. The force assigned to any point will be commensurate with the importance, size, and vulnerability of the target involved. In effect we shall have a series of strong antiair-raid squadrons, attached to particular industrial aggregates, power sources, government or military centers, urban population centers, and so on.

The fighters for home protection must possess extremely high rates of climb, great speed, exceptional maneuverability. They must be able to fire large-caliber missiles—or discharge the kind of "rocket torpedoes" which I shall describe below. Their effectiveness, in other words, must reside in an ability to move swiftly for the delivery of one or a few knockout blows, rather than in sustained combat. Combat planes, facing long air duels far from their home bases, need a variety of calibers of guns, large loads of ammunition, big fuel supplies—all of which calls for substantial size. But the "captive" pursuit, being right over its base, able to alight for refueling and renewed ammunition stores, can be fairly small. It may be compared to the unit in a mosquito fleet in home waters.

It may really be considered as a species of antiaircraft fire, except that the projectile has wings and the intelligence of a man to direct the trajectory. This is the force, logically, with which antiaircraft artillery, balloon barrages, and other passive defense appliances would be integrated. A single commander in any locality would in that way have full charge of all the defenses against aerial threats. Naturally he would be kept apprised of approaching friendly and hostile forces and the operations in which they are engaged.

For administrative purposes the local-defense forces should be divided into zones, each possessing adequate repair and supply bases for maintenance of equipment. The range of the captive aircraft need not exceed 500 miles; a 200-mile combat radius will give the airplanes sufficient duration for climb, attack, and return.

As we have already explained, strategic reconnaissance over enemy territory must be made by battleplanes, since reconnaissance means combat. But defensive reconnaissance will be made by planes especially designed for the purpose. Nearly everything else must be sacrificed for speed. Once these planes contact the enemy they should be able to maintain vigilance over the intruder while remaining outside the range of his fire. This can be accomplished because the reconnaissance plane, being practically stripped of combat and bombing power, can convert these savings into superior speed.

The Interior Transport Force will compass aerial equipment for moving supplies, troops, and service personnel along interior lines, making scheduled as well as special emergency runs. Reconnaissance will be intimately related to the interceptor activities.

## Co-operation Force

There is less need for detailed description of the Co-operation Force for task assignments with the Army and the Navy, since this is the aspect of aerial warfare in the present conflict best apprehended by American observers. Some of them have been impressed with this phase to the point of allowing a secondary aviation function to obscure their understanding of the primary function of air power.

All aircraft and personnel of this command must be available for instantaneous use with any army corps or naval force in any theater of war. That will provide maximum resiliency and unlimited use of the total striking power where and when needed. Permanent and integrated attachment to a particular segment of the Army or the Navy, to a specific locality, or to a given set of surface commanders, would obviously tend to immobilize large portions of this force. Hence it is ruled out.

In my view the co-ordinated aviation should be trained, organized, and deployed to permit assignment at a moment's notice to *any* army or fleet. To tie them into special surface units as members of a permanent combine would be as wasteful and inept as attaching specific cruisers or destroyers permanently to one battleship, or tying up specific units of the

Navy exclusively with specific Army divisions or coastal-artillery posts. In short, the surface Co-operation Force must be a single and separate aerial unit under the main air force, equipped and ready for service with land or sea forces anywhere in the world. It would be a reservoir from which the High Command can draw air power of the requisite strength and military character to help solve particular tactical problems faced by a composite task force. Naturally, once assigned to any task force such aviation would come completely under command of the chief of such combined force.

Aviation support of naval operations, beyond that available through the fleet and Marine Corps air arms, would be provided from the central pool of the Co-operation Command. Units assigned to such co-operative tasks would hold about the same position in relation to the Navy that the Marines now hold in relation to the Army when called on to co-operate in some joint tactical enterprise. The same will hold true in respect to aviation support for Army action. Indeed, the Co-operation Command would be the link which ties the air force (operating in a different element) to the surface forces, very much as the Marine Corps of the Navy serves as a link between the Navy (operating in its own medium) with shore forces and shore tasks.

This command would comprise both short- and long-range aircraft, especially designed and trained for supporting actions with ground forces. Their military characteristics would be approximately the same as in existing planes, but with great enhancement of fire power, bomb load, and radius of operation. For the sake of emphasis, we should recall in this context the penalties which all the belligerents paid for failure to make their co-ordinated aviation equal in range to the whole theater of any campaign. The constant struggle for intermediate bases (in an arena like Libya, for instance) has

INTERNATIONAL NEWS PHOTO

LONG-RANGE INTERCEPTOR FIGHTER. This Bell Airacuda represents a great engineering achievement. But its designation as "convoy fighter" is erroneous, since that requires different disposition of armament. With its maximum fire power directed forward, it really offers a preview of an effective long-range interceptor fighter.

LONG-RANGE INTERCEPTOR FIGHTER OF THE IMMEDIATE FUTURE. The author's concept of the lines of development in long-range interceptors. Engines, pilots, and gunners are all located inside the fuselage in an armored nacelle. There are retractable gun turrets in the tail, above and below. Comprehensive array of artillery firing forward is set into the wings. Large-caliber guns or "rocket torpedoes" can be fired through the propeller hubs and the nose of the fuselage. The propellers are driven by remote transmission.

RECENT VERSION OF THE FLYING FORTRESS B–17E. War has proved the contention that fire power, not speed, is the true defense of a bomber. Note the turrets above, below, and in the tail, indicating improved fire power as compared with earlier models.

IN THE BRITISH AIR COMMAND NERVE CENTER. Far underground, safe from air bombers, senior RAF officers watch the movements of their own and enemy aircraft as plotted on a map by girl operators constantly receiving information from all sources. This is only one tiny corner in the complex nerve center of British air power. The unified American air forces, likewise, must have a citadel serving as headquarters of operations for mastery of the "air ocean."

hampered war effort in all parts of the world. All nations have erred in this respect. The one possible exception is Japan, which seems to have made some progress. In any event, the Japanese fighters and torpedo planes showed sufficient range to provide support to bombers and invading forces across the full width of the South China Sea—roughly 700 miles. This would indicate a sustained range of some 1800 miles for those types of planes.

Location of the Co-operation Force units would correspond, as far as possible, to the disposition of Army and Navy establishments. In the training period, joint exercises and maneuvers would thereby be facilitated.

Dive-bombers, an important element in this force, would be armed with machine guns, cannon, naval torpedoes, "rocket torpedoes," as well as bombs, and able to tackle a variety of targets, including tanks, fortifications, battleships.

The aircraft geared and trained for joint tasks with our naval forces would, of course, include long-range torpedo planes to bring support to surface vessels far out at sea. It is not generally realized, even by experts, that planes can release far larger and more deadly torpedoes than would be practical from surface vessels, since planes merely *drop* their missiles, whereas ships have to *fire* them. For that reason land-based torpedo planes represent potentially a more formidable defense against naval threats than torpedoes fired by destroyers or ship-borne planes. It has been established that the torpedo planes which attacked the *Repulse* and the *Prince of Wales* were based on land—which may explain the devastating effect of the torpedoes.

The Coastal Command fits naturally into the Co-operation Force. Indeed, the planes for co-operation with fleets would in effect constitute a coastal-defense force.

Liaison officers from the surface services would, it goes

without saying, be permanent members of the Air Staff, and air officers would be on the Army and Navy staffs.

This summary of our air forces under an autonomous Air Department served by autonomous Air Ordnance and Supply is offered without any pretense of completeness or finality. My purpose is merely to give the reader the sense and "feel" of true air power expressed through appropriate equipment

--------------------------------- 5 ---------------------------------

THROUGHOUT THE history of war, there has been a race between offensive and defensive weapons. Every major advance in offensive power has stimulated defensive thinking, and the other way around, so that the pendulum has swung from one extreme to the other. No sooner did a nation consider itself immune by reason of its defenses, than weapons and techniques for cutting through those defenses emerged.

The career of air power has been no exception. At the end of World War I the fighter plane, essentially defensive, seemed master of the skies. But soon the improvement of armor and armament on bombers left the pursuit plane in the lurch. It was this that led General Douhet and others to pin their strategic hopes on a self-sufficient bomber. In the years immediately preceding World War II, however, the pendulum began to swing in the other direction as combat planes were improved. This race between offense and defense is now in full swing.

The armament factor, in both types of aviation, lags far behind the aerodynamic factors. Bombers, being larger, offer greater possibilities for installation of bigger and more powerful cannon. To contend with this, the pursuit plane must em-

ploy weapons other than cannon to preserve its present compactness and agility. As far as machine guns and cannon are
concerned, the modern fighter has practically reached its
point of saturation; witness the tiny Spitfire carrying twelve
machine guns on its wings. Furthermore, because of the high
relative speeds, the moments for firing are few and fleeting.
Weapons are called for to enable the attacking plane to discharge maximum destructive force in minimum time. Pursuits
should therefore be equipped with some type of large projectiles released at point-blank, in the way that a destroyer
attacks a battleship with a torpedo.

As far back as March, 1934, writing in *U. S. Air Services,* I pointed out that "attack by pursuit planes of bombardment aviation must be entirely changed. That means
that entirely different armament should be used." Specifically, I recommended aerial torpedoes. The reference was
not to the naval torpedoes of the type now launched by airplanes skimming the surface of water against surface targets,
but to torpedoes launched *in the air against air targets.* To
avoid confusion I have designated these as "rocket torpedoes."

At the same time the article recommended development of
nonrecoil large-caliber guns of 75 and 120 mm. I actually constructed and fired 82-mm. guns years ago. Armed with such
guns, with rocket torpedoes or both, combat planes will become real "destroyers of the air," prepared to "sink" bomber
"battleships" many times their own size, once they succeed
in penetrating the defensive fire. They would, in fact, apply
against big approaching battleplanes the same principle a destroyer or submarine employs against a battleship. Rather
than engage in an artillery duel, in which the bomber has the
advantage, the fighter will aim to utilize its speed and maneuverability to approach the enemy at close range, discharge
its rocket torpedo or other missiles in bulk, and get away.

There are indications, at this writing, that the Russians have already developed and used rocket-propelled torpedoes against tanks. The technique will unquestionably be extended against flying targets at any and all altitudes. Battleplanes will be torpedoed in the air just as ships are torpedoed in the sea. Conservatism and congenital shortsightedness stymied such developments by American aviation as long as its ordnance depended on ground services. The emancipation of air ordnance from Army and Navy and its unification under independent leadership will speed up the emergence of new weapons for fighter planes.

The same holds true for other vital creative effort, some of which has been hinted at in this chapter. Unhampered *thinking* along air-power lines will finally become possible, and the mechanism for implementing such thought in terms of swift action will at last be available.

Every intelligent observer of the course of the present war is aware that real aerial protection is not merely a question of planes and guns. It affects practically every area of a nation's life: the distribution of its industries, the availability of air-raid shelters, the vulnerability of its architecture. There is an "aviation angle" to every mine and factory, railroad and canal, bridge and tunnel. The air-attack potential enters into the construction of schools, theaters, fuel and ammunition dumps, and every other type of building. The Bureau for Civil Air Defense will unavoidably concern itself with this phase of our physical existence.

The hazards of the present excessively centralized industrial and power resources are obvious. Consider such extreme cases as those provided by the American manufacture of bomb sights and other precision instruments for aviation, or of airplane engine production, at the outbreak of the war. A few tons of explosives well placed on a relatively few plants might have paralyzed all our airplane output! Despite the sacrifice in economy, decentralization of American industry in general, and war industries in particular, cannot be avoided. The values of dispersion and of both natural and artificial camouflage must hereafter be considered in planning factory construction.

Certainly military and defense enterprises must not be left dependent on large-scale power resources which, by reason of their size, can be crippled by one blow. Every such industry should be broken down into relatively small units scattered through the nation, each absolutely self-contained, fed by its own power plant constructed far underground, beyond the reach of enemy bombs. Each of them should be provided with multiple railroad sidings and with bombproof warehouses holding large reserves of material against the day when communications might be interrupted. Aerial transport, if only as an emergency auxiliary service, is a minimum requirement.

Civilian architecture will inevitably be affected by the air age. Materials for roofing and other purposes will be increasingly selected with reference to resistance against explosive and incendiary bombs. The location of rooms will be conditioned, more and more, by the bombing potentials. I venture to guess, for instance, that gathering places which do not require daylight—such as motion-picture theaters, ballrooms, and banquet halls used largely at night, certain restaurants and meeting halls—will be built underground as natural air-raid retreats. That tendency, together with advances in air conditioning and ventilation may invert all our architectural concepts; "skyscrapers" may be built downwards instead of only upwards.

Merely to cite at random a few of the elements that enter into preparedness for air war today is to show that it is all-important for the Air Department to take a hand in such matters. Only for the aviation-minded will solutions to such problems seem natural and unforced; only they can provide complete answers to air-defense questions. The Department's consent would be necessary for all housing structures. Regulations must be particularly firm with regard to public utilities, water reservoirs, highways of all sorts.

The Air Department would, in addition, have to assume responsibility for the vital job of educating the American public on the problems of air power and the civilian role in countering attack. This job of making every American aviation-minded should have been undertaken in time of peace. There is no reason why it should be postponed any longer. The eagerness of certain military leaders to prevent establishment of autonomous air power has unfortunately led them to "play down" aviation and engender public complacency. While the OCD, for instance, was pleading for anti-air-raid measures and volunteers, Army and Navy spokesmen ridiculed the idea of air raids on the U.S.A. Aviational education, now and in the future, must begin in the schools and must permeate every home. Just as hygiene is now regarded as a public function, extending into every nook and cranny of the individual American's life, so aerial defense—the larger hygiene of national security—must be integrated with the everyday life of our population.

As I have tried to emphasize throughout this volume, we must reorient public opinion as well as install certain technical and organizational changes. For generations Navy and Army prestige has been paramount. A feeling of dependence on the Navy, especially, has been inculcated in every American almost from the cradle. Those emotions corresponded to the military realities of the epoch. But a new epoch is upon us. Popular psychology must be revised to throw an effulgence of glory around our air power. This is necessary not for any childish reasons of honor, but because the public's attitude toward a given weapon has a direct effect upon the development of that weapon. The Air Service must fire the imagination of our young men, must channel creative and inventive talent into the aeronautical domain, must draw the best personnel into its manifold divisions, from research to administration, from construction to combat.

The Roman Empire at the apex of its glory flourished in the era of land power. Every Roman was a soldier. The British Empire flourished in the age of sea power and every true Briton, though he might never go to sea, was a sailor in his emotions and loyalties. Even thus our own United States, in the new epoch of air power, will flourish only on the basis of matchless air power. Even thus every American—man, woman, and child—must be an airman in his heart.

# CHAPTER XII

# VICTORY THROUGH AIR POWER!

## 1

THE WAR in the Pacific—the war America can and will win —has begun most inauspiciously. Pearl Harbor, Manila, Hong Kong, Singapore, and Java are milestones of disillusion. The underestimate of Japan's strength and ingenuity was the least of the illusions. The greatest was the overestimate of the role of sea power. Within a few weeks after the attack on Hawaii, the Pacific floor was littered with Allied and Japanese warships—all but a few of them killed off by airplanes. The $400,000,000 naval bastion at Singapore turned into another Maginot Line. Neither sea forces nor ground forces could turn off invasions launched under the shield of superior aviation. The desperate cries for help from every front called neither for ships nor troops nor tanks, but only for planes— more planes and better planes.

But illusions die hard. Probably more hammer blows of disaster will be needed to end the paralyzing illusion that this is, despite everything, a naval war; that old-line fortifications can protect outposts of empire; that routine strategists of World War I vintage can handle a modern total conflict. The terrible losses of these cruel months will not have been in vain if they help to clear the mind of America of the debris of such bankrupt military concepts.

How soon and how decisively we win the war will depend on how soon and how completely we face the fact that today air power must be the backbone of any successful strategy.

330

This revolution in national thinking is essential before we can proceed to mobilize the men, the ideas, and the weapons for victory.

In the Justice Roberts report on Pearl Harbor the most ominous passages were not those pointing to negligence and lack of co-ordination. These are human failings which can be quickly remedied. The really sinister passages were those indicating quite clearly that the responsible officers did not take the threat of air assaults seriously. There was even evidence that the commanding personnel regarded the presence of a strong fleet in Pearl Harbor as a safeguard against air raids!

Those men were ignorant of what every airman and most laymen knew by that time; namely, that only air power can fight air power. They did not realize that the presence of battleships was an invitation to aerial attack. In the preceding years of war, they had failed to detect the clear pattern of a race between sea power and air power in which aviation relentlessly pursued naval forces all over the globe—and consistently won when it caught up with its quarry.

If this represented merely the state of mind of a few officers stationed in Hawaii it would be too trivial to bother with. We could treat the whole matter as an unfortunate accident. But those men were typical of the pervasive mentality in the older services generally. The same discount of air power, the same inability to understand the aerial lessons of the war, have been evident in the words and acts of the whole American military hierarchy.

A month after Pearl Harbor we had new proof that the lesson had not penetrated the orthodox military mind. In asking Congress for additional tens of billions of dollars, a ranking naval officer declared that, among other things, the investment would help America "gain command of the sea by

destruction of the enemy's seagoing forces." The assertion
amounted to a public confession of arrested strategic thinking. Yet it was accepted without protest by our legislators,
press, and public opinion.

To get some inkling of the emptiness of that threadbare
naval promise, we need only assume that we actually succeed
in annihilating "the enemy's seagoing forces." Then let us
inquire whether that miracle would, in fact, give us "command of the sea."

Would it enable our battle fleets to steam boldly into
Japanese waters and bombard the Mikado's harbors, submarine bases, and coastal fortifications? Certainly not. As
long as Japan has reasonably effective air power, such intrusion within the radius of its shore-based aviation would be
suicidal.

With the Japanese fleet counted out, would we proceed to
cut Nipponese communications with the Asiatic mainland, as
we could have done in an earlier military epoch? Would our
triumphant battleships venture into the Japan Sea, the narrow waters off Formosa, and the stretches of sea off Japanese-
held coastal points in China? Not if a few bright Boy Scouts
were around to tip off our admirals that they were inviting
destruction by enemy land-based aviation.

Would the victorious fleet be able to retrieve losses in
places like the Philippines, Malaya, the Dutch Indies, the
islands off Australia? Again the answer is no. With hostile
aviation firmly anchored on such points, the surrounding
waters would be strictly forbidden to our surface craft, no
matter how many vessels we owned.

The fact is that destruction of Japanese sea power would
leave us approximately where we were, as long as Japan re-
tained sufficient air power to control the skies. Our magnificent Navy would be obliged to keep at a respectful distance

from all seas dominated by the enemy's air strength. For reasons that we have analyzed on other pages, aircraft from "floating bases" would not enable the Navy to overcome genuine land-based aircraft.

And thus the promised "command of the sea" through the employment of naval forces shakes down to a meaningless phrase. It is valid only if preceded by command of the air. But—and there's the crux of the matter—once we have such aerial command, the Japanese "seagoing forces" are counted out anyhow; they become so many targets to be picked off at leisure even as the *Repulse* and the *Prince of Wales* were picked off.

This does not mean, of course, that advocates of autonomous air power crave to "abolish armies and navies." It does mean that air power has achieved primacy in modern warfare. It does mean that the first and decisive arena of modern conflict is neither on land nor on sea but in the skies, in the "air ocean." Those who do not grasp these elementary truths are unsuited to plan the strategy and the equipment for victory in the present era.

It is useless and frivolous to expect the necessary *aerial strategy* to be evolved for us by men whose ideas are rigidly set in older molds. The most we can expect from them is aviation as a supplement to old-line surface strategy, when we need all-out plans to eliminate the enemy's air power and enforce full mastery of the skies. Everything else is secondary and follow-up procedure: the exploitation of air ascendancy down below.

A brilliant infantry general is as unfitted to solve purely aerial tactical problems as a brilliant dentist is to perform an abdominal operation. It is no reflection on the surface strategists to recognize that they are in a strange, unexplored country when they venture into the sphere of modern avia-

tion. Real aerial strategy calls for men as thoroughly "sold"
on air power as a typical admiral is "sold" on sea power, as
convinced of its decisive role and potentialities for growth
as General Mitchell was convinced of it.

There is some danger that we may fool ourselves into be-
lieving that an older breed of military mind can be reformed
and adjusted to the new situation. That would be rank self-
delusion. A totally new strategy can never be developed and
put into effect by those who created the old one which
proved fallacious or inadequate. Military conceptions, after
all, are not put on and taken off like different cloaks for different climates. Strategy is the expression of a man's mind,
the embodiment of his whole military philosophy and convictions. A new approach to the problem of achieving victory under totally new conditions implies a new type of
mind. It calls for leadership by new enthusiastic men rather
than by reluctant and disgruntled converts.

Those associated with the old strategies cannot, even if
they would, suddenly turn their brains inside out because of
something that happened at Crete or over Britain, in Pearl
Harbor or at Singapore. We must have new men and an organization within which they can make fullest use of their
creative energies.

———————————————— 2 ————————————————

ADMITTEDLY IT IS risky business to deal with immediate aspects of the war, at a time when events move so much faster
than printing presses. Yet it is possible to make certain broad
generalizations on the strategic picture.

The irony of our war with Japan is this. Although the body
and heart of the enemy are closer to our American mainland
than any of his outlying limbs, we are grappling with those

limbs and cannot strike at his heart. We have come to grips
with Japan in the Philippines and Malaya and the Nether-
lands Indies, which represent, in terms of safe roundabout
supply routes, distances from seven to twelve thousand miles.
This despite the fact that the enemy lives only a fraction of
that distance from our back door: a scant three thousand
miles from Alaska, some two thousand miles from bases in
the Aleutian Islands.

What might have been—and what ultimately must be—a
conflict across 3000 miles has resolved into a conflict across
12,000 miles!

And the most melancholy part of the tale is that our inability to strike directly at the enemy across the shortest and
most expeditious distance is not due to inherent flaws in the
technique of warmaking. It is the result of a flaw in our intellectual vision. In Chapter V we repeated words written by
General Mitchell in 1929: "Alaska is really the key point to
the whole Pacific." With every advance in aviation, the
prophetic wisdom of these words has become more evident
to those with eyes unblurred by inherited illusions.

To grasp the strategic layout, think of Japan as a great oc-
topus. Its body and its vital organs are in the Nipponese
Islands proper. Its tentacles stretch out across thousands of
miles—into China, Malaya, the Indies, the Philippines, Guam,
Wake. Others are reaching out toward Australia and New
Zealand.

If we were able to strike at the heart of this sprawling
beast, at Japan itself, and knock it out there, all the tentacles
would instantly fall limp. They would relax their grip on
victims already crushed or struggling to survive. But because we lacked the revolutionary boldness to prepare the
appropriate strategy and weapons, we have no alternative
but to attack the tentacles one by one.

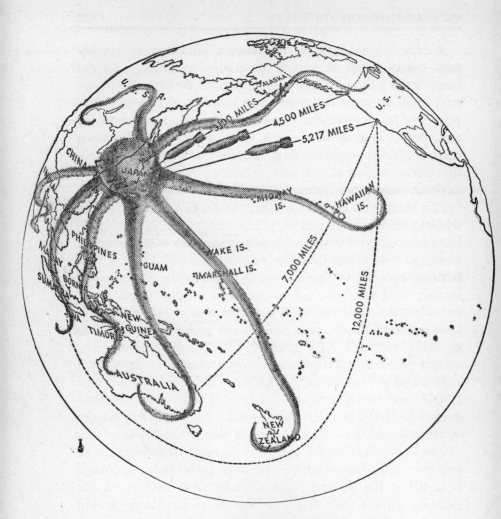

AIR POWER IGNORES THE TENTACLES

We are now engaged in the complex, laborious, and costly task—costly in life as well as materials—of hacking away at each of the tentacles. Americans, heirs to the greatest industrial civilization in the world, are reduced to fighting with primitive weapons in swamps and jungles, matching man for man and seeking to smother the enemy by the bulk of American bodies and machines. It is as though we had deliberately cast aside our natural advantages, discarding the very weapons that reflect our industrial and technological supremacy.

Our most optimistic hope seems to be to lop off these extensions of Japanese power, mile by mile, island by island, knowing full well that the maddened animal will throw out new tentacles every time we cut off old ones. Thus we are battling on a twelve-thousand-mile front, with a cumbersome strategy that calls for the formation and equipment of armies of millions of men, the construction of tens of billions of dollars' worth of naval tonnage, all of it protected by swarms of "Army planes," "Navy planes," and "Marine planes" conceived primarily to assist surface operations.

In effect we are trying to take over command of the entire Pacific basin—half a world!—piecemeal, in order that, thus entrenched, we may then prepare to carry the war to the vital organs of the octopus in the Japanese homeland.

The course envisaged can be surmised from the kind of construction upon which our present Army-Navy command is lavishing the billions at its disposal. It is implicit in the gigantic armies and vast amounts of mechanized ground equipment being projected, and in the colossal fleets of merchant ships scheduled for production. It is clearly implicit in the huge program of naval construction, much of it scheduled for completion only in 1948, and relatively little of it available in full force before 1945.

The plan apparently is to retrieve lost ground in the Pacific, mile by mile—to reconquer every island and every base that may have been seized by the enemy. Unaware that the old strategic manuals of Admiral Mahan have been invalidated by air power, our military masterminds are evidently gearing machinery to disentangle one Japanese tentacle after another. It is as though a bow-and-arrow army, having been routed by gunpowder, sought to win back lost ground by throwing in yet more bows and arrows.

I submit that it makes no sense. The sooner we supplement this strategy by preparing for direct aerial assault on the heart of the enemy the better. In the meantime let us give the present strategists all they ask for in the conduct of the immediate phase of the conflict. Having been caught without guns, so to speak, we must make the best possible use of more primitive weapons. But that should not stop us from forging the new weapons without delay.

It is not impossible that the present roundabout and exorbitant strategy may succeed. The enemy, like ourselves, has not yet exploited to the full the potentialities of the new weapon. As long as there are bridgeheads in Hawaii, Australia, and New Zealand, providing lines of communication outside the range of Japanese land-based aviation, we can continue trying to reinforce our strength at the ends of Japanese tentacles, across seven, ten, or twelve thousand miles vulnerable to hostile surface and undersea attacks throughout the journey. The detour will be necessary to evade contact with Japanese air power. But the military conjuncture at this writing does not offer too much ground for optimism.

If even a fraction of the materials and man power and creative genius now earmarked for expansion of the old weapons in line with the old strategy were diverted to true air power, we could construct the machinery and perfect the organization for the shortest and most direct road to victory.

There are those who denounce such a proposal as "gambling" with the nation's security by "venturing into the unknown." The truth is that the orthodox strategists—dependent on their surface lines of communication—are the real, if unconscious, gamblers. They are staking the whole war on the hope of beating Japan in a race for bridgeheads and way stations. Do they not understand that their own assumptions and their own preparations concede in advance that if that race is lost the whole war is lost?

Within their own restricted circle of vision they are right: if we lose those bridgeheads and thus find ourselves unable to carry shore-based aviation across the oceans on ships, we shall suddenly find ourselves entirely isolated, quarantined. Our whole prodigious investment of unnumbered billions in ships and short-range aviation, predicated on a war that begins and ends with surface lines of communication, must then be written off as a total loss.

Air power would have to pick up the job from there. Does it not seem, therefore, simple common sense to begin immediately to gear air power for that job. The reckless gamblers are those who, whatever their motives or psychological fixations, seek to prevent air power from undertaking preparations. Specifically it is imperative that we undertake immediate construction of a fleet of superbombers of the Douglas B-19 and Glenn Martin Flying Boat *size*. These have a range of nearly 8000 miles. Japan is within a 3000-mile radius of Alaska. Such an aerial armada will have an adequate margin of range for maneuvering and tactical operation over the targets. The present B-19 and Glenn Martin, having been designed years ago without benefit of recent aeronautical experience, leave much to be desired in the matter of military characteristics. But the experience gained in the course of their construction, the aerodynamical advances made in the meantime, and the lessons learned by our aerial strategists in the present war will enable superb American designers and able production men to put this type of plane into production at once. When these bombers leave the production line and take to the air, they will be true dreadnaughts of the sky.

The American aviation industry can now surpass the best available elsewhere. Mr. Glenn L. Martin stated in his company's house organ for February, 1942, that his firm "can build a 250,000-lb. flying ship, able to carry 80 tons of bombs or cargo to Europe at a speed of more than 300 mph *at any time that there is a demand for it*. The preliminary designs have already been worked out." I have italicized and now proceed to repeat the telltale words: "At any time there is a demand for it." It is not technique but strategic thought that lags so sadly in our country.

The human mind is strangely flustered by the unaccustomed. The same people who do not consider it remarkable or "extreme" to build giant battleships costing a hundred million dollars are bewildered by the idea of building superbombers, at a cost of between one and two million dollars, although from an engineering standpoint it is a much less difficult and less ambitious undertaking. The superbombers and superfighters under discussion, we may be sure, will cease to be "visionary" and "fantastic" as soon as they are in production.

While these bombers operate from the primary base on Alaska, their accompaniment of convoy fighters could start from Aleutian bases a thousand miles farther west. At the outset the convoy combat planes would therefore be of considerably shorter range. The two types together would give us a well-balanced striking force, with the military characteristics described in the preceding chapter, fit to attack Japan, not evading but seeking combat, just as great naval armadas used to do in the days before the advent of aviation.

If the construction of this aerial striking force begins in 1942, it could safely be planned for action in 1945. And if aviation is given the right of way on all deficit materials, tools, and labor, the whole process can be tremendously speeded up. If some naval leaders object that this would be "too late," remember that their own construction program for mile-by-mile struggle cannot reach its apex until 1948. Should the war be won in the interim, Americans will regret neither the investment in a long-range air-force program for 1945 nor the investment in a naval program for 1948.

Even while the minimal air-power project as outlined, on the basis of aviation types already in existence, is in progress, work must be begun on the succeeding phase, with even larger bombers, of at least 10,000 miles' range and convoy or combat planes of the necessary reach. By making possible aerial attack directly from the American mainland, with additional protective combat planes joining the attacking force from Alaska and the Aleutian Islands as the aerial battle fleet passes this region on its way to Japan, it would constitute our next line of defense in the skies, and a further enhancement of aerial insurance. Thereafter we would enter into the third stage, wherein, with a 15,000-mile range at our disposal, we could achieve mastery of the skies all over the globe. This is the concomitant of a war that is global in its sweep.

I am quite aware that these recommendations, though made with detailed and intimate knowledge of their practicability, will be received skeptically by those whose imaginations are muscle-bound. I recall that when I first offered to build a fully automatic bomb sight, I was assured that it was impossible because ballistic tables cannot be reproduced graphically or mechanically. But it was done!

When I proposed the first low-wing monoplane for training, I was told that it could not be built and, in any case, would be impractical because pupils would kill themselves. Today our training is done exclusively in monoplanes.

When amphibian planes were doing only 125 miles an hour, aerodynamics indicated that they might be built with speeds exceeding 200 miles. I was told, however, that this could not be done either. Yet a plane which I so constructed and flew myself broke the world's speed record for amphibians in 1935 at 230 m.p.h.

I was given solemnly to understand that a pursuit plane equipped with the radial air-cooled engine could not possibly do more than 300 miles, no matter how much power was put into it, since the drag of the engine alone would be prohibitive. I proceeded to design such a plane, and today it flies over 400 miles per hour.

My personal experience is merely typical of the sneering skepticism faced by men in the aviation industry and by aviation personnel in our military forces when they try to overcome the barriers of conservatism and frozen ideas. Men of the aviation industry are so accustomed to being told that "it can't be done" that we are almost cynical about it. Before critics shrug away our national opportunity, let them recall how bizarre and "utopian" the German *Blitzkrieg* projects sounded to the "Maginot Line" General Staff of France; how Crete demolished the terrestrial strategists' claim that air power cannot by itself conquer and hold territory; how the claims that battleships cannot be sunk by aircraft and that Singapore is impregnable have been disproved. Let them ponder on the recent words of Viscount Trenchard, Marshal of the Royal Air Force. The strength of the Germans, he wrote, derives from the fact "that they have ruthlessly discarded outworn naval and military traditions, have allotted to air power its proper share in their plans, and have remolded their naval and military technique to suit the conditions of the air age."

———————————————— 3 ————————————————

IMMEDIATE PREPARATION for direct aerial attack on Japan, and ultimately on Germany as well, does not imply a cessation of the struggle with the forces now at hand. The new organization for a single and autonomous air force will also enable us to make more effective the present equipment and the aircraft already projected. As a penalty for backward thinking, we find ourselves forced to fight along the old lines. Because our weapons are ill-conceived, we have no alternative but to defend every inch of ground and sea now exposed to enemy attack—instead of cutting off enemy power at its source. But even that process can be facilitated.

The most important thing that an Air Department could do immediately, while launching the program for long-range combat, is to release our existing aviation from its anachronistic dependence on surface transportation. At this stage of aeronautical science it is ludicrous that our aircraft should be taken apart and loaded on ships, then dragged across vast ocean areas in constant dread of attack from undersea, on the surface, and from on high.

The same aircraft can be readily modified to enable self-delivery to Hawaii and Iceland and, through a series of jumps, to Africa. It would require only minor adaptations of most fighter planes now in inventory or scheduled for early production to give them over 3000 miles of sustained flight; and there is not a bomber extant which could not be equipped with additional emergency range. Nearly 200,000 aircraft are planned for production in 1942–43. If the greater part of these, as well as the craft already built, were equipped with a minimum range of 3000 miles, avenues of operation now closed to us would suddenly be wide open. The terrible drain on our heavily burdened shipping facilities would cease.

The folly of shipping aircraft which could be made to fly under their own power is truly bizarre. Due to the bulk of airplanes, only a fraction of the tonnage of a cargo ship can be utilized. At a generous estimate, a 10,000-ton freighter can transport a hundred pursuits. To assure its safety in transit, it must be adequately protected against teeming threats on, below, and above sea level. It must move with an escort of warships in battle trim, under swarms of defensive airplanes brought along on the Navy's "floating bases," which in turn must be protected by land-based aviation from intermediary bases.

A handful of airplanes conducted slowly, inertly, to some scene of action by a convoy many times larger than the total combat power of the cargo! If the naval units, carrier-based aviation, gasoline, man power, and other elements entering into the undertaking were converted into direct striking air power, they would give us not only vastly greater offensive value but the kind of power that could be hurled directly at the vitals of the enemy country.

Insofar as it can be done, therefore, it is obvious that all available aviation for use at a distance from our shores would be given the range for self-delivery by a separate air force. As many as necessary could then fly under their own power to outlying bases such as Hawaii or Iceland, straight from the assembly line. The release of maritime shipping tonnage for other purposes, as well as the quicker and safer transfer of aviation, would thereby be accomplished. And what applies to delivery of the planes themselves applies to all the essential materiel for their sustained operation, since most of it can likewise be transported by air.

Obviously, it is immensely important for us to maintain the current battles in the Pacific and Atlantic arenas alike, with the weapons now at our disposal. "Air-power enthusiasts" do not wish to call the battles off. Airmen in particular are eager to keep the Axis as busy as possible, so that its energies may be diverted in other directions while we rush the construction of requisite long-range striking forces. One of our significant advantages at this writing is that both Japan and Germany have their hands full with relatively short-range tasks which may hamper if not postpone their concentration on aerial weapons for direct attack on the United States. It is an advantage which we derive from our superior wealth, resources, and production potentials.

In fine, we see even the present strategy enhanced through intelligent application of aviation principles. It can be converted into a telltale *delaying action,* winning for us valuable time. But we airmen do not have faith in that strategy as a road to final victory.

The island-to-island type of war involves water gaps approaching 1700 miles. Shore-based fighter aircraft, if they are to participate in the actions, must therefore have an operating radius of some 2000 miles. But that is already nearly 70 per cent of the radius necessary for direct attack on Japan from Alaska, so that it makes more sense to aim at the larger and more direct goal. If long-range aircraft for shore-to-shore conflict is to be built at all, why adhere to the roundabout 12,000-mile front instead of the 3000-mile front that can be opened quite as readily? By the longer route, if and when we finally reach the last way station to Japan, we shall have to negotiate a water barrier anyhow, and one that requires air power of nearly the same range as the Alaska-Japan jump.

In any event, the present strategy does not contemplate such long-range aviation. It obviously counts on retrieving the chain of islands with the aid of ship-based aviation. In the initial stages, with Japan far from its primary or home base, this procedure may succeed. As we approach closer to the ultimate goal, however, we shall face the full weight of the enemy's land-based planes, especially his land-based torpedo planes.

Any possibility of conquering the enemy by ship-borne aviation is out of the question, for reasons we have already analyzed. Regardless how wishful-thinking admirals may stack the cards, theoretically, in their own favor, our position remains impossible as long as we must depend on ship-borne equipment against an enemy based on shore.

Any program of victory, anything that involves more than defense and stalling tactics, must return to the fundamental principle of air power. It must be geared to move first, to assume control, to land air-borne troops, to get all necessary aerial reinforcements moving under their own power—with navies and armies following up the advantage to clinch the victory by actual occupation and possession. That holds true whether the objective is an intermediary base or the final objective.

Sea power received its most telling blow at Norway, when Germany, in defiance of Britain's massed naval strength, invaded the Scandinavian peninsula. Because the blow shocked our naval men out of their somnolence, they seem unable to forget the Nazi method of co-ordinating land, sea, and air services in that particular engagement. They think they are being "modern" if not actually "revolutionary" in treating the Pacific campaign as though it were a series of Skagerraks and Norways. In fact, they are imitating without understanding. They forget, for one thing, that the Skagerrak was narrow enough to permit Germany to take aerial control. Only when we have aviation capable of establishing such control across the water gaps between the Pacific steppingstones will the picture become analogous.

Whether in the Atlantic or in the Pacific, we shall ultimately face the necessity of striking at the sources of the power which we wish to crush—that is to say, Japan and Germany proper. The localized battles at in-between points are important. As we have already seen, the loss of bridgeheads like Australia would practically quarantine us on the West. If Hitler were to succeed in taking the British Isles, the Azores, Iceland—the two latter points close enough to America to enable him to attack us with the kind of bombers already at his disposal—we should be similarly quarantined on the Atlantic side. But the main problem is to seek and find a road to the heart of the enemy.

Referring to the more limited British problem, Air Marshal Trenchard wrote:

"Air power cannot play its part in helping us win the war unless we maintain unswervingly the policy of the offensive and concentrate steadily and consistently on building up a bomber force which, while always available if required for defensive operations in support of the other services, has suitable aircraft and suitable trained crews in adequate numbers to sustain the offensive against our primary enemy, to wear down German resistance from within, and play a major part in creating that situation without which no Allied army can ever hope to force its way into Germany."

These words are even more pertinent to the United States. In a war based on long-range aerial strategy we face the Axis as an equal—even with an edge of superiority deriving from our greater resources. In the orthodox strategy upon which we now seem embarked, however, we are overwhelmingly at a disadvantage. Both Japan and Germany operate on the surface on *interior* lines of communication, enabling them to mobilize force almost instantly at any front where it may be needed. The United States, working on *exterior* lines, cannot do this. We must have every front covered at all times, and therefore need naval forces and armies many times in excess of the enemy's.

From whatever angle we examine our position, therefore, preparation without further delay for all-out and direct aerial attacks on the enemy's primary bases is not only preferable, but, in my view, our main hope. Our task is to hold the enemy on land and sea with minimal forces, to conserve our resources—and to channel our main energies and economic wealth for massing in the air for a decisive all-out offensive.

Admittedly it is a view not easily accepted by skeptics and congenital conservatives in the military sphere. To date, such people have moved toward that view only under the impetus of enemy surprises and disasters for ourselves and our friends. Are we really a tired nation, too lackadaisical to think for ourselves? Must we remain content to turn the crank of mass production and spew out vast amounts of backward equipment in imitation of the enemy's weapons? Can we not find among ourselves men with the courage to launch an advanced, modern strategy—and to assume full responsibility for their mental daring? Shall we remain helpless in the hands of military leadership which fears to tackle anything that has not been haloed by precedent? Such an attitude, unfortunately, leaves the initiative forever in the hands of the adversary.

Day-to-day events are forcing the truth upon the most reluctant minds. The sinking of a dreadnaught by an airplane demolishes delusions about battleships being invulnerable to air power. The clear helplessness of valiant surface defenders when the skies are held by the foe shakes the traditional faith in armies. But the process of trial-and-error is too slow in the present life-and-death struggle. The American people must somehow cut through the psychological obsessions at the top.

Our current war program is based on certain assumptions which have the prestige of age and past success. They were wholly valid in their time. Today we owe it to ourselves and all humankind, in its hour of supreme danger, to review those assumptions in the light of the new conditions. To intensify a false strategy is not to remedy it. If we are headed in the wrong direction, we cannot get where we want to go by stepping up the speed.

If, for instance, it becomes clear that battleships have lost their former importance and their traditional initiative, we accomplish less than nothing by doggedly building yet more of them. We must ask ourselves whether the mammoth production effort on which we are now engaged may not conceivably be channeled in a wrong direction. Must we really, through sheer inertia and fear of breaking with the past, continue to build more hundred-million-dollar targets for enemy aviation to destroy? Must we persevere in the complex absurdity of building airplanes to protect navies against airplanes, so that those navies may do the work which the airplanes can do far more quickly, more economically, and without dependence on the support of another service?

We must muster the intellectual courage to act on our reason, and not merely to react to disaster. It is not only a problem of substituting one weapon for another. That will avail us nothing if our thinking remains bogged down in past assumptions, if our leadership remains old-fashioned. What I am urging is not a minor operation on our military system, but bold surgery.

— 4 —

THERE CAN be no doubt that the native common sense of the American people will assert itself in time to switch our major strategy onto the wings of modern warfare. As the Pacific Ocean struggle unfolds; as Germany reaches out for our advance bases in the Atlantic, off Europe and Africa; as Germany resumes its eastward drives in the attempt to enclose Asia in a great Nazi-Nipponese pincers—it must become increasingly clear to the average man that the global war is resolving into a struggle, in the first instance, for dominance in the air.

And somewhere in the course of this mental enlightenment Americans must become deeply aware that this fact is all to the good—*that it is a virtual guarantee of victory.*

The same people who now fluctuate between apathy and despair will suddenly feel the pressure of their own untapped strength. They will thrill to the realization that precisely because this is essentially an aerial war, we Americans can have the upper hand. Recognition that the conflict must be won or lost in the "air ocean" is being brought to us in the language of frustration and defeat on the surface of land and sea. But the bigger message is one of inevitable triumph.

It bears repeating that Americans are the natural masters of the aerial weapon and therefore the destined victors in a technological contest. Americans invented this air weapon. They have never developed it destructively. But now that it has been turned against them, they will reclaim their technological priority. More than any other people Americans are the natural children of the machine age. Once fully alive to their advantage, they may be expected to take the initiative in this war. They will no longer wait to be stunned and bewildered by enemy surprises or content to let the enemy establish all the "precedents." They will know in their bones that they cannot risk a mood of doubt and timidity in this dynamic air-power epoch. They will settle on a policy of audacity, with men of great vision and uninhibited imagination at the controls.

The war prospects are melancholy in the extreme, as long as they are viewed from the angle of armies and navies. The gloom dissipates as soon as the landscape of events is surveyed from the eagle's view of real air power. Optimism based on wishful thinking is an opiate. As Homer Lea, the great American military theorist, warned in 1909: "The self-deception of a nation concerning its true militant strength increases at the same ratio as its actual militant capacity decreases." But optimism deriving from clear-eyed perception of what must be done and *how to do it* is a reservoir of strength.

In this sense the advocates of unstinting and self-contained air power are the only ones who have a warrant for optimism. They alone can implement their hopes with the sureness and precision of engineers. Convinced that they are witnessing the last naval battles in human history, they are not "let down" by naval impotence or naval reverses. Knowing that the loss of this or that area of land or ocean is a temporary episode, with the real decision still to be fought out in the skies, they cannot be discouraged by defeats which in former times would have spelled final doom.

We have already heard, and may be fated to hear again, the dire warnings of terrestrial-minded military experts that should Australia and New Zealand and the British Isles fall to the Axis, the United States would be finished. We would then, they cry, immediately become a fourth-rate nation condemned to slavery. Their fears are genuine—because to them the impotence of a fleet, its inability to carry war to enemy shores, seems an end beyond which lies the darkness of utter hopelessness. Such military disasters, the tragedy of which we do not for a moment underestimate, will not overtake us, if air power is given full rein at once. But even if they did overtake us, they would not spell doom to us airmen. We would regard them as passing stages in a planetary conflict which cannot end as long as we possess air power to battle for mastery of the skies. The outcome thus still depends on our own vigor and wisdom in preparing the requisite aerial strategy and aerial weapons.

This book has been in large part a chronicle of American error and shortsightedness and stubborn orthodoxy. But its moral is not despair. On the contrary, its message is one of soaring hope, as summed up in the title—*Victory Through Air Power*.

America's aerial potential, as compared to that of the Axis, is so clearly greater that in the race for supremacy in the skies victory is assured. We must, however, bear in mind that the differential is being rapidly reduced as the Germans and the Japanese lay hands on new sources of supply. Hence the immense importance of acting now, when the advantages are still overwhelmingly on our side. Tomorrow it may be a race between approximate equals; today our margin of superiority in materials, productive forces, and brains is still large enough to guarantee success.

Air power is the American weapon. It will not fail us, if only we unchain it and provide immediately the minimal conditions for its unhindered development. I know that I speak for all my colleagues in the aeronautical legions of the land—our gallant pilots, designers, engineers, and manufacturers, the aerial strategists and the humblest aeronautical mechanics—and especially for the millions of American young people born into the air-power age and attuned to its dynamic rhythm, when I say that we airmen feel frustrated by the artificial restraints. We are eager to serve and ready to act when our beloved America says the word.

# A NOTE ABOUT THE AUTHOR

MAJOR ALEXANDER P. DE SEVERSKY was born in Russia in 1894. At the age of ten he went to military school and subsequently to the Russian Naval Academy where, in 1914, he was graduated a lieutenant of the Russian Navy. After seeing some service with a Russian destroyer flotilla in the Baltic Sea through the winter of 1914–15, he was selected for duty with naval aviation and sent to the Military School of Aeronautics at Sebastopol, Crimea, where he was graduated as a military aviator. He then returned to the Baltic Sea and completed a Naval postgraduate course in aeronautics and received a degree as a naval aviator. Thereupon he was attached to the naval aviation forces of the Baltic Sea. During the following three years he saw active combat service, first in bombardment aviation and then in pursuit; in 1917 he was appointed Chief of Pursuit Aviation of the Baltic Sea. Despite the fact that he lost his right leg in 1915 while on a bombardment mission, he returned to active duty with an artificial limb. Through his daring military exploits he became the leading Russian ace of the Naval Air Force and received all the honors that his native land could bestow on him, including the Gold Sword and the Order of St. George, the highest military award.

In 1918, as a result of his technical contributions to the progress of aviation, he was selected as a member of the Russian Naval Aviation Mission to the United States. After Russia dropped out of the war, he offered his services to the United States Government and was appointed aeronautical engineer and test pilot for the government, in which capacity he served until the Armistice. In 1921 he acted in an advisory capacity to the late General William E. Mitchell during the latter's demonstration of the ability of aircraft to sink battleships. As a result of this work, he was appointed consulting engineer to the War Department by the Secretary of War, a great honor for a young man not yet an American citizen. In 1927 he became an American citizen and was commissioned a major in the U. S. Air Corps Specialist Reserve the following year.

Major Seversky designed the world's first fully automatic bombsight. In 1931 he founded the Seversky Aircraft Corporation, now Republic Aviation Corporation, of which he was President and Director for more than seven years. This company has been engaged in building some of America's best pursuit airplanes. He designed and built the fastest amphibian plane in the world, the first low-wing basic training airplane for the U. S. Army Air Corps, and is responsible for the development of American pursuit airplanes in their present form. He also pioneered in high-altitude combat tactics by developing and building the first turbo-supercharged, aircooled-engine fighter. He has made numerous other contributions to our air defense. His advanced ideas and long-range views in connection with the technical development of aeronautical equipment have been fully substantiated by the events of the present war.

Major Seversky holds numerous world's speed records and in December of 1940 he was presented with the coveted Harmon Trophy by President Roosevelt for his outstanding achievements in the field of aviation for the year 1939. He is considered one of our greatest experts on the tactics and strategy of aerial warfare. His ability in that respect has been demonstrated by the accuracy of his forecasts in the course of the current war. In particular his public predictions as to the time the war would begin, the ability of Great Britain to resist invasion, the events in Crete, the Russian-German conflict, and, finally, his analysis of the Pacific theater of war have been truly remarkable.